Rocket Man: Nuclear Madness and the Mind of Donald Trump

**Edited By:
John Gartner
Steven Buser
& Leonard Cruz**

CHIRON PUBLICATIONS • ASHEVILLE, NORTH CAROLINA

www.ChironPublications.com

Interior and cover design by Danijela Mijailovic

Printed primarily in the United States of America.

ISBN 978-1-63051-591-1 Limited Edition Paperback

ISBN 978-1-63051-588-1 paperback

ISBN 978-1-63051-589-8 hardcover

ISBN 978-1-63051-590-4 electronic

Library of Congress Cataloging-in-Publication Data Pending

Table of Contents

Is Trump Psychologically Fit to Command the Nuclear Arsenal or is He a Danger?

Introduction   9

Images from Hiroshima and Nagasaki, August 1945   15

Chapter 1   23
The Erratic President
-Harry Segal, Ph.D. Dept. of Psychology, Cornell University

Chapter 2   27
DEFCON 2? Nuclear Risk is Rising as Donald Trump Goes Downhill
-John Gartner, Ph.D., Founder, Duty To Warn

Chapter 3   35
If President Trump Were Airman Trump, I Would Not Certify Him Psychologically
Fit to Handle Nuclear Weapons
-Steven Buser, M.D., Psychiatrist, Former Major, USAF

Chapter 4   41
If Trump Were a Policeman I Would Have to Take Away His Gun
-David Reiss, M.D., Psychiatrist in Private Practice

Chapter 5   47
If Trump Was Entering the Military, He Would Not Receive a Security Clearance
-William Enyart, Former U.S. Congressman from Illinois and Retired General,
U.S. Army National Guard

Images from the United States Strategic Bombing Survey, 1945   53

Chapter 6   57
A Man with No Humanity Has the Power to Destroy Mankind
-Lance Dodes, M.D., Boston Psychoanalytic Society

Chapter 7   61
Trump's Sick Psyche and Nuclear Weapons: A Deadly Mixture
-Gordon Humphrey, former Republican Senator of New Hampshire

Chapter 8 65
Facing the Truth: Trump Wields the Power of a Predatory Narcissist and May Destroy Us All
-Jacqueline West, Ph.D., New Mexico Society of Jungian Analysts

Chapter 9 71
Trump's No Madman, He's Following the Strongman Playbook
-Ruth Ben-Ghiat, Department of History, New York University

Building Your Own Bomb Shelter (1950's Photo Images) 75

Will the "Dealmaker" Make a Deal or Start a War? 79

Chapter 10 81
The Gospel of War Presidency
-Richard Painter, Former Chief White House Ethics Lawyer and Leanne Watt, Ph.D., Psychologist in Private Practice

Chapter 11 107
The Greatest Danger to America is Her Commander in Chief
-Joe Cirincione, President, Ploughshares Fund

Chapter 12 115
Bluffing Us Into the Nuclear Abyss? What October 1962 Teaches Us About Nuclear Risks Under Trump
-James Blight and Janet Lang, Department of History, University of Waterloo

Images from the Cuban Missile Crisis 121

Chapter 13 125
One Week in August: How a Self-Made Nuclear Crisis Exposed Donald Trump's Psychopathology
-Seth Norrholm Ph.D., Department of Psychology, Emory University

Chapter 14 133
The Bully-in-Chief: Trump and Kim Jong-Un Could Destroy the World to Prove Who Has the Bigger Button
-Philip Zimbardo, Ph.D., Stanford University (emeritus) and Rosemary Sword, Private Practice

Chapter 15 139
American Carnage: The Wars of Donald Trump
-Melvin Goodman, Department of Foreign Relations, Johns Hopkins University

Chapter 16   143
Taking Trump's Finger off the Nuclear Button
-Tom Z. Collina, Director of Policy, Ploughshares Fund

1950s Civil Defense Pamphlet (Photo Images)   149

Chapter 17   153
Is Donald Trump a Fascist?
-Bård Larsen, Historian, Civita

Chapter 18   161
The Relentless Victim: How Donald Trump Reinforces North Korea's Narrative
-Paul French, Freelance Writer

Chapter 19   167
Trump and North Korea: The Offer for Talks Was Impulsive, but Could it Work?
-Stephan Haggard, Director, Korea-Pacific Program, University of California, San Diego

Chapter 20   173
The Art of the North Korea Deal: If Trump Can Understand Kim's Fears, We Can Have
Peace on the Korean Peninsula
-Harry Kazianis, Director of Defense Studies, The Center for the National Interest

Chapter 21   181
Madman or Rational Actor? Kim Jong-un's Nuclear Calculus
-Ken Gause, Director, International Affairs Group CNA Corporation

Chapter 22   191
Nuclear Deterrence and Leadership Behavior: How Presidential Actions Raise
or Lower the Risk of War
-James E. Doyle, Ph.D. Former Nuclear Nonproliferation Analyst,
Los Alamos National Laboratory

Chapter 23   205
Extinction Anxiety and Donald Trump: Where the Spirit of the Depths Meets
the Spirit of the Times
-Thomas Singer, M.D.

Afterword   213
Visions of Apocalypse and Salvation
-Leonard Cruz, Editor-in-Chief, Chiron Publications

Contributing Authors   221

Is Trump Psychologically Fit to Command the Nuclear Arsenal or is He a Danger?

Introduction
Everyone on Planet Earth is Trump's Hostage

By John Gartner

In 2016, mental health professionals began to speak out *en masse* to warn the public about a dangerously disordered president. In what came to be known as the Duty to Warn movement, tens of thousands of us signed petitions, wrote articles, held meetings across the country, and marched in the streets. You can dismiss it as partisan politics if you like, but partisan politics have been around since the founding of the republic, and never before in history, anywhere in the world, has the mental health community felt a "duty to warn" the public about a leader who is so grossly ill that he represents a mortal threat to life, liberty, and the American way of life.

It's not only professionals. The majority of Americans tell pollsters that President Trump is mentally unfit for office.[1] One reason *The Dangerous Case of Donald Trump: 27 Psychiatrists and Mental Health Experts Assess a President* was an instant New York Times best seller (the first time I have ever seen an edited academic book on that list), was that most Americans already knew there "was something wrong with him" but hungered for the validation and insight that only experts could provide.[2] But while there was a great demand for this information, there was also a short supply because of a 1970s-era ethical principle, The Goldwater Rule, which forbade psychiatrists from diagnosing a public figure they hadn't personally interviewed. Elsewhere, I and others have argued that The Goldwater Rule is antiquated. Since the introduction of the *Diagnostic and Statistical Manual* in 1981, the field switched to using observable behavioral criteria to form diagnoses. So, if you can observe a patient, or talk to "informants" who do, you can form a valid diagnosis. And Lord knows, we've all observed enough aberrant behavior from the president to fill a psychiatric textbook.[3] As an ethical matter, The Goldwater Rule is superseded by an ethical

---

[1] Jessica Kwong, "Most Americans think Trump is psychologically unfit to be president," Newsweek, March 30, 2018.

[2] Bandy Lee (editor), The Dangerous Case of Donald Trump: 27 Psychiatrists and Mental Health Experts Assess a President, New York: St. Martin's Press, 2017.

[3] Bandy Lee, Edwin Fisher, Leonard Glass, "The Goldwater Rule has been turned into a silencing mechanism aimed at those who would speak out," Boston Globe, February 26, 2018; John Gartner, "Psychologists have a duty to warn the country about Trump: We can no longer pretend he's stable,"

principle that trumps The Goldwater Rule: our mandated "duty to warn" the public when they are in imminent risk of harm.

Whether or not you choose to diagnose Trump, it's clear he exhibits behaviors that make him dangerous, and in no area is that danger more extreme than in the area of nuclear war.

Polls show most Americans don't trust President Trump with the "nuclear button," afraid that "Trump might launch a nuclear attack without justification."[4] Americans have lived with nuclear anxiety since the 1940s, but only senior citizens can remember what it was like to look Armageddon in the face. Not since the 1962 Cuban Missile Crisis has nuclear war looked so conceivable. One man of dubious sanity, recklessly brandishing his "bigger button," has the unilateral power to kill us all.

Trump holds a nuclear gun to the world's head. This is not dystopian fiction. It is our reality in 2018.

Every book is a snapshot in time, but writing a contemporaneous book about Trump creates a unique problem. His position can change radically, and then change back again, within a single day. Like battleships, books can't turn around quickly to adapt to breaking news, and once they're published, there's no second draft.

This book evolved out of a conference on "Presidential Mental Health and Nuclear Weapons," hosted by Tom Steyer at the National Press Club in Washington, D.C., in February of 2018. In the summer of 2017, Trump had been threatening "fire and fury like the world has never seen." Seth Norrholm, focusing on "one week in August" documents Trump's ratcheting up of nuclear tensions with threats and taunts, like calling Kim Jong-un "Little Rocket Man," and threatening to "totally destroy the nation of North Korea." When the D.C. conference was organized, it looked as if we were at DEFCON 2, just one step away from DEFCON 1— "imminent nuclear war." With the exception of our optimists, Harry Kazianis and Stephan Haggard, most of our 25 authors, writing from their diverse perspectives as psychologists, psychiatrists, foreign policy experts, politicians, former military, historians, and journalists, sound a note of extreme alarm.

As I was editing the completed chapters in March 2018, Trump announced that John Bolton, along with Mike Pompeo—two überhawks—would replace the more moderate Rex Tillerson and H.R. McMaster as national security advisor and secretary of state. The adults in the "adult day care center" who were allegedly going to tackle Trump if he lunged for the nuclear football were gone,

---

New York Daily News, May 12, 2017.

[4] Emily Guskin, "Most Americans don't trust President Trump with the "nuclear button," Washington Post, January 23, 2018.

replaced by men who seemed more inclined to block for him, rather than tackle him, as he runs to war.

Suddenly, nuclear war seemed not only possible, but maybe even probable. Only weeks before, Bolton had penned an op-ed arguing for a first strike against North Korea. Bolton was known to be much like Trump: aggressive, erratic, dishonest, and looking for a fight. One of our contributors is Richard Painter, a former Republican and Bush administration ethics lawyer who is now a Democratic candidate for U.S. Senate in Minnesota. Paraphrasing Reagan, I would say Painter didn't leave the Republican Party, *it left him*, when it chose to rally behind the most unethical president in history. Painter told *Business Insider*: "John Bolton was by far the most dangerous man we had in the entire eight years of the Bush Administration. ... Hiring him as the president's top national security advisor is an invitation to war, perhaps nuclear war."

Many chapters were returned to the authors with directions to rewrite them to incorporate comment on Bolton and Pompeo.

As the chapters were being copy-edited, on April 8, 2018, Trump announced a summit with Kim Jong-un. The announcement was so impulsive it took virtually everyone by surprise, including the president's own advisors. When the idea was first proposed by South Korea's national security advisor, Chung Eui-yong in an Oval office meeting, "Trump accepted on the spot, stunning not only Chung and the other high-level South Koreans who were with him, but also the phalanx of U.S. officials who were gathered in the Oval Office," wrote *The New York Times*.[5]

Still, one had to admit the shocking gamble offered hopeful possibilities for peace, even if also entailed potential risks for failure, and the buzz was that Trump could win the Nobel Peace Prize. Counting their chickens before they were hatched, the administration even minted a commemorative coin in advance of the historic summit. Our book release date corresponded with the very week of the proposed summit. Some of the contributors contacted me in a panic: "If we cry the sky is falling while Trump is winning the Nobel Peace Prize, we're going to look like fools," wrote one who proposed we delay or even cancel release of the book.

I assured our authors that our looking foolish was the best possible outcome we could hope for. Never in my life have I prayed more earnestly to be wrong. I would rather have egg on my face than radioactive ash in the air, along with millions of dead. I've been a fool for far lesser things.

---

[5] Peter Baker and Choe Sang-Hun, "With Snap 'Yes' Trump Gambles in North Korea," New York Times, March 10, 2018.

But my gut told me not to count Trump's Nobel chickens before they hatched. Trump is a master of the 360-degree turn. He starts with an extreme position, like ending DACA. He then feints toward a more reasonable position, telling Congress he will sign any DACA bill lawmakers can agree on. And then, he tacks back to crazy—blowing up the DACA negotiations after a rare bipartisan agreement had been struck, landing him right where he started.

As I write this introduction over Memorial Day weekend of 2018 and our chapters head towards galleys, Trump has canceled those talks as abruptly as he started them. "Based on the tremendous anger and open hostility displayed in your most recent statement," Trump wrote to Kim, the meeting would be "inappropriate at this time." And once again, he rattled the nuclear saber: "You talk about nuclear capabilities, but ours are so massive and powerful that I pray to God they will never have to be used."

"After weeks of chumminess, we appear to be back to 'fire and fury,'" wrote *Slate*.

But if Kim was displaying "tremendous anger and open hostility," it was in response to provocations by Bolton, as well as Pence and Trump. On April 29, Bolton told CBS News that he envisioned North Korea following the "Libya model" of disarmament, knowing Kim's greatest fear was that if he gave up his nuclear weapons, he would lose his deterrent and leave himself vulnerable to regime change. As our Korea experts like Ken Gause and Paul French point out, survival of the regime is an existential struggle for which Kim will sacrifice everything and everyone. He will not *go gently into that good night*. After Gaddafi gave up his nukes, he ended up not only deposed, but shot dead in a ditch—Kim's worst nightmare. It was exactly the wrong thing to say, or the right thing if your aim was to sabotage the negotiations, as some have speculated Bolton wanted to do all along.

One of our authors, Stephan Haggard, titled his article, "If Trump can understand Kim's fears, we can have peace on the Korean peninsula." He may be right, but that's a big "if," because it presumes Trump has a capacity for empathy. The enormous importance of that "if" is highlighted by our authors James Blight, Janet Lang, and James Doyle, who point out that it was JFK's ability to empathize with Khrushchev, to see the crisis from his point of view, that narrowly avoided catastrophe in the Cuban Missile Crisis. But even for Trump, who is known to be empathetically challenged ("I hear you," read his clutched crib notes when meeting with the Parkland mass shooting survivors), is it possible to be more tone deaf? If you're trying to make a deal, saying, "Put down your weapons so we can kill you," is a bad opening bid and fits into what Paul French describes as a decades-long narrative of North Korea as a "relentless victim" at the hands of evil American aggression. Even if you argue Kim is a rational actor, as Ken Gause does, it would be irrational for him to surrender his nuclear weapons to an adversary who appears to be plotting his demise.

And then both Trump and Vice President Mike Pence made things worse by tripling down on the "Libya model." "As the president made clear, this will only end like the Libyan model ended if Kim Jong-un doesn't make a deal." But oops, Gaddafi ended up dead in a ditch *because* he made a denuclearization deal with the U.S., in North Korea's view.

In response, Choe Son-Hui, a North Korean vice foreign minister, called Pence "a "political dummy." "As a person involved in the U.S. affairs, I cannot suppress my surprise at such ignorant and stupid remarks gushing out from the mouth of the U.S. vice president." He has a point.

If we needed further proof that Bolton does not want to give peace a chance, he was the voice in Trump's ear urging immediate withdrawal from the summit. Like the decision to hold the summit in the first place, the decision to cancel it was impulsive and took his own administration by complete surprise. "National security adviser John Bolton was a key figure in persuading President Trump to withdraw from the summit—a move that blindsided Secretary of State Mike Pompeo," wrote the *Washington Examiner*.[6] The sudden decision also stunned North Korea, South Korea, our allies, and virtually every member of the administration other than Bolton.

Ironically, literally hours before the summit was canceled, in a confidence-building measure, Kim had destroyed a nuclear test site—a concrete first step in the direction of denuclearization. Kim took a step forward, and we stepped back. It sure doesn't look like the behavior of a nation seeking peace.

This morning the news is that the summit may be back on. By the time we print the book you are now reading, who knows? But Trump's chaotic process gets to the heart of the problem. Round and round he goes, and where he stops nobody knows. That's why we begin our book with Harry Segal's chapter on "the erratic president." Trump's wild instability makes the survival of the planet feel like a jump ball.

Some authors, like Steve Buser, David Reiss, and William Enyart argue that if Trump were not president, he would not be granted a security clearance or pass a fitness-for-duty evaluation to even handle nuclear weapons because of the disturbing behaviors he displays. While others like Lance Dodes, Gordon Humphrey, Jaqueline West, Philip Zimbardo, Rosemary Sword, and I argue that the president is not only unfit, but deeply, diagnosably, and dangerously psychologically disturbed.

---

[6] Diana Stancy Correll, "John Bolton persuaded Trump to cancel summit with Kim Jong Un: Report," May 24, 2018.

In contrast, historians Ruth Ben-Ghiat and Bard Larsen, argue Trump is not mad, but rationally and systematically following the strongman's handbook for dissolving democracy and seizing autocratic power.

Either scenario makes war seems likely. As Melvin Goodman, Richard Painter, and Leanne Watt argue, Trump's own psychology, that of his advisors, and even the clergyman who runs the administration's weekly Bible study, worship the glory of war.

Others look at the problem from a policy perspective. Joe Cirincione points out that Trump's policies of advocating an expansion of our nuclear arsenal and touting the useful value of "low-yield" nuclear weapons make the tactical use of nukes seem within acceptable normal limits and, thus, more likely to be used. All of this screams out for some check on the president's unilateral authority to launch nuclear weapons. Tom Collina argues for the necessity of a bill, currently stalled in Congress, that would require an act of Congress for a nuclear first strike.

This is a disturbing book. You may not want to read it. As a nation, we're exhausted, and we just can't take any more stress. We're suffering from an adrenaline overdose, careening from one scandal and outrageous violation of democratic norms to another.

We don't know how this hostage crisis will end, but there is an ominous sense of foreboding that it won't end well. Trump triggers the very deepest of all anxieties, what Tom Singer calls "extinction anxiety," fear for the demise of our species. At the deepest recess in our brains, we envision the worst: The Doomsday Clock is chiming, and the bell tolls for us all.

If what these experts have to say scares you, don't shut down. Take action. The 2018 election may be our nation's last chance to set limits on this president before mass destruction is loosed upon the planet. The terrifying truth is that it may already be too late.

Images from Hiroshima and Nagasaki, August 1945

Hiroshima

The devastation wrought upon the city of Hiroshima left indelible marks on our individual and collective psyches that the passage of more than seventy years has not erased. The shirtless airman cleaning and loading the atomic bombs offers strange juxtaposition to the utter destruction rained down on the citizens of the city.

To appreciate the scale of the mushroom cloud that rises from an atomic bomb, notice the beautiful Chūgoku Mountains rising up in the background of the devastation. The tallest peaks of this range reach an elevation of 5,600 feet. The mushroom cloud rose to six times that elevation (30,000) or higher. Imagine even more debris from a modern nuclear warhead rising into the atmosphere and dispersing. The consequences of thermonuclear warfare are on the scale of the results of the meteor strike on the Yucatan peninsula that ended the Paleozoic period when dinosaurs became extinct.

Nuclear Weapon of the "Fat Man" type, the kind detonated over Nagasaki, Japan, in World War II. H-bomb is 60-inches in diameter and 128-inches long. The second nuclear weapon to be detonated, it weighed about 10,000 pounds and had a yield of equivalent to approximately 20,000 tons of high explosive. *Los Alamos Scientific Laboratory. Harry S. Truman Library & Museum*

A "Fat Man" test unit being raised from the pit into the bomb bay of a B-29 for bombing practice during the weeks before the attack on Nagasaki. *Photo from U.S. National Archives, RG 77-BT*

Enola Gay after Hiroshima mission, entering hardstand. It is in its 6th Bombardment Group livery, with victor number 82 visible on fuselage just forward of the tail fin. *Public domain, via Wikimedia Commons*

At the time this photo was made, smoke billowed 20,000 feet above Hiroshima. Six planes of the 509th Composite Group participated in this mission; one to carry the bomb *Enola Gay*, one to take scientific measurements of the blast *The Great Artiste*, the third to take photographs *Necessary Evil*, the others flew approximately an hour ahead to act as weather scouts, 08/06/1945. Bad weather would disqualify a target as the scientists insisted on a visual delivery, the primary target was Hiroshima, secondary was Kokura, and tertiary was Nagasaki. *Public domain, via Wikimedia Commons*

Effects of the atomic bomb on Hiroshima. View from the top of the Red Cross Hospital looking northwest. *Public domain, via Wikimedia Commons*

Battered religious figures stand watch on a hill above a tattered valley. Nagasaki, Japan. September 24, 1945, 6 weeks after the city was destroyed by the world's second atomic bomb attack. *Public domain, via Wikimedia Commons*

Hiroshima on Honshu Island lies in ruins as a result of August, 1945 atomic bombing that hastened Japanese capitulation. *Harry S. Truman Library & Museum*

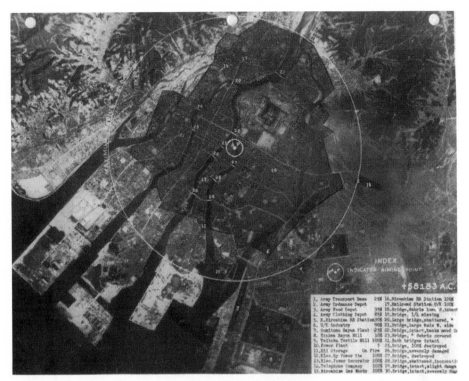

A photo prepared by U.S. Air Intelligence for analytical work on destructiveness of atomic weapons. The total area devastated by the atomic strike on Hiroshima is shown in the darkened area (within the circle) of the photo. The numbered items are military and industrial installations with the percentages of total destruction. *Photo from U.S. National Archives, RG 77-AEC*

An overview of the destruction of Hiroshima, undated, circa August-September 1945. *Photo from U.S. National Archives, RG 306-NT*

The Enola Gay returns to Tinian Island after the strike on Hiroshima. *Photo from U.S. National Archives, RG 77-BT*

Hiroshima Aftermath, cropped version with writing of Paul Tibbets. *Public domain, via Wikimedia Commons*

Nagasaki

The mushroom cloud over Nagasaki shortly after the bombing on August 9. *Photo from U.S. National Archives, RG 77-AEC*

Nagasaki's Mitsubishi Torpedo Plant, said to be the world's largest, following the atomic bomb explosion. *Harry S. Truman Library & Museum*

Ground view of Nagasaki before and after the bombing; radiuses in increments of 1,000 feet from Ground Zero are shown. *Photo from U.S. National Archives, RG 77-MDH*

Chapter 1
The Erratic President

By Harry Segal, Ph.D.

What if our president has a major mental illness? Donald Trump has been called a megalomaniac, a sociopath, a man suffering from a malevolent narcissistic personality. All three may be accurate, but those labels mean nothing to the general public. So to explain Trump's mental illness, let's move away from jargon and diagnosis, and instead focus on his behavior in terms we can all understand. What seems most obviously wrong is how *erratic* he is—this is the one quality that runs through the weave of his personality like a thread. The word comes from the Latin *error* which means "to wander." In the ancient world so dependent on sailing, to wander meant to wander off course, and so the English words *to err*, and *error* carry the meaning of being wrong.

When you call someone *erratic,* this word actually moves closer to its original meaning because you're describing someone lurching from one behavior to another almost randomly. A chess player or an army general might surprise you with a move that you didn't expect, but you wouldn't call them erratic—you would simply say they did something unexpected. But calling someone erratic implies the person isn't in control of his actions; that you can't trust him because you don't know what he's going to do. You can't trust a car that operates erratically—sometimes it starts, sometimes it doesn't—but it's even worse with a person because erratic behavior can include lying, betrayal, impulsive reactions, and violence. And what's most disturbing: The erratic person is often as surprised by what he does as you are.

The types of behavior that prove him erratic are things like tantrums, reversals, lying, betraying, and risky behaviors:

<u>Tantrums:</u> It began with his very first press conference as president, attacking the media and insisting the crowds for his inaugural were larger than observed. There was his anger at the press after the white supremacist march in Charlottesville, Virginia. Confirmed reports from inside the White House say he often needs to be calmed down by staff when he reacts to bad news or, more frequently, bad press.

<u>Reversals:</u> Politicians often change their positions or *evolve* into new ones, but that's different from the almost dizzying speed that Trump can reverse course. Sen. Lindsey Graham of South Carolina has famously referred to the "Tuesday Trump" who agreed to sign a bipartisan immigration bill but changed

his mind on Friday. He has fired countless people days after characterizing reports of their imminent departure as "fake news," and he fired David Shulkin, his Department of Veterans Affairs secretary, by tweet literally hours after telling him he was doing a good job in a private meeting.

Lying: Trump's lying has been documented since his presidency began, sometimes posting long tweets with no true statements. I remember being struck in the first month of his presidency when he was asked on Air Force One about National Security Advisor Mike Flynn having been caught lying to Mike Pence about communications with the Russians. Without batting an eye Trump, looking concerned, said, "This is the first I've heard of it." Turns out he had known for the past week, but his lying about it was immediate and convincing.

Betraying: The most obvious acts of betrayal have been in his three marriages. His encounter with pornographic film star Stormy Daniels and his extended affair with Karen McDougal demonstrate his betrayal of his wife, Melania. Michael Wolff describes Trump's pleasure in seducing attractive wives of his "friends,"[1] and he was famous in the real estate world for breaking contracts, underpaying construction companies, not to mention cheating the subscribers to Trump University. Of course, con games depend on betrayal.

Risky Behaviors: Certainly, Trump's sexual behavior, self-described and reported, has been so risky he put lawyers in place ready to impose nondisclosure agreements on women to cover his tracks. Yet his behaviors in business are no better. He reportedly lost a billion dollars building casinos in Atlantic City. (As comedy writer Steve Skrovan once asked, "What kind of genius *loses* money owning casinos?") And while there is no hard evidence of it yet, journalists report that Trump engaged in money laundering with Russian and other foreign entities as a way to shore up his at times faltering real estate empire. Wolff reports Trump promised Melania that he would lose the election, and I think he was counting on it for fear that his illicit financial dealings would come to light.

By contrast, most adults achieve some level of *psychological maturity* that involves, among other factors, having a moral compass, self-consistency, delaying gratification, and self-regulation, all traits conspicuously lacking in Trump

Moral Compass: Internalizing a value system, based on the Golden Rule of treating others as you would want to be treated, leads to principles of honesty and loyalty. If you keep promises whenever possible, that helps you to resist betraying someone for your own gain; if you believe in being honest with yourself, then you won't hide your destructive intentions with a phony rationalization.

Self-Consistency: A moral compass creates a kind of coherence to our lives. If you make choices based on honesty and respect for others, you create a

24

pattern that becomes its own guide. This doesn't mean you'll always do the right thing, but if you act out of dishonest self-interest, you'll feel some regret or anxiety afterward because you'll have acted *uncharacteristically*.

Delaying Gratification: Freud argued that civilization came about because human beings learned to trade immediate gratification for later gratification. Premed college students give up parties to master organic chemistry, but they're doing it for the delayed gratification of getting into medical school. Only by refusing to be a slave to your desires can you actually choose when to give in to them.

Self-Regulation: This is a crucial step after delaying gratification—can you allow yourself to feel angry, excited, jealous, and ashamed without feeling overwhelmed or impulsively acting on these feelings? Some people give in to all of these feelings and desires; others may wall off their emotions as a way of controlling them. (Trump is a good example of the first; Mike Pence a good example of the second.) Neither strategy leads to psychological health or happiness.

By having no moral compass, no consistency of values, an inability to defer immediate gratification, or to regulate his emotions and reflect on them, he is always at the mercy of his aggressive impulses and his appetites. This explains the tantrums, the reversals, the lying, the betraying, and his risky behaviors. This is why mental health practitioners consider him mentally ill. This is why he is the erratic president.

Some erratic people seek relationships with others whom they implicitly or explicitly asked to provide external *walls* to keep them from misbehaving—it's as if they wish to borrow the other person's moral compass. Former President Bill Clinton relied on his grandmother and then his stalwart wife, Hillary, to provide some limits to his erratic, impulsive behavior (see John Gartner's underappreciated book on Clinton[2]). And how many alcoholics have relied on long-suffering spouses who try to keep them sober?

Trump has at times relied on his daughter Ivanka to provide such a ballast (it's reported that he ridicules his sons), or on Hope Hicks, until recently his longtime media aide, but it's the generals he has leaned on the most to protect his reputation as a "great man." Although I was pleased to know Trump had established a troika of Mattis, McMaster and Kelly, hoping they would serve as a force against Trump's potentially reckless behavior, I knew they wouldn't last. *This is because the strategy of using other people to rein in one's own impulsive behavior is doomed to failure.* It represents a compromise—a wish to stay erratic AND the wish to become stable. The erratic component always wins in the end.

So where do things stand? News that Trump now feels "unfettered" and is confidently acting on his "gut" is a dangerous sign that he has rid himself of the external barriers to his disturbed behaviors. His policies have become more

25

erratic, promising to leave Syria on one day, while planning a retaliatory strike the next. His invitation to meet with Kim Jong-un with no prepared negotiations was made on the spur of the moment. What happens if Kim Jong-un ridicules Trump in a meeting? What if the Mueller investigation turns up evidence of criminal wrongdoing? What if his wife divorces him? Any of these actions might stir up powerful shame, and, to distract from that shame, he could set into motion reckless, impulsive reactions with dire consequences to the safety of our democracy and of the world. And given the immense power of his office, including nuclear weapons, those consequences could threaten our very survival.

Trump's erratic behavior is a hallmark of his mental illness, one that is putting all of us at risk. This is why so many mental health providers are finding it is their duty to warn the public before it's too late.

References

1. Wolff, M. (2018) *Fire and Fury: Inside the Trump White House*, New York, New York, Henry Holt.

2. Gartner, J D. *(2009) In Search of Bill Clinton: A Psychological Biography*, New York, NY. St Martin's Press.

Harry Segal graduated with a BA and MA in English Literature from Columbia (1990); He received a Ph.D. in English Literature Yale University and second doctorate in Clinical Psychology from the University of Michigan in 1990. He completed a post-doctoral fellowship in the Department of Psychiatry, University of Michigan Medical School, and joined the psychology faculty at Cornell in 1998. His work has focused on the clinical assessment of narrative and, more recently, models of the self. His publications include empirical studies on adolescent suicidality and depression, borderline personality disorder, and theoretical work on the creative process in fiction.

Chapter 2

DEFCON 2:

Nuclear Risk is Rising as Donald Trump Goes Downhill

John Gartner, Ph.D.

Surveys show that the majority of Americans believe that Donald Trump is psychologically unfit, and they worry about his control of nuclear weapons.[7] But what the public needs to understand is that Donald Trump's mental health is not static. It is deteriorating, and he will continue to get worse and worse for four reasons, all of which have great bearing on this issue of nuclear risk.

Because nuclear war is not *imminent* we have not yet reached the military's highest-rated DEFense readiness CONdition: DEFCON 1. But if we are indeed "locked and loaded," as President Trump has repeatedly tweeted, then arguably we have reached DEFCON 2: "Armed Forces ready to deploy and engage in less than 6 hours."[8] But regardless of what our current DEFCON rating might be, the forces of psychic gravity are pulling Trump, and thus all planet Earth, in only one direction—toward DEFCON 1.

Troubling evidence of cognitive decline is one reason for this dire prognosis. If you compare interviews Donald Trump did in the 1980s and 1990s to more recent interviews, the magnitude of the decline is striking.[9] In the past, he not only spoke in complete sentences, he spoke in polished paragraphs, using sophisticated vocabulary and complex thought. More recently, his vocabulary is thin. His reasoning is loose. He repeats himself over and over again. He's actually impaired in his ability to finish a sentence or a thought without derailing into some kind of irrelevancy.

For example, below is an interview Trump had with David Letterman in the 1980s:

"It's a shame what's happening. Japan, Saudi Arabia, Kuwait, they're all, everybody's taking advantage of the United States. People know that if certain

---

[7] Jeremy White, "Majority of Americans think Trump is 'unstable,' Fox News Poll shows." The Independent, September 1, 2017; Emily Guskin, "Most Americans don't Trust Trump with the "nuclear button," Washington Post, January 23, 2018.

[8] Wikipedia, "DEFCON" https://en.wikipedia.org/wiki/DEFCON

[9] Sharon Begley, "Trump used to be more articulate. What could explain the change?" STAT, May 23, 2017.

people are running a country, that it won't happen. I mean when you look at Japan not paying for the defense, we're defending Japan. We're losing billions and billions of dollars. We're fighting for AIDS help and for farmers and for this and that, and it's a shame. The Japanese folks who I respect greatly, but they're not treating us fairly. They're really not treating us fairly. Kuwait, Saudi Arabia, they're not paying us anything for the services we're rendering and I think it's a disgrace.

Contrast that with a recent public speech:

You know what irks me, look, having nuclear, my uncle was a great professor and scientist and engineer, Dr. John Trump at MIT. Good, good genes, very good genes, okay, very smart, Wharton School of Finance, very good, very smart. You know if you're a conservative Republican, if I were a liberal, if, like, okay. If I ran as a liberal Democrat, they would say I'm one of the smartest people anywhere in the world. It's true, but when you're a conservative Republican, they try, oh, do they do a number. That's why I always thought of went to Wharton, and was a good student. Went there, went there, did this, built a, you have to get my credentials all the time because we're in a little disadvantage, but you look at the nuclear, the thing.

A picture is worth a thousand words. This is a clear dramatic example of cognitive decline when comparing Trump to his own base line.

Seventy of us from Duty to Warn were part of a group that sent a letter to the president's former physician, Dr. Ronny Jackson imploring him to give Trump some kind of cognitive screening during his annual physical.[10] Indeed, Dr. Jackson gave the president the Montreal Cognitive Assessment, a screening tool for dementia. Trump passed, bragging that his performance supported his claim to be a "stable genius." "Let me tell you, those last ten questions are hard," Trump said, adding, "There aren't a lot of people that can do that."[11]

Actually, anyone who is older than 6 and not grossly demented can do that. It's important to be clear about what we do know and what we don't know about the president's cognitive health from this result.[12] We know Trump can identify a rhinoceros. He can draw a clock. He can repeat three number backward, which means that he is not frankly or grossly demented. It does not rule out predementia, the early stage of a disease such as Alzheimer's. So, while he's not ready for the nursing home, that doesn't mean he's ready for the White House.

---

[10] Jen Christensen, "Doctors want Donald Trump's head examined," CNN, January 16, 2018.

[11] Allan Smith, "Trump boasts at RNC dinner about his prefect score on mental health exam," Business Insider, February 2, 2018.

[12] Erich Fromm, The Heart of Man, New York: American Mental Health Foundation, 1964, 84; John Gartner, "What is Trump's psychological problem?" Huffington Post, June 9, 2016.

The simplest explanation is that we're seeing someone who is on the downward slope of cognitive decline. He hasn't reached the bottom yet, but Trump is rolling downhill, and gravity only works in one direction. While we don't know the biological etiology of this process, the most likely explanation would be the early stages of Alzheimer's, the disease his father was diagnosed with when he was fifteen years older than Trump is now. Most likely, his father was also in an undiagnosed state of predementia years before it was so grossly apparent that it warranted formal diagnosis.

What that means is that Trump is going to get worse in his ability to think, comprehend, speak, read, pay attention, delay his impulses, and make appropriate judgements. In a nuclear emergency, where seconds can count, someone with predementia is not going to have the cognitive capacity to process and evaluate information properly. He won't be able to think clearly even *inside the box*, much less *outside the box*, as Kennedy had to do to resolve the Cuban Missile Crisis. That's the first area in which we're more at risk because of Trump's deterioration.

When that proverbial 3 a.m. phone call comes, will Trump be able to fully comprehend what is happening? Will he be able to rapidly sift through and evaluate the veracity and the wisdom of the information and advice he receives? Will he be able to cognitively turn the problem upside down, see it from his adversary's point of view, and predict how that adversary might interpret and react to our actions? I think the answer is no.

The second source of Trump's psychological deterioration has to do with his personality disorder. Trump suffers from malignant narcissism, a diagnosis first introduced by Erich Fromm, a refugee from Nazi Germany, to explain the psychology of dictators. We all know Trump is narcissistic. He claims to know more about everything than anyone, merely from watching cable news, and only he can fix it. He requires constant praise and has empathy for no one but himself.

But malignant narcissism is far more toxic and dangerous than mere narcissistic personality disorder because it combines narcissism with three other severely pathological components: paranoia, sociopathy, and sadism. When combined, this perfect storm of psychopathology defines the "quintessence of evil," according to Fromm, the closest thing psychiatry has to describing a true human monster.[13]

Trump's many wacky conspiracy theories, as well as his demonization of the press, minorities, immigrants, and anyone who disagrees with him, are all signs of paranoia. In Trump's inner world, he is a perpetual victim of attacks by bad people who deserve to be counterattacked.

---

[13] Nicholas Gass, "Trump tries to clarify his 'I love war' comment", Politico, September 7, 2016.

The third component of malignant narcissism is sociopathy, a diagnosis that describes people who constantly lie, violate norms and laws, exploits other people, and show no remorse. They have no moral limits. Their moral code is the law of the jungle.

The fourth component of malignant narcissism is sadism. Trump has been a bully since he was a child. He takes gleeful pleasure in harming and humiliating other people. He is undoubtedly the most prolific cyberbully in history. I had the distasteful job writing an introduction to a book about his tweets and had to read hundreds and hundreds of his toxic vicious tweets, spewing contempt and hatred against all the "liars and losers" who have rubbed him the wrong way.[14]

Because Americans are optimistic, many shared the hope that once Donald Trump got the nomination or won the election, he was going to pivot and become more presidential. But Erich Fromm warned us to expect the exact opposite (as did I, in a little-read 2016 article in the *Huffington Post*). [15]When malignant narcissists gain power, it affirms and inflames their grandiosity. Intoxicated by drinking their own Kool-Aid, they feel omniscient and invincible. They also become more paranoid about naysayers who question or try to impede their great work. And because they are antisocial—now imbued with immense power, they are determined to ruthlessly destroy anyone who gets in their way. Indeed, their sadistic side takes satisfaction in doing so, in the most destructive and degrading way possible. Because Trump has no empathy or concern for anybody but himself, he will feel no remorse for the people he kills. In fact, because of his sadism, a part of him will savor the chaos, destruction, and enjoy subjugating those weaker than himself

Leaders of this type revel in dramatic acts of destruction that demonstrate and enhance their power. It's the rare malignant narcissistic head of state who does not start a war. "I've had a lot of wars of my own. I'm really good at war. I love war…, but only when we win,"[16] Trump told the audience at a campaign rally. We run the risk of starting a war, against our own interests, because Trump is attracted to the thrill of war and savors his imagined victory.

Now, when you take the natural trajectory of malignant narcissism, which is to deteriorate, and then add cognitive deterioration, you accelerate the process. When somebody begins to deteriorate cognitively, the disagreeable, unwanted, problematic features of the person's personality get worse. Specifically, when people are in a state of predementia, research shows that they become more

---

[14] Pam Belluck, "Personality changes may be early signs of dementia, experts say," New York Times, July 24, 2016.

[15] Erich Fromm, The Heart of Man, New York: American Mental Health Foundation, 1964, 84; John Gartner, "What is Trump's psychological problem?" Huffington Post, June 9, 2016.

[16] Nicholas Gass, "Trump tries to clarify his 'I love war' comment", Politico, September 7, 2016.

impulsive, egocentric, paranoid, aggressive, and irritable, and less conscientious.[17] Since these are all personality traits that Donald Trump had to begin with, it's a safe bet that he will continue to get progressively worse in these respects.

To make matters worse, Erich Fromm said malignant narcissists live on the boundary of sanity and insanity, and as they deteriorate, they become psychotic. If we look at what Donald Trump said in the first few days of his presidency, in contradiction to the easily verifiable and observable facts, he insisted that he had the biggest crowd size in history and that Barack Obama was bugging his offices—classic grandiose and paranoid delusions. So, we run the risk that Donald Trump may make a decision about nuclear weapons in a state of psychosis, under the influence of paranoid and grandiose delusions.

The third factor that increases our nuclear risk is the stress of the Mueller investigation. It's clearly driving Trump crazy. What we need to understand is that the Russia probe is pushing Trump toward pushing the nuclear button, because it would solve all of his problems. In a *Wag the Dog* scenario, it would distract from his wrongdoing and rally the country behind him as a wartime commander in chief (naysayers who decry his true motivations will be branded unpatriotic). Because the Mueller investigation seems to make him feel like a cornered animal, pushing the button will transform him from feeling like a hunted victim into an omnipotently destructive conqueror. As a general rule, malignantly narcissistic leaders crave war because it makes them feel powerful, redresses their grievances, and gives them the pleasure of destroying their enemies, both real and imagined.

Finally, the fourth reason that Trump is getting worse is that the human guardrails who were supposed to keep him from running America off the road, and over the cliff, are being purged one by one. One of the reassuring falsehoods America told itself about Trump was that he would surround himself with "the best people," or at the very least, rational, experienced adults, who would serve as brakes on his worst impulses. They would be the guiding hands of reason, restraint, and reality. But as I warned in 2016, these types of personalities are incorrigible. Trump cannot, and will not, be restrained. When his advisors try to direct Trump, "he spits the bit out of his mouth," said conservative commentator Tucker Carlson. "There is no one in this White House who can say no to this president," said Republican strategist Steve Schmidt. We are quickly descending to the point where no one in the White House would even dream of it, no matter how dangerous, aberrant, incoherent, or deranged his ideas and behavior become.

One by one, the adults are being extruded from the adult day care center, as Senator Bob Corker of Tennessee dubbed this White House. The "moderating

---

[17] Pam Belluck, "Personality changes may be early signs of dementia, experts say," New York Times, July 24, 2016.

forces eager to restrain the president from acting impulsively have resigned or been fired," wrote the *Washington Post*, leaving the lunatic to run the asylum, unfettered.[18] "Now he knows how the White House operates, and he'll operate it himself," said former Trump staffer Michael Caputo.

Trump is replacing those adult advisors, mostly with Fox News commentators with whom he has *chemistry*, who share his extreme ideology and his preference for aggressive action over thoughtful deliberation. "The president is replacing aides who have tended toward caution and consensus with figures far more likely to encourage his rash instincts and act upon them," wrote the *Post*. "The president is in an action mood and doesn't want to slow-roll things," said White House press secretary Sarah Huckabee Sanders "He's tired of the wait game," as if too much restraint has been the president's problem, instead of too little.[19]

Trump unbound, or "unhinged" as the *Washington Post* put it, is most frightening in the nuclear sphere, where a president has free rein to unilaterally launch at any time, for any reason, in just ten minutes. What would the adults do then? According to Gabe Sherman of *Vanity Fair*, Republican politicians, speaking in 2017, "imagined General Kelly and Secretary Mattis had conversations about, if Trump lunged for the nuclear football, what would they do? Would they tackle him? I mean literally, physically restrain him?"

But these new advisors seem more likely to egg him on to make a play with nuclear football than they would be to physically tackle him before he can touch it. Trump's new *war cabinet* includes people like John Bolton and Mike Pompeo, ideologically driven "über hawks" who are "known for agreeing with Trump." Like Trump, Bolton is known to be an aggressive, impulsive, and confrontational bully by temperament, as well as ideology. Bolton strongly pushed for the Iraq war when he served in the Bush administration, a decision he still defends. He has ripped up the Iran nuclear deal to (which Iran is adhering) and in the past he has advocated launching a first strike against Iran. And just a few weeks ago, Bolton published an op-ed in the *Wall Street Journal* making a case for a first strike against North Korea. "John Bolton was by far the most dangerous man we had in the entire eight years of the Bush Administration," former Bush ethics lawyer Richard Painter tweeted. "Hiring him as the president's top national security advisor is an invitation to war, perhaps nuclear war."[20]

---

[18] Phillip Rucker and Bob Costa, "Tired of the wait game: White House stabilizers gone, Trump calls his own shots," Washington Post, March 31, 2018.

[19] Phillip Rucker and Bob Costa, "Tired of the wait game: White House stabilizers gone, Trump calls his own shots," Washington Post, March 31, 2018.

[20] Ben Brimelow, "Former Bush Official says John Bolton was "by far the most dangerous man we had in the entire eight years," Business Insider, March 22, 2018.

These four sources of Trump's mental deterioration should send chills of terror up our spines. We are not in a static situation, but rather a deteriorating one, and as every day goes by, we are at greater risk of nuclear annihilation.

Trump might push the button because, at a moment of crisis, he lacks the cognitive capacity to objectively and critically analyze data, look at a standoff from an adversary's point of view (since he appears to have no empathy, even when he was cognitively intact), or fashion creative alternatives to war. He might push the button because at times he appears to be in a true psychotic state, operating under the influence of grandiose and paranoid delusions, believing either that he is an invincible conqueror or that his adversary is imminently planning to attack, when he is not. He might push the button because he is angry, impulsive, and determined to show the world who is boss by employing the ultimate power—as perverse as it sounds, Trump would revel in being the center of chaos and destruction. In a *Wag the Dog* scenario, he might push the button in a conscious cynical calculation that, while millions might die, war would distract from the Mueller investigation and rally his base behind him as commander in chief, and consolidate his power. He might push the button because he is egged on to do so by his über-hawk war cabinet, who may throw gasoline on Trump's fire when they should be throwing buckets of cold water. Most likely it, if doom awaits us, it will be some combination of these factors, coming together in a perfect storm, that will take us to DEFCON 1.

In my opinion, Donald Trump is sick, and he is getting worse. As he goes further downhill the risk of Armageddon skyrockets. The time to panic is now.

John Gartner, Ph.D. is a psychologist in practice in Baltimore. He taught in the Department of Psychiatry at Johns Hopkins University Medical School for 28 years. He is the author of *In Search of Bill Clinton: A Psychological Biography* and *The Hypomanic Edge: The link Between (a Little) Craziness and (a Lot of) Success in America.* He has also published in *Psychology Today, The Washington Post, Baltimore Sun, USA Today, NY Daily News, Politico, The New Republic, Huffington Post, Salon, Worth,* and *Talk.* He graduated from Princeton University (magna cum laude), received his Ph.D. from University of Massachusetts, and completed his postdoctoral fellowship at New York Hospital-Cornell University Medical Center He is the founder of Duty To Warn.

The "Baker" explosion, part of Operation Crossroads, a nuclear weapon test by the United States military at Bikini Atoll, Micronesia, on July 25, 1946. The wider, exterior cloud is actually just a condensation cloud caused by the Wilson chamber effect and was very brief. There was no classic mushroom cloud rising to the stratosphere, but inside the condensation cloud the top of the water geyser formed a mushroom-like head called the cauliflower, which fell back into the lagoon. The water released by the explosion was highly radioactive and contaminated many of the ships that were set up near it. Some were otherwise undamaged and sent to Hunter's Point in San Francisco, California, United States, for decontamination. Those which could not be decontaminated were sunk a number of miles off the coast of San Francisco.
Public domain, via Wikimedia Commons

Chapter 3

If President Trump Were Airman Trump, I Would Not Certify Him Psychologically Fit to Handle Nuclear Weapons

By Steven Buser, M.D.

As a psychiatrist in the Air Force, one of my duties was to evaluate military personnel to determine whether or not they were psychiatrically "fit for duty." This involved examining the individual to rule out the presence of any mental health condition that would preclude them from meeting the strenuous demands of military life. When I was asked to evaluate military members who worked with nuclear weapon systems, there was even more concern about the individual's fitness for duty, and the standard to which the person was held was higher. These personnel were certified under a higher level of psychological standards detailed in a program known as the *Nuclear Personnel Reliability Program*, or *PRP* for short. When I saw patients for a clinical evaluation who worked with nuclear weapons, they came with a large red "PRP" stamped on the front of their medical chart. This alerted me to the need for a higher level of psychological readiness associated with handling or being in the vicinity of these extremely dangerous weapons.

On one occasion a young man I evaluated was suffering severe depression accompanied by suicidal thoughts and admitted to hearing voices directing him to kill himself and others. I asked what his job was, and he replied, "Loading nuclear warheads onto Air Force bombers." My concern soared, and had it not been for the required PRP, he might have continued loading warheads while suffering psychotic symptoms. Instead, this young man was safely hospitalized and his access to nuclear weapons removed.

The Air Force provided me with very clear guidance about what was expected when conducting an evaluation of military members in the Nuclear PRP system. Department of Defense Directive 5210.42 states: "Only those personnel who have demonstrated the highest degree of individual reliability for allegiance, trustworthiness, conduct, behavior, and responsibility shall be allowed to perform duties associated with nuclear weapons, and they shall be continuously evaluated for adherence to PRP standards." [21]

---

[21] DODD 5210.42 Nuclear Weapon Personnel Reliability Program (PRP), May 25, 1993; Section D, Paragraph 3.

What if we were to apply the same psychological standards that every military member must meet in order to work with nuclear weapons to President Trump? Would our president be certified as "safe to be around nuclear weapons" under those PRP standards?

If President Trump were instead "Airman Trump" and stationed at the same Air Force base where I was stationed, and he was assigned to work with nuclear weapon systems, could I certify Airman Trump as safe around these weapons? Suppose I also had reliable outside information that Airman Trump was involved in sexually abusive behavior toward women, that he had regularly engaged in cyber-bullying on Twitter, that at times he appeared paranoid about being surveilled by others and often complained of being persecuted unjustly, and that he had a history of making highly distorted if not frankly untruthful statements. Would I allow Airman Trump to work around nuclear weapons? My definitive answer is ABSOLUTELY NOT, certainly not without further psychological evaluation. The great irony is that the entire nuclear chain of command, from the airman in the missile silo to the chairman of the Joint Chiefs of Staff are all held to the highest standards of psychological stability, while the president of the United States, the very person who holds his or her finger on the nuclear button, is not.

Suppose the president woke up tomorrow morning and decided to launch a nuclear attack against North Korea or any other adversary. Those missiles would be in the air within five minutes of issuing the order. Under our current system, such an order would be a fully lawful order that must be followed by all military personnel in the nuclear chain of command. Once those missiles are in the air, they cannot be recalled or aborted. The consequences of such an act could easily lead to a full-scale exchange of nuclear weapons from other nuclear armed countries. The destruction would not only have immediate catastrophic consequences for the recipient of president's attack but could have far-reaching planetary consequences. A large exchange of nuclear weapons would lead to what scientists call a "nuclear winter," blocking out the majority of light reaching the Earth's surface, leading to enormous famine and potentially the extinction of the human species. In light of the stakes, that is far too much power to vest with any single person, particularly in the absence of any psychological standards to which the president is held.

On January 13, 2018, at 8:07 a.m. every cell phone in the state of Hawaii rang out with a loud tone with the following message coursing across the screen in all caps:

"BALLISTIC MISSILE THREAT INBOUND TO HAWAII. SEEK IMMEDIATE SHELTER. THIS IS NOT A DRILL."

It was a full thirty-eight minutes before a second alert was sent out notifying people of the mistaken alarm. For over a half hour, one and a half million residents of Hawaii didn't know if they had just a few minutes to live and were left thinking about how they should spend their remaining moments on Earth—which loved ones they should reach out to, or where should they hide in vain hopes of surviving?

Fortunately, that emergency text message was a false alarm, and though it terrified many people, it was caught in time to avoid triggering any catastrophic retaliation. Trump was reputed to be on the golf course, unaware of the entire incident. But what if the next false alarm isn't caught so quickly? When seconds count, can we trust Donald Trump, at 3 a.m., to accurately assess the information he is being given? Can we trust his judgment, impulse control, or even his ability to distinguish reality from fantasy? Will he have the skills to finesse a delicate Cuban Missile Crisis type of situation?

But even in the absence of a sudden crisis, Trump represents a nuclear threat. He casually threatens the use of nuclear weapons while taunting Kim Jong-un as "little Rocket Man," almost daring him to launch. We live in a dangerous world, and it is reasonable to expect that the commander in chief to not add to the dangers unnecessarily. The president swears an oath to "preserve, protect and defend," which can reasonably be understood to include protecting our nation's inhabitants.

There are a number of safeguards we could put in place that would substantially improve the safety and security of the American people as well as the inhabitants of other nations.

There is currently a set of bills pending in Congress, House Bill 669 and Senate Bill 200, collectively known as the *Restricting First Use of Nuclear Weapons Act of 2017* sponsored by Representative Ted Lieu (D-California) and Senator Edward Markey, (D-Massachusetts). The bill would prohibit any president from launching a first-strike nuclear attack without the consent of Congress. The president would still be able to order a counterattack without congressional consent if another country attacked us first with nuclear weapons, but it would prevent the president from beginning a nuclear war without congressional consent. This bill would effectively be like placing a *safety* on our nuclear guns. It is hard to imagine what reasons either political party could invoke for opposing legislation that would prevent this president or any president from acting hastily in ways that could begin an unprovoked nuclear war. This bill would introduce a crucial safeguard for our nuclear forces.

A second straightforward reform that would also increase our security involves the current two-person authentication system that is in place for most of our nuclear command and control systems. If a military member wishes to take a significant action on a nuclear weapon such as repairing, loading, arming, or launching a nuclear weapon, there is a requirement that at least two personnel execute that action. This is true for all actions with nuclear weapons except for one—the decision of a president to order a nuclear attack. Solely on a president's authority a planet-ending attack can be launched. This is a situation that clearly calls for a more stringent confirmation. Why would we not want one more person confirming a decision that has the potential to end civilization? The ranks of those serving as a second confirmation could be filled by a cabinet-level official like the attorney general or the secretary of state or even a federal judge. It would be someone to say "Yes, Mr. President, I agree that a nuclear attack is a reasonable decision." The gravity of this action is too heavy and too dangerous for any one person to bear. The world's fate should not be taken so lightly.

The third common-sense initiative to improve the safety of the American people is House Bill 1987 also known as the *Oversight Commission on Presidential Capacity Act*. This bill is sponsored by Representative Jamie Raskin (D-Maryland). It provides a means by which the Congress could obtain an evaluation of a president who shows substantial signs of medical, psychological, or cognitive difficulties. Clearly, it would be essential to ensure any such examination undertaken remained strictly nonpartisan and would most likely require multiple evaluators to reach a consensus. Regardless of the details of how such an examination would be conducted, there is little justification for ignoring strong signs of impairment should they appear. This would provide another safeguard against a dangerous decision being undertaken by an impaired president.

One potential source of impairment is organic cognitive decline. The topic of presidential fitness and cognitive decline has always been a legitimate issue, but as life expectancy rose during the last century and the complexities of the job increased, this issue became profoundly important. For the executive branch to function effectively and without exposing the American people to undue danger, the president must possess stable mental faculties without deficits. In a 1994 article titled *Presidential Disability and the Twenty-fifth Amendment: A President's Perspective*, former President Jimmy Carter warned that our country is in "continuing danger" from the possibility that a president could become disabled "particularly by a neurological illness."[22] It is widely believed that President Reagan began to show signs of cognitive decline during his last term. Reagan's son claimed in his memoir, *My Father at 100*[23], that there was something different with President Reagan by the third year of his first term. The possibility of a president's cognitive decline presents a substantial risk to U.S. security.

The office of the presidency demands an occupant with the highest degree of mental reliability and trustworthiness. The American electorate may not always choose a leader who sufficiently carries these qualities. It is vital that we have adequate psychological safeguards and standards in place to add a measure of security to our nuclear command and control systems. The American people and indeed the world deserve the reassurance that these safeguards would provide.

Adequate standards and safeguards to protect the American people from a president whose mental capacities have deteriorated are dangerously lacking. The complex daily demands of running this country make this a vitally important issue, but in the event of a nuclear crisis when the stakes are the highest, our current lack of adequate standards and safeguards could have catastrophic consequences. As it now stands, the one man who can unilaterally order a nuclear strike couldn't pass the PRP standard of psychological fitness. This glaring oversight must not be ignored.

Steven Buser, M.D. trained in medicine at Duke University and served 12 years as a physician in the U.S. Air Force. He is a graduate of a two-year Clinical Training Program at the C.G. Jung Institute of Chicago and is the co-founder of the Asheville Jung Center. He has worked for over 20 years in private practice psychiatry. He currently works in the field of addiction medicine and serves as Publisher of Chiron Publications.

---

[22] Jimmy Carter, "Presidential Disability and the Twenty-fifth Amendment: A President's Perspective," JAMA, 1994; 272(21):1968; doi:10.1001/jama.1994.03520210082027.

[23] Ron Reagan, My Father at 100: A Memoir. Viking, 2011.

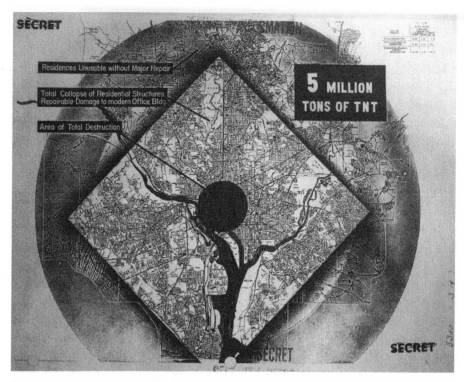

Secret map used to explain to the members of the Congressional Joint Committee on Atomic Energy (JCAE) the effects of the newest weapon developed by the United States, the hydrogen bomb, by superimposing the effects on a map of Washington, D.C. *National Archives*

Chapter 4

If Trump Were a Policeman I Would Have to Take Away His Gun

By David Reiss, M.D.

I've performed thousands of evaluations in my career as a psychiatrist. If I were being asked to evaluate Trump's fitness for duty as commander in chief there are behaviors that would trouble me.

After many months of sabre rattling marked by juvenile name calling and implicit threats of nuclear war, President Donald Trump *popped in* to the White House press briefing room to announce he would have a face-to-face summit with the North Korean dictator. There was no description provided of any thought process, rationale, new developments, or governmental or political process that led to the dramatic reversal of Trump's previous statement that talks with North Korea would be futile. In fact, just hours before Trump's announcement, Secretary of State Rex Tillerson had said that such talks were "unrealistic." Further, within 24 hours, the administration "walked back" Trump's announcement, suggesting that a summit would not occur until certain conditions were met by North Korea—conditions that have virtually no chance of being accepted. Yet in subsequent days, there was the implication that a meeting would occur—with no further explication of any specific conditions. The only explanation for this objectively bizarre turn of events is impressionistic thinking: at times, it *feels right* to Trump for him to threaten North Korea; on this particular day, it met Trump's emotional needs to impulsively announce a summit with no planning or forethought. Of course, this cannot be compared in any manner to Nixon's *surprise* announcement of his iconic visit to China—which was a very carefully planned diplomatic initiative, with Secretary of State Henry Kissinger having held secret meetings with Chinese representatives in preparation for the "surprise" announcement.

Regardless of what you may think about the wisdom of this hastily agreed to summit, as someone with thirty years of experience performing fitness for duty evaluations, what strikes me as alarming is not the policy, but the thinking process, or lack thereof, behind it.

That's a big problem

> *Every Fitness-for-Duty evaluation involves assessing the <u>problem-solving</u> ability of the person, relevant to specific job duties; which includes gaining an understanding of the <u>thought processes</u> that are used in the process of problem-solving.*

In performing a Fitness-for-Duty Examination, the bottom line of what I am charged to determine is whether or not psychiatric impairment interferes with the ability of the person being evaluated to function safely and effectively at their assigned duties. One of the most important aspects of the examination is the evaluation of the person's thought processes: the ability of the person to think logically and rationally; the ability of the person to evaluate situations objectively; and the ability of the person to problem-solve in a manner appropriate to the situation. To use an example most relevant to the question of the Fitness-for-Duty of the POTUS: when I evaluate a law enforcement officer who has fired a weapon, I ask: "What was going through your mind during the incident? What was your thought process from the time you perceived that there was a danger or risk to the time you fired your weapon? During that time, what did you think about, or did you respond rather *automatically*? What emotions may you have experienced? What alternatives did you consider? What was your goal? What risks did you consider? At what point, did you determine, consciously or *automatically* that firing your weapon was necessary? If you find yourself in a similar situation again, would you act in the same manner or differently? Would you be more or less prone to fire your weapon? Has this incident changed or impacted how you perceive your role and your responsibilities?"

Trump's public statements have provided little, if any, transparency to his inner thought processes. Extremely frequently and most typically, Trump will begin with a statement regarding his perception of a situation (a perception that may or may not contain verifiably false information) and then proceed to providing a conclusion or an opinion regarding the *necessary* course of action, with little verbalization of the logical analysis or thought processes that led from point A to point B.

Often, rather than providing any information as to alternatives that he considered and reasons for accepting or rejecting those alternatives, any *explanation* of Trump's process of problem solving will be nothing more than a (frequently rambling) discourse regarding his feelings, his emotions, and his (frequently grandiose) perceptions of his abilities. Perhaps Trump has a logical internal problem-solving thought process—if so, he has not revealed that process; perhaps Trump's conclusions are impulsive responses rather than well-considered analyses of alternatives. Perhaps Trump has little or no ability to perform problem solving or an evaluation of options other than by relying upon *impressionistic* (i.e., emotion-based) thinking.

One possible explanation for this apparent paucity of thought is a neurological impairment, and one would want to rule out organic cognitive decline.

Older subjects require additional attention to the possibility of age-related cognitive issues. During a Fitness-for-Duty Examination (as well as during any general psychiatric or medical examination for any reason), there should be routine screening of every person over 65 years of age regarding their cognitive functioning. Screening is often possible while spending over an hour conversing with a patient while taking a comprehensive history of both recent and past events. The interview may reveal concerns that suggest that a formal screening protocol should be employed. However, if there is detection of any indications or suggestions of even mild cognitive impairment, especially for persons in positions of significant responsibility for the welfare of others, a referral for a full battery of neuro-psychological testing in order to definitively determine the person's level of functioning and level of impairment should be completed. A full battery of neuro-psychological testing is also indicated if there are available reports of significant concern from other involved parties (family, other medical personnel, supervisors, coworkers, etc.)

In that regard, there is public information that, in and of itself, suggests the need for a comprehensive neuropsychological evaluation of Donald Trump:

1. There are obvious differences between Donald Trump's recent public presentations and those recorded in the past, specifically regarding his speech pattern, language content, vocabulary, tendency toward repetitiveness, frequency of self-references, ability to stay on topic, etc.

2. There have been public observations made and concerns expressed regarding Donald Trump's cognitive status by multiple people who have personally known him and via observations recorded in the media. Of course, the significance of those observations may be distorted due to lack of context, and/or benign or malicious motivation of the reporting party, etc.

Thus, those observations are <u>not</u> at all diagnostic, but they <u>do</u> serve as data that leads to the conclusion that a comprehensive evaluation is indicated—to determine <u>whether</u> those observations are of neuro-psychological significance. Clinically, such reports and observations essentially carry the weight of concerns expressed about a patient that might be expressed to a physician by family members; concerns that would need to be seriously <u>considered</u> by the evaluating physician.

Any positive findings or (reliable) history regarding possible cognitive impairment requires a referral for formal neurological and neuro-psychological testing, including a complete physical examination, appropriate laboratory data, formal neurological evaluation, an MRI of the brain and comprehensive neuropsychological testing to evaluate emotional state, cognitive impairment, and personality structure—and if at all possible, comparison of the results of those procedures to previous baseline data.

Thus, based on what we know from the public record, any competent Fitness-for-Duty Evaluation would include a full neuro-psychological battery of tests.

The Case of Donald J. Trump:

Of extreme significance in the case of Donald Trump, at least as evidenced by his public statements, speeches, interviews, tweeting, etc., is that Trump appears to be a person who relies very heavily (if not almost exclusively) upon what is often referred to as *impressionistic thinking.*

Impressionistic thinking is the internal process of arriving at conclusions and decisions regarding practical and behavioral responses to events and circumstances based upon the person's emotional mind-set and emotional needs of the moment, as opposed to objectively considering all relevant data and facts in a logical, rational, and consistent manner.

We are all susceptible to impressionistic thinking. Developmentally, before we have full command of language and analytical thought processes, we rely heavily upon our internal emotions and observations of the emotional expressions of others to assess and respond to different situations. Neuro-psychological studies indicate that separate areas of the brain process different types of information. In general, (in most right-handed people), logical, cognitive analysis takes place largely in the left brain while emotionally driven reactions and responses emerge largely from right-brain functioning. Complex neurological processes integrate the totality of information, but learning must occur for this to occur optimally.

As a person matures, he or she (hopefully) learns to put emotional responses (i.e., impressionistic, emotional, right-brain responses) into appropriate context. This does not require that emotions should be ignored, but rather the task is to gain an understanding of the nature and fallibility of emotions and emotionally driven conclusions and decisions, and to be able to modify emotionally driven responses based upon a logical and rational assessment of objective data. It is relatively easy for any person to fall back into impressionistic thinking in stressful situations.

Maturity and sound judgment require that decisions and behaviors take into account emotions but are not ruled by emotional needs or preferences. A mature person steps back and evaluates their ideas and conclusions to determine if they are consistent with fact and logic and realizes that if that is not the case, further analysis and reconsideration is in order.

There is a close relationship between narcissistic pathology and reliance upon impressionistic thinking— but I will defer that discussion to others, as it goes beyond the issue of fitness-for-duty being addressed in this chapter.

However, it must be recognized that there can be a malignant interaction between tendencies toward impressionistic thinking and any physiological or neurological deterioration of cognitive functioning (whatever the cause, reversible or degenerative).

That is, in a person who already relies heavily upon impressionistic thinking, any physiologically/neurologically based deterioration of cognitive processes exponentially amplifies the risk of responding to problems with illogical or irrational responses, especially during stressful situations. If Trump has organically based cognitive decline, we would expect no improvement on this front, and in fact we should expect further deterioration.

At least based upon Trump's public statements and behaviors, since the time of his announcement of his candidacy and the Republican debates: 1) there is no public evidence of any improvement of problem-solving or decision-making abilities; 2) there has been no change in the absence of transparency to logical problem-solving thought processes; while, 3) there is considerable suggestion of a continuation, if not deterioration, of Trump's ability to verbalize and exhibit the capacity for sound, logical and consistent problem solving and decision making.

As I write this, without having performed any evaluation of Donald Trump, clinical knowledge leads to the conclusion that the blatant factual inaccuracies and illogical/irrational arguments presented by Trump may represent intentional lying, ignorance, results of dyslexia, consequences of cognitive impairment (acute or acquired; reversible or degenerative), incipient or emerging psychotic/paranoid pathology, and/or pathological reliance upon impressionistic thinking.

Even if I had personally interviewed Donald Trump, I can say with near certainty that I would not provide an opinion regarding which of the potential *differential diagnoses* are applicable without first ordering and reviewing comprehensive medical, neurological, and neuro-psychological consultations and testing.

But I can also definitively report: If Donald Trump were a police officer who had been referred to me for a Fitness-for-Duty evaluation, and the information I had available included public observations questioning the cognitive competence of the officer; and that the officer had offered written descriptions of the events that occurred including as many inaccuracies as are present in Trump's pronouncements; and especially if within the interview, I observed apparent impressionistic thought processes as discussed above, my recommendation would be removal of the officer from any position of responsibility pending a complete evaluation.

That is, I would advise that pending a complete neuropsychiatric evaluation, it should be considered likely and "within reasonable medical probability" that without intervention or treatment, 1) Trump's embrace of inaccurate/irrational standpoints will not improve; and, 2) it is more likely than not that under additional stress, the level of dysfunction will increase.

This is not to say that it can be predicted or assumed that every action taken by Trump will be inappropriate or dangerous. Failing a Fitness-for-Duty evaluation indicates that within reasonable medical probability the risks of inappropriate or dangerous behavior are too high to certify the person to return to their normal duties. It is not a prediction that a police officer will act inappropriately; it is a finding, on a psychiatric basis, of an unacceptable risk of inappropriate behavior. For example, considering the situation described above, I certainly cannot predict that Trump's gambit regarding North Korea will fail (for the sake of the country and the world, I hope that is not the case). Nonetheless, the data available strongly suggest that—pending additional evaluation—the risk of a dangerous outcome due to distorted thought processes is unacceptable.

The recommendations discussed above would be in reference to withholding from duty single officer possessing one handgun. Obviously, an impaired and armed law enforcement officer could cause significant risk to the safety of many others. However, regarding President Donald Trump, we are referring to the most powerful man in the world who has direct and immediate access to the nuclear codes, and who could pose a threat to all of humanity—and yet based upon the public data currently available, pending comprehensive neurological and neuro-psychological consultations and testing, particularly regarding his abilities to think logically and to safely and rationally execute problem solving tasks, Donald Trump would not pass a psychiatric Fitness-for-Duty examination to be released to return to duty due to an unacceptable risk of dangerous behavior due to psychiatric im-pairment.

David M. Reiss, M.D. obtained a B.S. degree in Chemical Engineering and his M.D. from Northwestern University, followed by a psychiatric residency at U.C. San Diego. For over 30 years, he has maintained a private practice in California performing medical-legal evaluations and providing psychotherapeutic and psychopharmacological treatment. Dr. Reiss has been a psychiatric hospital Medical Director and continues to be an attending psychiatrist at hospitals in the New York/New England area. Dr. Reiss has worked with the media for 10 years, writing and being interviewed many times regarding issues directly and indirectly related to mental health and psychosocial/political phenomena.

Chapter 5

If Trump was entering the Military, he would not receive a Security Clearance

By *Maj. Gen. (retired) William L. Enyart*

A young lieutenant colonel who nearly always can be seen walking one step behind President Trump is responsible for carrying the *football*—the black briefcase containing the nuclear launch codes. It is this soldier's sworn duty to follow a lawful order should his commander in chief intend to launch any or all of our nuclear weapons. The president of the United States, who is the constitutionally named commander in chief, is the ultimate superior officer.

Civilian control of the military enjoys a long tradition in our country and is enshrined by the language of Article II, Section 2 of the United States Constitution. Although all but fifteen of our presidents from George Washington to Donald Trump have served in the military, some rising to the rank of general, the concept of civilian control of the military is a preeminent symbol of our democracy.

As a retired general, former legislator, and one who has taken that constitutional oath of office three times, I am extremely concerned about whether our nation can continue to rely on the concept of civilian control of the military. Serious discussions are taking place in public and behind closed doors about the emotional and mental stability of our current commander in chief. Were it not for the fact that I am now retired from the military, Articles 88 and 89 of the Uniform Code of Military Justice would forbid me from the use of critical language or actions toward the president. The truth of such statements provides no defense for a soldier who fails to comply with these articles. This is why you will not hear criticism from those who currently serve in uniform. However, I am retired and I have regained my First Amendment rights of freedom of speech.

President Trump has shown a remarkable lack of judgment. He has attacked the bravery of a fellow Republican, Senator John McCain who is a retired Navy aviator and former prisoner of war. He has questioned the patriotism of a Gold Star family Khizr and Ghazala Khan and he has threatened North Korea with nuclear destruction, to name but a few. Such conduct shows that he lacks self-control and he is not circumspect even when it comes to complicated geopolitical issues. Our nation faces a significant threat based on the flaws displayed by Mr. Trump.

During the course of my civilian legal career while serving in the Illinois National Guard, I represented several clients who were denied security clearances before the judges of the Defense Office of Hearings and Appeals. Let me assure you that based on Mr. Trump's record of bankruptcies, refusals to pay lawful debts, multiple actual or very probable adulterous relationships, a tangle of Russian business activities and associates that lacks transparency, President Trump would most certainly be denied a security clearance. The great irony that President Trump has underscored is that the commander in chief, who is not subject to the UCMJ, may behave in a manner unbecoming of an officer and gentleman and that conduct is not constrained by the same expectations that would be applied to anyone in the military, or, for that matter, anyone seeking or holding a security clearance.

One of the purposes of the clearance process is to ensure that no foreign power has material that could be used to blackmail anyone. Among the allegations that found their way into the infamous "Steele dossier," the most explosive, shocking, and controversial were those related to potential sexual "kompromat" the Russians may have on Mr. Trump. The charges seem so bizarre and tawdry that, just on the face of it, they seem like a "hit job" to many. However, those of us who have had to deal with the Russians can tell you that obtaining and using sexual "kompromat" is standard operating procedure for the Russians, and they are very good at it.

As a case in point, I offer my own experience while participating in military exercises in Kiev, Ukraine, in 2005. In July of that year, freedom was in the air, and Maidan Square thronged with happy young people celebrating the broken shackles of the former Soviet Union. Although the U.S. was at war in the Middle East, the threat of military conflict in Central and Eastern Europe seemed a thing of the past. With the Soviet Union dissolved, the Warsaw Pact had collapsed, and NATO was absorbing Poland, Lithuania and many of our former Warsaw Pact enemies. Even Ukraine, the former bread basket of the Soviet Union, was on track to eventually join NATO. There appeared to be no danger of war in Central and Eastern Europe.

I was one of fifteen officers and noncommissioned officers, experts in our fields, overseeing war games intended to validate the Ukrainian War College, change the Ukrainians from their Soviet-era mindset, and test how far divorced the Soviet-trained senior military staff had become from Russia. The exercise involved 250 soldiers from twenty-two NATO nations. The Russians were furious. The Moscow evening news featured a California Army National Guard colonel commanding the exercise on the front page. The news report alleged that NATO was preparing for war against the motherland. I was one of two other colonels charged with the operational aspects of the exercise. Unbeknownst to my fellow colonels, I had just been nominated for promotion to general. The news of this nomination, like all nominations to the rank of general, was a closely guarded secret.

Unlike a field exercise, a staff exercise like the one we conducted in the summer of 2005 typically begins by 7 a.m. and ends by 5 p.m.; this left us time in the evenings to enjoy Kiev. Like other central European cities, Kiev is beautiful in the summer despite the crowded buses belching foul-smelling diesel fumes. We were cautioned to always travel in pairs, to refrain from intoxication, and to avoid fraternizing with locals of the opposite sex. We were reminded that we were an emblem of America and our conduct should not tarnish our country's image.

I partnered with my deputy commander, Lt. Col. Byron von Hoff, a career National Guardsman who was 55, a year older than I. He was at the end of his career and had nothing to lose by telling the truth, the kind of qualities that often make for the best officers in the military. Byron, who'd been drafted 21st by the New York Mets in the 1966 professional baseball draft, is one of those in the best officer category. His pitching career ended after an injury in his fourth year in the minors. His injury didn't prevent his full-time Guard career, which began shortly after he left professional baseball.

Byron (at six feet three inches, 210 pounds, graying hair, glasses and vaguely high school coach appearance) and I (at five-foot-eight, 165 pounds, and with the posture of a former high school football linebacker turned military officer) made a contrasting pair as we strolled through the throngs of young people enjoying the summer evenings. The cafes were full. The summer evening light lasted late in the northern latitudes of Eastern Europe. It seemed that no one in Kiev, other than us, could possibly be older than 25.

We weren't the only Americans in Kiev. There was a marriage market at our hotel. A ballroom at the hotel filled with small tables and at each a young, usually attractive, woman lured an assortment of American men. It cost $200 to get in. If you found one you liked, you could take her home with a guarantee that she'd stay married to you for at least three years. The cost? A few thousand dollars to the marriage brokers and the new wife's travel expenses. The men? Late middle-aged Americans with enough money to buy a new bride every few years.

Byron and I quickly fell into the habit of changing out of our NATO forest pattern BDU's (battle dress uniforms) after duty and strolling down Khreshchatyk, the main boulevard, eventually dining in one of the street-side, open-air cafes.

One evening while we dined at a restaurant I pointed out two very attractive young women sitting just behind us. As we rose to leave, Byron excused himself to go to the bathroom, and I told him I would meet him at the entrance gate. As I waited, I was startled by the approach of one of the women who'd been seated near our table; she was a striking blonde whose features reminded me of a movie star.

"What are you doing?" she asked in nearly perfect English.

"Waiting for my friend," I replied.

"What are you doing then?" she asked.

"Going back to my hotel."

"May I come with you?"

"No!" I replied in a polite but unequivocal manner.

"Why not?"

"I'm married."

"So?" she pressed on.

I supposed she was a prostitute and probably an expensive one at that. Thirty years earlier during the Vietnam War, when I was a young airman, a girl came darting out of an alley and propositioned me; it was the only other time in my career this had happened. I tried to put an end to the exchange with the lovely Eastern European woman.

"No. You are very beautiful, but you are not coming to my hotel," I said. She cast a look of disbelief that I was rejecting her offer, smiled, and walked away. Seconds later Byron reappeared.

"You're not going to believe what just happened," I said, and recounted my short exchange with the young Eastern European woman.

Two nights later, at the same café, two young women seated at the same table behind Byron and me made a similar approach after we paid our bill. As we made our way down the sidewalk, one of the women asked, "Would you like to go discoing with us?"

"No, thank you," I replied.

"Why not? It will be fun."

"We're married."

"So?"

"You are quite pretty, but we can't do that," I said, and the young women walked off disappointedly. Byron and I chuckled as we ambled back to our hotel imagining that we had become James Bond-like figures.

About five days later, I was alone in the elevator heading to my eleventh-floor room when the elevator stopped and the door opened. I automatically stepped out and saw two wide-eyed, white-shirted, neck-tied men who had the distinct appearance of intelligence officers. I scanned to my right and saw a roomful of TV monitors with similarly dressed men sitting at consoles, wearing earphones, and watching monitors conducting surveillance.

Without turning, I stepped back onto the elevator, saying, "Oops, sorry, wrong floor," and resumed my journey to my floor. That was the only time the elevator stopped on that floor during my stay in Kiev.

Three days later I was homeward bound, our mission a great success, particularly since no soldiers had gotten drunk or gotten into trouble, and our forces had created no international incidents by virtue of our conduct.

More than a decade later, I recounted this to a couple of FBI counter-intelligence agents. The agents, after I regaled them with the story, told me: "That's the honeypot trap. They lure you into a compromising situation. Get you on video and blackmail you. They then own you." I then realized the women weren't prostitutes but almost certainly Russian spies.

I went on to be promoted to brigadier general (one-star), then major general (two-star), and after retirement was elected to Congress, where I served on the House Armed Services Committee. About a year after leaving Congress I was invited to give closing remarks at a symposium on the future of Iraq being held in Washington DC and sponsored by a nonprofit think tank. Following my closing presentation and a spate of television interviews, a handsome young man approached me, handed me his business card, and extended an invitation to meet him for coffee. He explained that his government understood how influential think tanks, like the one I had just addressed, could be in forging US foreign policy. With just the right amount of flattery, he let me know he wanted to explore my thoughts on foreign policy. His business card showed the charming young man's job was that of deputy military attaché at the Russian embassy.

I declined to meet him, but I did jot down my recollections of the conversation. Soon after that encounter I reached out to the FBI counterintelligence agents and learned about the honeypot trap. I was left wondering if my refusal of two very attractive young women a decade earlier had led the Russians to see if the offer of a charming, handsome young man might prove more successful.

Did the Russians know that I was on track for promotion to general soon after I returned from Kiev in 2005, or do Russian operatives simply cast a wide net as an investment in the future of various American personnel who may rise to positions of power and influence?

Was Mr. Trump ever the target of a honeypot trap? Knowing the Russians, it would be unlikely if they hadn't dangled women in front of Trump when he visited Russia and Eastern Europe. Knowing Trump's well-publicized sexual behavior, it seems unlikely that he could refuse such a tantalizing offer. My personal experience combined with a long civilian career in law lead me to conclude that the allegations in the Steele dossier, including the charges of potential sexual kompromat are not as improbable as they might seem. Perhaps in time those allegations will be confirmed, but if Donald Trump were undergoing a standard security clearance investigation, any credible suspicion of such kompromat would be enough to sink his application. Period.

The fact that President Trump is now privy to our nation's greatest secrets, not to mention that he has command and control of our nuclear arsenal, is a repudiation of the due process our lowest-ranking military members and federal employees must undergo to obtain and hold onto a security clearance. It is an affront to countless military and civilian personnel who have undergone the extreme vetting required to receive promotions in military service and those who have been granted Top Secret clearance that a man who would be unable to get past the initial security screening sits as the commander in chief of our great nation.

Maj. Gen. (retired) William L. Enyart served as an enlisted airman during the Vietnam War and subsequently in the Army National Guard for nearly thirty years. He retired from the military in 2012 as the commander of the 10,000 soldiers and 3,000 airmen of the Illinois National Guard, whereupon he was elected by the voters of southern Illinois's 12th Congressional District to serve in the 113th Congress, where he served on the House Armed Services Committee. He left Congress in 2015. He is an alumnus of the Harvard University Kennedy School of Government U.S. Russia Relations Senior Executive Course, the George Marshall Center Counterterrorism Senior Executive Program, the U.S. Army War College, Southern Illinois University School of Law and Southern Illinois University-Edwardsville. Now in private life, he is an attorney in private practice.

Images from the United States Bombing Survey, 1945

United States Strategic Bombing Survey, 1945
What do you do after destroying two heavily populated cities in Japan? You commission a study of course. This survey of the effects of the nuclear bombs detonated in Hiroshima and Nagasaki spell out in blunt, though somewhat uninformed fashion, what can be expected from an atomic bomb. *Harry S. Truman Library & Museum*

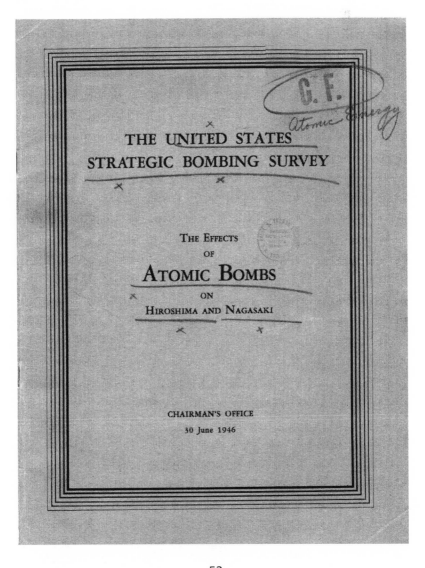

THE UNITED STATES
STRATEGIC BOMBING SURVEY

THE EFFECTS
OF
ATOMIC BOMBS
ON
HIROSHIMA AND NAGASAKI

CHAIRMAN'S OFFICE
30 June 1946

I. INTRODUCTION

The available facts about the power of the atomic bomb as a military weapon lie in the story of what it did at Hiroshima and Nagasaki. Many of these facts have been published, in official and unofficial form, but mingled with distortions or errors. The United States Strategic Bombing Survey, therefore, in partial fulfillment of the mission for which it was established, has put together in these pages a fairly full account of just what the atomic bombs did at Hiroshima and Nagasaki. Together with an explanation of how the bomb achieved these effects, this report states the extent and nature of the damage, the casualties, and the political repercussions from the two attacks. The basis is the observation, measurement, and analysis of the Survey's investigators. The conjecture that is necessary for understanding of complex phenomena and for applying the findings to the problems of defense of the United States is clearly labelled.

When the atomic bombs fell, the United States Strategic Bombing Survey was completing a study of the effects of strategic bombing on Germany's ability and will to resist. A similar study of the effects of strategic bombing on Japan was being planned. The news of the dropping of the atomic bomb gave a new urgency to this project, for a study of the air war against Japan clearly involved new weapons and new possibilities of concentration of attack that might qualify or even change the conclusions and recommendations of the Survey as to the effectiveness of air power. The directors of the Survey, therefore, decided to exam-

ine exhaustively the effects of the atomic bombs, in order that the full impact on Japan and the implications of their results could be confidently analyzed. Teams of experts were selected to study the scenes of the bombings from the special points of emphasis of physical damage, civilian defense, morale, casualties, community life, utilities and transportation, various industries, and the general economic and political repercussions. In all, more than 110 men—engineers, architects, fire experts, economists, doctors, photographers, draftsmen—participated in the field study at each city, over a period of 10 weeks from October to December, 1945. Their detailed studies are now being published.

In addition, close liaison was maintained with other investigating units. Cooperation was received from, and extended to, the following groups:

The Joint Commission for the Investigation of the Atomic Bomb in Japan.
The British Mission to Japan.
The Naval Technical Mission to Japan.

Special acknowledgment is due to the medical groups of the Joint Commission, whose data and findings have been generously made available to the Survey. On medical aspects of the bombings, the Joint Commission was the chief fact-finding group; it will present its definitive report in the near future. In other fields, however—particularly the study of physical damage and the impact on community life—the Survey collected its own data and is the primary source.

TABLE OF CONTENTS

	Page
I. INTRODUCTION	1
II. THE EFFECTS OF THE ATOMIC BOMBINGS	3
A. The attacks and damage	3
1. The attacks	3
2. Hiroshima	5
3. Nagasaki	9
B. General effects	15
1. Casualties	15
Flash burns	17
Other injuries	17
Radiation disease	18
2. Morale	20
3. The Japanese decision to surrender	22
III. HOW THE ATOMIC BOMB WORKS	24
A. The nature of the explosion	24
B. Heat	25
C. Radiation	25
D. Blast	28
E. The atomic bomb compared with other weapons	33
IV. SIGNPOSTS	36
A. The danger	36
B. What we can do about it	38
1. Shelters	38
2. Decentralization	41
3. Civilian defense	41
4. Active defense	43
5. Conclusion	43

HIROSHIMA–from the top of the Red Cross Hospital looking northwest.

NAGASAKI… "like a graveyard with not a tombstone standing…" Nagasaki Prefecture Report.

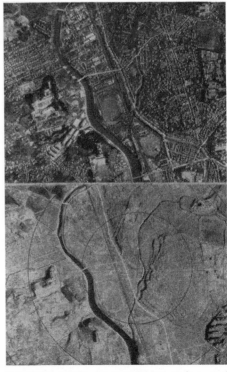

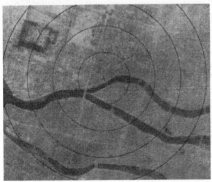

HIROSHIMA before and after bombing. Area around ground zero. 1,000 foot circles.
A. A. F. Photos

GROUND ZERO AT NAGASAKI–Before and after bombing.
A.A.

PROTECTION AGAINST RADIANT HEAT. This patient (photographed by Japanese 2 October 1943) was about 6,500 feet from ground zero when the rays struck him from the left. His cap was sufficient to protect the top of his head against flash burns.

Chapter 6

A Man with No Humanity
Has the Power to Destroy Mankind

By Lance Dodes, M.D.

The power to kill millions of people, nearly all of whom would be innocent civilians, by starting a nuclear war must rest with a person who possesses certain essential personality characteristics. These characteristics are not rare. Indeed, they are basic human emotional capacities present in the great majority of people. Unfortunately, Donald Trump possesses none of them. Far from normality, Mr. Trump seems to meet every single criterion of the official *Diagnostic and Statistical Manual of Psychiatric Disorders* (the *DSM*, 5th edition) for the diagnosis of "Antisocial Personality Disorder" (refs: *DSM and Dangerous Case book*). This severe disorder may also be described by the common terms *sociopath* or *psychopath*. It refers to a history of failure to conform to social norms, deceitfulness, impulsivity, pathological aggression, reckless disregard for the safety of others, irresponsibility, and lack of remorse. Beyond this, Mr. Trump has a dangerous degree of instability, with a well-known history of rage reactions and denial of reality when it differs from his wishes. Under the stress of reality not meeting his wishes, his inability to tolerate reality slides into what appears to be psychosis, as in the many instances of his insistence upon imaginary events even long after they are shown to be absolutely false. This combination of severe sociopathic traits coupled with inability to maintain a consistent view of reality makes Mr. Trump unqualified and incompetent to have power to control weaponry of any sort.

In the following, I consider each essential attribute required for safety in controlling weapons of mass destruction.

1. Stability

There must be an ability to stay calm in a crisis or under stress. Rage outbursts are especially dangerous. Mr. Trump is well known to have rage reactions, and to act precipitously on them, as in firing the Director of the FBI after hearing his testimony before Congress. Such enraged episodes cannot be minimized as isolated incidents because they arise from his personality. A person with a disturbed narcissistic need to always be both powerful and right will predictably become enraged at challenges to his views or power. But as the leader of a country, such challenges are the norm. Mature, emotionally healthy leaders respond to challenges with a carefully considered strategic reply. We see examples of this kind of normal response every day from world leaders, including past Presidents of the United States. Responding by threatening to "wipe out" a country whose leader is insulting, as Mr. Trump did, indicates his extreme personal fragility and, with that, his great risk of using the nuclear arsenal.

2. Empathy

With the lives of millions at stake, there must be an ability to recognize and empathize with the feelings and experiences of others. Individuals and nations, including allies, will always have different perspectives and goals. To function normally, a leader must be able to understand and appreciate the views of others, even if he does not agree with them, in order to work with differences and create a useful dialogue (diplomacy). Throughout his life, Mr. Trump has shown the inability to empathize with others that is central to sociopathy. He has a history of lying and cheating others, and his repeated and often obvious lies since taking office are signs of both his disdain for other people and his indifference to the harm he causes them by being dishonest. A long history of racism and bigotry shows a fundamental failure in the normal capacity to recognize the humanity of others. A dramatic, recent illustration is Mr. Trump's need for a cue card reminding him to say, "I hear you," when speaking with a group of grieving young people. Empathy is a crucial quality in nuclear negotiations, especially during a crisis. A leader needs to be able see a conflict through his adversary's eyes and use that understanding to craft a solution both leaders can accept. Because Mr. Trump has shown an incapacity for genuine empathy, the risk of nuclear war goes up.

Lack of empathy is the counterpart to an intense need to insist upon one's greatness and power. The never-ending need to prove one's superiority means that the lives, feelings, and concerns of others are unimportant—indeed, others are ultimately to be used only for one's own purposes. Having a near-psychotic need to be better than everyone else regardless of the harm caused to others defines a person who is unsafe to have power over nuclear weapons.

3. Ability to learn from others

A person vested with the power to launch a war must be aware that he is not always right and certainly must be aware that he is not all-knowing, a capacity that Mr. Trump has repeatedly shown himself to lack. Inability to hear the views or arguments of others, and to change one's own view, means that decisions are based on a personal closed belief system. Without the benefit of knowledge from many others, ignorance about the complexity of the world persists, and one-sided personal misinterpretations of events and consequences are more likely. To say of multiple national and world problems as Mr. Trump did, "Only I can solve it," shows both near-psychotic narcissism and dangerous inability to be aware of one's own lack of knowledge. Upon taking office Mr. Trump reportedly asked why he cannot use nuclear weapons if the country has them; this reflects ignorance well beyond that of the man on the street, as well as a remarkable inability to have heard the concerns of many over decades. His ignorance is consistent with his pathological view of himself as a "genius" who does not need to learn from others.

4. Wisdom

The combination of all the above capacities allows for wisdom. Wisdom about human life requires a normal degree of human empathy (with its consequent absence of cruelty, bigotry, cheating, and lying to others). It requires enough humility to know that one is imperfect and to therefore be willing to learn from others. It requires emotional stability without rages. It requires the ability to tolerate disappointment and accept mistakes without needing to distort reality to fit an inner need to be right. Mr. Trump possesses none of these qualities.

Accordingly, Mr. Trump is a profound risk to the nation and the world. His deeply disturbed emotional need for greatness and power, when coupled with his unconcern for the feelings or rights of others, makes him a profound risk to the very democratic structure of the United States. His unparalleled history of attacking judges who disagree with him and his dictator-like expectation that public officials, such as the FBI director, pledge loyalty to him personally rather than allegiance to the Constitution, are examples of the existential threat he poses to democracy.

For the same psychological reasons, Mr. Trump presents a profound risk to launch nuclear weapons. His personalizing events, inability to hear the views of others, unstable rage reactions coupled with loss of awareness of reality make him likely to start a war when international challenges occur. Rather than seeking diplomatic solutions in consultation with American experts in foreign policy, he has reacted by feeling personally challenged and even insulted by the views of leaders of other countries. His disturbed emotional state makes him the gravest danger to our country and the world since at least the darkest days of World War II.

References

1. APA (American Psychiatric Association. (2014) *Diagnostic and Statistical Manual of Mental Disorders, 5th Edition* Arlington, VA.
2. Lee, B X, Lifton, R (Eds). (2017) *The Dangerous Case of Donald Trump: 27 Psychiatrists and Mental Health Experts Assess a President*, New York. Thomas Dunne Books.

Lance Dodes, M.D. is a Training and Supervising Analyst Emeritus at the Boston Psychoanalytic Society and Institute and retired assistant clinical professor of psychiatry at Harvard Medical School. He is the author of many journal articles and book chapters about addiction, and three books on the subject. He has been honored by the Division on Addictions at Harvard Medical School for "Distinguished Contribution" to the study and treatment of addictive behavior and elected a Distinguished Fellow of the American Academy of Addiction Psychiatry. He contributed the chapter "Sociopathy" to the recent bestselling book, *The Dangerous Case of Donald Trump.*

Chapter 7

Trump's Sick Psyche and Nuclear Weapons: A Deadly Mixture

By Gordon Humphrey

"Donald Trump is impaired by a seriously sick psyche. His sick mind and reckless conduct could consume the lives of millions. The threat of nuclear war is steeply on the rise." These are the words I used in writing to the members of New Hampshire's congressional delegation, urging its members last August to co-sponsor HR 1987, the Raskin bill, which would create a panel that could be called on to evaluate the president's mental fitness under the Twenty-fifth Amendment.

Since then, the danger of catastrophe has grown. Increasingly, the president surrounds himself with advisors who are likely to incite his reckless impulses rather than restrain them. Trump's firing of Secretary of State Rex Tillerson and National Security Advisor H.R. McMaster and his replacement of those sober officials with Mike Pompeo and John Bolton, men both hawkish and aggressive, means that Trump is freer to indulge his worst instincts.

The turbulence at the highest levels of the administration reflect Trump's helter-skelter mind. One of the nation's most eminent jurists, Theodore Olson, in a March 26, 2018, interview, described the turbulence as "beyond normal bounds."[24] Olson, a prominent Republican, served as George W. Bush's solicitor general and in 2011 was awarded the American Bar Association's highest honor. "I think everybody would agree this is turmoil, it's chaos, it's confusion, it's not good for anything …,"[25] said Olson. According to the *Washington Post*, the White House earlier had sought to hire Olson to represent the president in matters under investigation by the special counsel.[26] Trump can hardly call Olson a "fake" critic.

But it is the president's reckless threat of nuclear war that is the most convincing evidence of his mental unfitness and the need to transfer his powers to the vice president through the implementation of the Twenty-fifth Amendment.

"North Korea best not make any more threats to the United States," the president fulminated on August 8th. "They will be met with fire and fury like the

---

[24] "Andrea Mitchell Reports," MSNBC, March 26, 2018.

[25] Ibid.

[26] Robert Costa and Carol D. Leonnig, "Star GOP, lawyer Theodore B. Olson declines offer to join Trump legal team," Washington Post, March 20, 2018.

world has never seen."[27] Senator John McCain, chair of the Armed Services Committee, criticized Trump's threat, saying, "All it's going to do is bring us closer to some kind of serious confrontation."[28]

Trump hurled his fire and fury fusillade between rounds of golf at his club in New Jersey. Were the secretaries of state and defense and the national security advisor consulted in the choice of words? No. Trump's belligerent outburst was off the cuff. The White House press secretary later confirmed Trump's words "were his own."[29]

Threatening nuclear war as though playing a hand of poker, when millions of innocent human beings unwillingly serve as the stakes, is more than dangerous and reckless in the extreme. It is utterly mad. No president of sound mind would do such a thing.

Having served on the Senate Armed Services Committee for twelve years, I remain keenly sensitive to the danger of accidental nuclear war. In a rapidly developing crisis, Trump's ignorance, belligerence, impulsiveness, and recklessness could trigger a nuclear exchange. That would mean death to probably millions of people in the blasts and millions more as radioactive fallout spreads in wide swaths around the world, disrupting economies, public utilities, the distribution of energy, food, and medicine, and triggering the breakdown of civil order and public health.

Trump's mental problems are compounded by astonishing ignorance. His ignorance of nuclear policy was evident early on. In a March 2016 *New York Times* interview, he suggested it was time to consider having Japan and South Korea acquire their own nuclear weapons to counter those possessed by North Korea, "You may very well be better off if that's the case," he said. [30]

Across more than sixty years, the U.S. has worked hard to limit the spread of nuclear weapons. That there are nine nuclear powers today is worrisome. Who can doubt there would be many more with even greater dangers of nuclear war absent that effort? Apparently, Donald Trump can!

That this erratic, ignorant president frequently ignores his senior advisors makes him even more dangerous. In September 2017, dismissing their warnings against insulting Kim, the president belittled him as "Rocket Man"[31] while addressing the United Nations, an insult that was not in the speech vetted for his delivery. A

---

[27] Jacob Pramuk, "Trump warns North Korea threats 'will be met with fire and fury'" CNBC, August 8, 2017.

[28] Interview on "Mac and Gaydos," KTAR, August 8, 2017.

[29] Glenn Thrush and Peter Baker, "Trump's Threat to North Korea Was Improvised," The New York Times, August 9, 2017.

[30] Maggie Haberman and David E. Sanger, "Donald Trump Expounds on His Foreign Policy Views," transcript of conversation, The New York Times, March 26, 2016.

[31] David Nakamura and Anne Gearan, "In UN speech, Trump threatens to 'totally destroy North Korea' and calls Kim Jong-un 'Rocket Man,' The Washington Post," September 19, 2017.

few days later, he upped it to "Little Rocket Man,"[32] and in January 2018, he launched another volley, saying his nuclear button is "bigger and more powerful"[33] than Kim's.

No healthy president would deliberately and repeatedly taunt a nuclear-armed dictator. But Trump is not healthy. The president's erratic conduct, his ignorance, belligerence, impulsiveness, and recklessness, and his readiness to wave off experienced counsel in favor of his gut instincts, constitute a grave danger to the safety of the United States and to the world. At a time when Trump-abnormal is so commonplace as to overwhelm the senses, one cannot say often enough: Trump is not normal. He is abnormal. He is burdened by an unhealthy mind. He is sick.

Should a layperson say such a thing? Yes. Citizens are not required to hold a doctorate in economics to form a judgment about the president's tax policies. They are not required to graduate from the Army War College to reach a conclusion about the president's defense policies. And citizens need not be mental health professionals to conclude the president's mind is dangerously afflicted.

The Twenty-fifth Amendment gives laypersons—the vice president and the fifteen members of the Cabinet—the power to transfer the president's authority to the vice president, should a majority, inclusive of the vice president, find the president "unable to discharge the powers and duties of his office." As an alternative, the Constitution empowers Congress to appoint a panel to pass judgment on the president's fitness. Nowhere do these provisions mention physicians, psychologists, or psychiatrists.

Precisely, what is the president's diagnosis? That is the wrong question. The question we must ask is: Can we depend on this president to rationally, responsibly, soberly, and sanely discharge the powers and duties of the office? Certainly, when the matter involves nuclear weapons, we are daily taking very grave risks in trusting an impulsive, reckless man heavily burdened by a sick psyche.

The vice president, Cabinet officers, and members of Congress should remind themselves they are not required to be physicians, psychiatrists, or psychologists; they are not required to render a diagnosis. Instead, they are charged to make a judgment about the president's mental fitness based on his conduct.

There is a mountain of evidence in the president's conduct over the last three years indicating he is afflicted with an unsound mind. Will the Cabinet and members of Congress continue to fail in their serious responsibilities? The safety of every American and millions of human beings around the world is in their hands.

They should act.

---

[32] Julie Hirschfeld Davis, "Is Trump All Talk on North Korea? The Uncertainty Sends a Shiver," The New York Times, September 24, 2017.

[33] Peter Baker and Michael Tackett, "Trump Says His 'Nuclear Button' Is 'Much Bigger' Than North Korea's," The New York Times, January 2, 2018.

Gordon Humphrey represented New Hampshire in the United States Senate from 1979 to 1990, serving on the Senate Armed Services and the Foreign Relations Committees, among others. In 1991, he returned home, fulfilling a two-term pledge made when he first ran for office. He regards himself as a Reagan Republican and left the party by registering as an independent the day after Donald Trump was elected president. Prior to public service, Gordon Humphrey was a pilot with a major U.S. airline. Earlier, after four years of military service, he attended George Washington University and specialized flight schools.

Chapter 8

Facing the Truth: Trump Wields the Power of a Predatory Narcissist and May Destroy Us All

By Jacqueline J. West, Ph.D.

Perhaps the most difficult feat when it comes to President Trump is facing, fully and honestly, just how deeply destructive and dangerous he is at his core. This truth is more than just inconvenient, it is terrifying. While the natural human tendency is to distort, distract, and defend against truths that scare us, our survival as a species may depend on facing this reality head on.

Trump presents an unusually intense profile of narcissism. Indeed, he is so often referred to as narcissistic that this diagnosis has become taken for granted in the media. But we need to wake up to the distressing reality that the particular form of narcissism that he evidences, Alpha Narcissism, has the potential to lead us into oppression and global destruction. It has the dangerous power to destroy.

Narcissism in general refers to a complex set of dynamics that range from healthy to disturbed, and these dynamics form several different profiles. Normally, when a child begins to develop a sense of "I am here—I can do it—I want it!" these natural, potentially healthy narcissistic dynamics are balanced with appropriate limitations, and the child learns how to tame, or integrate, the raw force of their omnipotence, exhibitionism, and grandiosity. With the containing and caring support and mirroring of emphatic caretakers, the child learns how to use these energies creatively to foster the emergence of self-esteem and creative assertion. These positive self-values give rise to the development of empathy for the other and the emergence of a young but growing conscience that, in turn, nourishes a capacity to form mutual relationships with others.

However, some children who are not met with sufficiently nurturing containment, or are met with clearly threatening or abusive caretakers, are cast into a state of threatened survival that leads them to divide the world into predator and prey. And defensively they become identified with the predator. In Trump's case, this view of the world was reinforced by his father who told his son over and over: "You need to be a killer and a king." The message was clear: There are two types of people in the world—the victors and the vanquished, and you must be the former.

The predatory narcissist is inherently what Jung called an "archetypal trickster." Trickster figures that appear in mythologies, folktales, and fairy-tales are well known to be amoral. They turn reality inside out—and upside down as suits them in the moment. We've seen them commonly portrayed as coyotes or ravens, as the wily

Brer Rabbit, or the cunning thief. Magical, compelling, and charismatic, they bring transformations that range from creative to destructive—at their whim. The con man is a victor, and the trusting suckers are his prey.

Adopting this identification in the first months of life, the child feels thoroughly antagonistic toward everything within himself as well as *outside* himself that is vulnerable, which amounts to everything and everyone who then, by definition, are prey. In effect, predation is defensively split from its opposite dynamic, prey, which must be disowned and avoided at all costs. Living in this kill-or-be-killed field, any hint of being one-down, any hint of vulnerability is experienced as utterly intolerable.

Imbued with the drive for predation, this pattern is recognizably psychopathic.

Once a child develops an early identification with the predator, and its psychopathic patterns, he proceeds to manage the world from within this profile. He employs grandiosity, omnipotence, and exhibitionism to tenaciously aim for domination. He MUST remain on top. Vulnerability is experienced as *out there* in *others*, not in one's self. In effect, the Predatory Narcissist, who is also at times referred to as an Alpha Narcissist, is so thoroughly centered on the self that authentic relatedness, empathy, and conscience are effectively short-circuited.

We have seen the enactments of this profile routinely as we experience President Trump. We regularly see how Trump's ever-active need for dominance requires unquestionable admiration and incessant acknowledgement of his power, and in order to gain this feedback, he routinely resorts to bold, disinhibited, egotistical displays that inflate his sense of himself, and a need to viciously defend against anyone who even hints at challenging his status.

It is generally the case that the more the Alpha Narcissist wins, charms, and gathers wealth and power, the more he wants— and the more he desperately needs. The intensity of the hidden needs, inherently tied to vulnerability, create a disturbing frailty in his *armor,* and his behaviors become more and more extreme in their magnitude, their urgency, and at times their shifting, contradictory, and slippery nature. This appears in Trump's incessant shifting of truth, his impulsive and thoroughly aggressive tweets that are, at times, followed by apparently unrelated disclaimers. These patterns portray—and induce—a chaotic, distressed reality.

As is characteristic of the Alpha Narcissist, fueled by the destructive side of the Trickster, Trump employs these forces to support his astute capacity to manipulate others. He seems relatively free of conscience, and while deeply identified with predation, Trump is free to ruthlessly rule over others, spinning reality to consistently support his dominations. He is especially adept with cunning, quick, and paradoxically charismatic moves that twist and turn reality in ways that suit his aim—or simply so confound reality that the aims of others are effectively canceled out. Meanwhile, his abundantly flaunted power exudes an uncanny charisma, a fascinating pull that entrances many people to fall into the sway of his manipulations.

Many of us are acquainted with the fairy-tale of Bluebeard. No question, it is a chilling tale, but it is also a tale very worth listening to: *It is a tale that informs us.* At times, stories paint pictures that take us into a felt sense of the reality we are facing. Bluebeard offers not only a profile of the psychopathic dynamics that inform Alpha Narcissism, but also invaluable clues about facing this predatory pattern. A very brief synopsis of the story leads us into reflections about these truths.

Once upon a time . . . A man arrived in the community seeking a bride. He effectively displayed his impressive wealth and power, though he had an odd and very disconcerting blue beard. He visited a well-established woman with two daughters, proposing marriage. In spite of their uncertainties about him, through his charm he convinced the younger daughter to marry him, and she and her sister moved into Bluebeard's castle. Soon, he announced that he was going for a journey. Handing his young wife the keys to his house, he invited her to explore each and every room *except* the utterly forbidden one at the end of the corridor. He added, "My orders are to be strictly obeyed, and if you should dare to open the door, my anger will exceed anything you have ever experienced."

After Bluebeard's departure, the young bride found herself increasingly curious about what was in the firmly forbidden room—so curious that she went to the door, paused for a moment, but then unlocked the door and stepped inside. She found herself facing pools of dried blood amid the hanging, dead bodies of Bluebeard's previous wives, each with their throats cut. Once she could recover her senses, she quickly left the room and only later noticed that the key to that particular room was stained with blood that could not be removed. When her husband returned and demanded she return the keys, he immediately knew she had disobeyed his orders and he proclaimed that she therefore would "take her place" in that same room. She pleaded for some time to "say her prayers" and, within the granted minutes, with the support of her sister, her two brothers arrived barely in time, and in short order they killed Bluebeard.

While Bluebeard is a fairy-tale, French in origin, written by Charles Perrault, it clearly portrays dynamics that appear cross-culturally and globally over centuries. There are two central themes in this story that are directly relevant to our endangered realities in America today. The preponderance of these very dynamics in the psyche of our nation and their intense embodiment in the individual character of our current president highlight its particular value for us—at this moment. First of all, the story aptly portrays the trickster at work; his *work* in this case is truly psychopathic. Bluebeard *is* a well-disguised, gruesome serial killer.

The arc of the story hinges on the young bride's curiosity. Commentaries about this story typically focus on the young bride's naivety, casting her curiosity as a potentially fatal flaw. I think this perspective is biased, if not chauvinistic. I see the young bride's curiosity leading her into a moment of *facing the reality* that pervades the castle. Had she not opened the door, Bluebeard would have killed her at his leisure, and she would have never seen it coming. What she discovered was the rawest of truths: Her husband was a predatory killer. She dared to inform herself about the reality she had entered; she stepped up to the risks involved. Calling upon her sister and her brothers for help, she freed them all from the dominance of destruction. I'd like to suggest that we can simultaneously hear this story objectively as a story about facing the destructive energies in others while subjectively we can hear it as a metaphor for relying on the strengths of one's various internal selves to join and support one's process of facing and de potentiating one's own internal predator.

Facing—truly facing—the Predatory Narcissist is clearly not a lightweight action whether this is objective or subjective. But the "moral" of this tale clearly suggests that it is an essentially life-giving creative act. It is an act that re-establishes balance and safety in the world.

Many of Trump's egotistical displays have been not only boisterous and threatening but have also explicitly featured blatant misogyny and repetitively expressed racism both nationally and internationally. When his deeply fueled aggression is focused upon an identifiable group, it is particularly damaging, wounding, and dangerous. Rejecting the relational values based on empathy, responsibility, and respect, Trump destroys the bonds between people, separating and alienating them from each other, casting them into insecurities and fears, leaving them exposed in his manipulative hands. His power is not only dangerous at a political level, but it is corrosive and oppressive at a personal *and* interpersonal level. Metaphorically, he kills off creative connections—one after the other.

Along with these metaphoric killings lies the horrifying possibility that Trump's entrenched drive toward destruction might cast him into unreflective action that could, at its most intense and/or impulsive activation, set off a nuclear war that could ultimately destroy life on this Earth as it is.

If we dare to open the forbidden door, like the young bride, what we see will make our blood run cold. But it could also save our lives. Bluebeard killed one woman at a time, but Trump could kill millions. There is ample evidence that Trump's Alpha Narcissism is leading us to our doom, threatening nuclear "power and fury like the world has never seen." We should believe him and boldly face the danger we are in.

References

Dougherty, Nancy J., and West, Jacqueline J. *The Matrix and Meaning of Character: An Archetypal and Developmental Approach*. London: Routledge, 2007.

Hurt, Harry III. As quoted in https://www.politico.com/magazine/story/2016/04/donald-trump-2016-campaign-biography-psychology-history-barrett-hurt-dantiono-blair-obrien-213835. 2016.

Zipes, Jack *The Great Fairytale Tradition: From Straparola and Basile to the Brothers Grimm*. New York: W.W. Norton & Company, 2001.

Jacqueline J. West, Ph.D. With a BS from Stanford University and a Ph.D. in Psychology from the University of California, she trained to be a Jungian Analyst with the Inter-regional Society of Jungian Analysts. She has served as President and Training Director of the New Mexico Society and as President of the North American Societies of Jungian Analysts. She is co-author, along with Nancy Dougherty, of *The Matrix and Meaning of Character: An Archetypal and Developmental Perspective* and has published several articles about Alpha Narcissism and the American psyche. She lectures and teaches widely on archetypal psychology and its interplay with art and politics.

In the 1950's, many nuclear tests were conducted. One of a total of 10 such locations was the "Central Nevada Test Area," in Hot Creek Valley. Project Faultless was detonated 3,200 feet underground on January 19, 1968 at 10:15 a.m. *Public domain*

Chapter 9

Trump's No Madman, He's Following the Strongman Playbook

By Ruth Ben-Ghiat

Many have sought to diagnose President Donald Trump, depicting him as a toxic narcissist or as delusional as a means of accounting for his destructive behavior and attachment to falsehoods that are often of his own making. While it's easy to see how such opinions of him take hold, I argue that it's the history of authoritarianism that provides the best framework for understanding Trump's words and actions. From Benito Mussolini onward, strongmen have ruled through a combination of seduction and threat, building up protective cults of personality and relentlessly pushing their own versions of reality until they are in a position to make them state policy.[34]

Far from being madmen, leaders such as Trump are opportunists and skilled manipulators whose ideas on specific policy issues may change without them ever deviating from their main goals: the accumulation and steady expansion of their own power and the desire to have their own will prevail over others, including other global players. His approach to nuclear policy and diplomacy may be seen within this larger frame.[35]

Trump's been remarkably organized and consistent since he appeared on the political scene on the issues that really matter to him: self-glorification; putting enemies and those who doubt his version of reality in their place by installing what I call a "culture of threat"; racial discrimination (the desire to protect whiteness); and admiration for foreign despots (except for the ones who he feels are his nemeses). Most of these themes are visible in his thinking about who should and should not have nuclear weapons and his ideas about how to check such weapons' proliferation.

Strongmen are nothing without their adulatory followers. They need an audience for their endless self-glorification: that starts with the security blanket

---

[34] Jonathan Chait, "New Reports Suggest that Trump Might Not Be A Liar at All, but Truly Delusional," New York Magazine, November 28, 2017.
http://nymag.com/daily/intelligencer/2017/11/new-reports-trump-not-a-liar-is-truly-delusional.html?utm_campaign=nym&utm_source=tw&utm_medium=s1

[35] This article is adapted from Ruth Ben-Ghiat, "Trump's No Madman, He Knows Exactly What He's Doing," The Washington Post, November 30, 2017.

they weave when they forge direct bonds with followers based on loyalty to their person rather than to any party or principle. Over one hundred years, rallies and moving images of the leader have been the most effective means of establishing these attachments and the aura of *specialness* around the leader. Trump has added Twitter to the mix, using his tweets as well as rallies to control the media cycle and to keep himself at the center of attention. He has also led his followers through a kind of emotional training that is foreign to democratically minded politicians, including telling them whom to hate.

These emotional bonds are the basis for Trump's indoctrination of his followers into his own universe of meaning, complete with its own standards for truth (i.e., truth is what he says it is). History shows the efficacy of such techniques for the creation of national enemies and the mobilization of support for wars against them, including through genocidal techniques and weapons of mass destruction. Having such bonds of faith intact is also insurance for Trump and authoritarians past and present against those sectors (the judiciary, the press) that uphold the values of evidence and investigation and may reveal his warmongering to be baseless or find wrongdoing that merits his removal. When Trump tells the country, "I am the only one that matters," and disregards expert opinion, as he's shown every intention of doing in nuclear negotiations with North Korea, he's not just channeling his inner narcissist or egomaniac, but a century of strongman practices that, in the past, have led to world wars, famines, and other disasters.[36]

The strongman likes to think he alone is indispensable to the nation, but in reality, he is nothing without his enablers, who accede to his every whim by knowing when to keep quiet or, occasionally, issuing tepid remonstrations that the leader knows are just a show. The GOP is playing the textbook role of *co-opted elites* who throughout history have convinced themselves that the leader will *calm down* once in office (the illusion of the Trump *pivot*), despite evidence to the contrary. After these elites have worked out the terms of their support, they usually back the leader no matter what he says or does, unless a serious economic downturn, coup, or military defeat looms on the horizon.[37]

In September 2017, when Trump recklessly told the United Nations General Assembly that America might have to "totally destroy[38]" North Korea unless it

---

[36] Trump made the comment, "Let me tell you, the one that matters is me, I'm the only one that matters because when it comes to it that's what the policy is going to be," regarding his lack of nominees for important State Department jobs, as reported in Jesse Byrnes, "Trump on Lack of Nominees: 'I Am the Only One that Matters,'" The Hill, November 2, 2017. http://thehill.com/blogs/blog-briefing-room/news/358573-trump-on-lack-of-nominees-i-am-the-only-one-that-matters.

[37] See, on elite co-optation, Sergei Guriev and Daniel Treisman, "How Modern Dictators Survive," National Bureau of Economic Research Working Paper 21136 (April 2015).

[38] David Nakamura and Anne Gearan, "In U.N. Speech, Trump Threatens to 'Totally Destroy North Korea' and Calls Kim Jong Un 'Rocket Man,'" The Washington Post, September 19, 2017.

denuclearizes, here's how leading Republican officials involved in Senate and House Foreign Relations committees responded to reporters: "Senate Foreign Relations Chairman Bob Corker hurried into an elevator. Senator Marco Rubio quickly ducked into the Capitol Visitor Center television studio. And Senate Armed Services Chairman John McCain shut down reporters' repetitive questions," wrote John T. Bennett of RollCall.[39]

Three months later, Trump's terrifying Twitter cockfight with Kim Jong-un over the size of their nuclear arsenals (Trump ended things on a macho note, tweeting that his button was "bigger & much more powerful") met with the same party-coordinated silence. "You keep asking that question, and I keep being too busy to answer it," commented Corker. The GOP has thus behaved according to plan, sticking with Trump through the allegations of Trump's sexual assaults, conflicts of interest, the Russia investigation, and even, seemingly, the threat of mass annihilation. Individual politicians may mutter that Trump is volatile and even deranged, but both parties of the Trump-GOP pact have acted in a highly rational and predictable manner if their behavior is placed in the context of the history of authoritarianism.[40]

Strongmen speak the language of force, not diplomacy, and they consider liberal notions of human rights as the province of the weak. Long before he was president, Trump had strong opinions on how to conduct foreign relations, in particular where nuclear weapons are involved. A 1987 interview with Ron Rosenbaum lays out his frightening views of how to denuclearize a country he sees as inferior. He takes the example of Pakistan, which at the time was receiving nuclear technology from France, much to Trump's irritation. As this quote makes clear, his idea of nuclear "diplomacy" goes well beyond economic sanctions to an engineered humanitarian crisis and the collapse of civilian society:

I'm saying you start off as nicely as possible. You apply as much pressure as necessary until you achieve the goal. You start off telling them, 'Let's get rid of it.' If that doesn't work you then start cutting off aid. And more aid and then more. You do whatever is necessary so these people will have riots in the street, so they can't get water. So they can't get Band-

https://www.washingtonpost.com/news/post-politics/wp/2017/09/19/in-u-n-speech-trump-warns-that-the-world-faces-great-peril-from-rogue-regimes-in-north-korea-iran/?utm_term=.39b0c6a71b26.

[39] John T. Bennett, "Republican Senators Mostly Silent After Trump's North Korea Threat," Roll Call, September 20, 2017.https://www.rollcall.com/news/politics/republican-senators-mostly-silent-trumps-north-korea-threat

[40] Tara Goldman, "I Asked 7 Republican Senators about Trump's Nuclear Button Tweet. They Seemed Unfazed," Vox, January 4, 2018 https://www.vox.com/policy-and-politics/2018/1/4/16848846/7-republican-senators-trump-nuclear-button-tweet

Aids, so they can't get food. Because that's the only thing that's going to do it—the people, the riots.[41]

Thirty years later, this brutal mentality has stayed with Trump, on this issue as on his views on race and so many other subjects. Although many see the president as mentally unstable, it would be wrong to underestimate his tenacity. He plays a long game, as in his bid for the White House, which he considered periodically over the years. He made his move (on the counsel of his racist advisor Stephen Bannon) only after eight years of Barack Obama's presidency and progress in gender issues had raised conservative white resentment to the right degree.

Trump may seem a fluke or an irrational agent of chaos, but he's better taken seriously as the American symptom of a cultural and political shift away from liberal democracy. Americans must see his see his method, rather than his madness, including about the existential threat posed by his approach to nuclear diplomacy. You might think only a madman would light the world on fire, but history shows us strongmen do it all the time.

Ruth Ben-Ghiat is Professor of History and Italian Studies at New York University. The recipient of Guggenheim, Fulbright, and other fellowships, she's an expert on fascism, authoritarianism, and propaganda. She writes frequently for the media on those topics and on Donald Trump. Her next book is *Strongmen: How They Rise, Why They Succeed, How They Fall* (Norton). She sits on the Board of Directors of the World Policy Institute.

---

[41]Ron Rosenbaum's 1987 interview with Donald Trump is reprinted in Ron Rosenbaum, "Trump's Nuclear Experience," Slate, March 1, 2016.

Building your own Bomb Shelter (1950's Photo Images)

Mutually Assured Destruction seems gentler when one believes a bomb shelter can help spare a person and their family. During the Cold War, there was a very superficial understanding of the consequences of thermonuclear war. The following series of photographs shows cartoon figures and a smiling woman in heels promoting the benefits of finding shelter in the event of a nuclear attack. As ill-conceived as these photos may seem today it is important to remember that today's nuclear weapons are substantially more powerful than those detonated in Japan. The *Little Boy* nuclear bomb dropped on Hiroshima released approximately 15 kilotons of energy (15,000 tons of TNT), and sent a mushroom cloud up to about 25,000 feet. The current B83?'s power is 1.2 megaton, equaling 1,200,000 tons of TNT. This is eighty times more powerful than the *Little Boy*. Bomb shelters might offer some immediate protection from the initial blast and release of ionizing radiation from the detonation of a modern-day nuclear bomb but would do little to mitigate the lasting impact of thermonuclear warfare. Most experts agree that a large scale exchange of modern nuclear warheads would release enough particles in the upper atmosphere to block most sunlight from reaching the planet's surface for years, causing widespread famine and extinction of numerous species.

The adult-orientated Survival Under Atomic Attack issued in 1950, pre-dated the release of "Duck and Cover" in 1951-52. *Public domain, via Wikimedia Commons*

TEMPORARY BASEMENT FALLOUT SHELTER

Drawing of a temporary basement fallout shelter. *National Archives*

Signs used to mark emergency shelters for nuclear and chemical warfare fallout in the United States. *Public domain, via Wikimedia Commons*

Photograph of a display of survival supplies for the well-stocked fallout shelter, 1961. *National Archives*

1950s fallout shelter. *Public domain*

Screenshot from "Duck and Cover" film, a 1952 movie. The "Duck and Cover" propaganda movie was probably one of the most famous of all the pieces of propaganda during the early stages of the Cold War. It was targeted at school children and was intended to install the constant fear of a nuclear attack from the Soviets. *Public domain*

Will the "Dealmaker" Make a Deal or Start a War?

Atomic bomb blast. *National Archives*

Chapter 10
The Gospel of War Presidency

By Richard Painter and Leanne Watt

A president who is dangerously unfit

Now, more than ever, Donald Trump is in need of a Twenty-fifth Amendment intervention. But the probability that this ultimate "check"—a corrective mechanism for an American president who is physically or psychologically unable to lead—will be utilized is highly unlikely.

Ratified in 1967,[42] the Twenty-fifth Amendment was created specifically for the nuclear age to assure a smooth transition when a president becomes incapable of leadership. With tensions flaring around the globe, there can be no doubt as to the fitness of the man or woman in possession of U.S. nuclear codes. The amendment grants legal authority to those closest to power—first, the vice president, followed by the secretary of state and other Cabinet members—to stage an intervention if a president is judged unfit to govern.

Based upon his patterned track record of behavior, we believe that Donald Trump is psychologically unfit to lead, having reached (and significantly exceeded) the level of impairment that our nation's leaders had in mind when they crafted the Twenty-fifth Amendment.[43] With a compromised House failing to stand up to Trump's improprieties,[44] this amendment has been our nation's only hope of stopping the devastating effects of the president's downward spiral.

But President Trump has virtually eliminated the possibility of the Twenty-fifth Amendment being invoked. With his removal of the only moderate Cabinet members, his current Cabinet is primarily composed of authoritarian[45] absolutists—

---

[42] Andrew Glass, "The 25th Amendment was Ratified Feb. 10, 1967," Politico, February 10, 2012, https://www.politico.com/story/2012/02/nevada-puts-25th-amendment-over-the-top-072700.

[43] Richard W. Painter and Leanne E. Watt, "The 25th Amendment Proves Why Donald Trump's Mental Health Matters," NBC News Think online, October 18, 2017, https://www.nbcnews.com/think/opinion/25th-amendment-proves-why-trump-s-mental-health-matters-ncna801666.

[44] Adam Entous, "House majority leader in 2016: 'I Think Putin Pays' Trump," Washington Post, May 17, 2017, https://www.washingtonpost.com/world/national-security/house-majority-leader-to-colleagues-in-2016-i-think-putin-pays-trump/2017/05/17/515f6f8a-3aff-11e7-8854-21f359183e8c_story.html?utm_term=.30093cea1ed5

[45] Hemant Kakkar and Niro Sivanathan, "When the appeal of a dominant leader is greater than a prestige leader," PNAS 114, no.26 (June 2017): 6734-6739, https://doi.org/10.1073/pnas.1617711114.

including a neoconservative "über-hawk"[46] and advisors who appear to favor domination over diplomacy. In service of their own ideological agendas and autocratic tendencies, our concern is that his obsequious Cabinet[47] will be eager to do Trump's unfettered bidding, rather than putting the brakes on his destructive choices.

In our 2017 article,[48] we established the behavioral and correlated diagnostic underpinnings of the president's demonstrated unfitness and dangerousness. Trump has a well-documented and long-standing pattern of easily observed actions and attitudes over the course of many decades that are consistent with the characteristics associated with two severe personality disorders in the Cluster-B family[49]—antisocial personality disorder (ASPD) and narcissistic personality disorder (NPD).

The presence of antisocial and narcissistic personality disorders means impulsive, dramatic, and unpredictable behavior that is resistant to change, even with treatment. ASPD symptoms include a disregard for the rights and safety of others, a tendency to break the law, lack of remorse, frequent lying, failure to honor financial obligations, interpersonal exploitation, risk-taking, and revenge-seeking in response to perceived slights.50 Hallmark NPD symptoms include phantasies about power, arrogance, an exaggerated self-importance, sensitivity to criticism, lack of empathy, a need for admiration and attention, entitlement, and exploitation with a need for personal gain.[51]

As an expert in presidential ethics and a clinical psychologist with an expertise in treating patients with personality disorders, respectively, the authors of this chapter have no relationship to President Trump. But due to our collective and relevant experience, we do believe experts have a professional and ethical

---

[46] Colum Lynch and Elias Groll, "Trump Taps Uber-Hawk Bolton as National Security Advisor," Foreign Policy, March 22, 2018, http://foreignpolicy.com/2018/03/22/trump-taps-uber-hawk-bolton-as-national-security-adviser/.

[47] Steve Benen, "Trump's first cabinet meeting was surprisingly creepy," MSNBC online, June 12, 2017, http://www.msnbc.com/rachel-maddow-show/trumps-first-full-cabinet-meeting-was-surprisingly-creepy.

[48] Painter and Watt, "Mental Health Matters."

[49] Mayo Clinic staff, "Personality Disorders: Symptoms and Causes," Mayo Clinic online, last modified September 23, 2016, https://www.mayoclinic.org/diseases-conditions/personality-disorders/symptoms-causes/syc-20354463.

[50] Mayo Clinic staff, "Antisocial Personality Disorder," Mayo Clinic online, last modified August 4, 2017, https://www.mayoclinic.org/diseases-conditions/antisocial-personality-disorder/symptoms-causes/syc-20353928.

[51] Mayo Clinic staff, "Narcissistic Personality Disorder," Mayo Clinic online, last modified November 18, 2017, https://www.mayoclinic.org/diseases-conditions/narcissistic-personality-disorder/symptoms-causes/syc-20366662.

responsibility to speak up when they notice behaviors that are troubling, suspicious, and harmful to the security of our nation.

As Donald Trump's legal and ethical failings receive closer scrutiny and the Mueller investigation closes in around the president, it is reasonable to expect that he is in an acute and constant state of distress. As his *perfection* façade crumbles, the pain of being exposed as a fraud on the world stage is unparalleled. In an effort to disrupt the unbearable agony of this unprecedented exposure, the president has become progressively more erratic, manipulative, and "belligerent."[52] Individuals with patterned behavior consistent with ASPD and NPD *act out* in more reckless and alarming ways when the threat of extreme humiliation and punishment becomes imminent.

Under relentless and intensified psychological pressure, a president with severe Cluster B behavior patterns will double down on the use of paranoid accusations, looking for easy scapegoats to blame—like the FBI or the Department of Justice—to try and maintain their perfection delusion.

But as the legal noose tightens and the president's desperation mounts, his use of blame as a manipulative distraction has become increasingly more dangerous. Trump's references to staging real showdowns with unstable boogeymen, such as Kim Jong-un of North Korea[53] or with the nation of Iran,[54] have swept the entire world into the president's drama, forcing everyone to experience the terror he's facing, but on a potentially catastrophic level. The gripping worry that the president, in a frenzied state, may ignite a war or even use nuclear weapons against North Korea or Iran is on the front burner for the majority of Americans[55] according to recent polls.

Disclaimer

In each of the following instances, we are only interested in the individual's state of mind at the time they made a statement, not the ultimate truth of what they said based on what we now know or might learn later. In each case, is this an

---

[52] Eliza Barclay, "The psychiatrist who briefed Congress on Trump's mental state: 'this is an emergency,'" Vox, updated January 6, 2018, https://www.vox.com/science-and-health/2018/1/5/16770060/trump-mental-health-psychiatrist-25th-amendment.

[53] James Cameron, "The high price of Trump's nuclear saber-rattling," Washington Post, December 7, 2017, https://www.washingtonpost.com/news/made-by-history/wp/2017/12/07/the-high-price-of-trumps-nuclear-saber-rattling/?utm_term=.ff9c11cb075f.

[54] Nicole Gaouette, "US and Israeli officials intensify the drumbeat against Iran," CNN online, April 27, 2018, https://www.cnn.com/2018/04/27/politics/us-israel-iran-dangers/index.html.

[55] Harriet Sinclair, "Most Americans Fear Major War Under Trump, Polls Show," Newsweek, October 19, 2017, http://www.newsweek.com/most-americans-fear-major-war-under-trump-poll-shows-688214.

individual capable of objectively analyzing facts presented to them, asking questions about what additional facts they might need before reaching a conclusion and recognizing uncertainty where it clearly exists? Or, is this a person who jumps to conclusions, allowing bias or ideology, rather than facts, to determine their conclusions, or otherwise, distorts the truth?

A war Cabinet that will not restrain him

The Twenty-fifth Amendment ship has likely sailed. But at the very least, when a country is in an acute state of crisis, with its president in the clutches of a profound psychological breakdown, a team of confidants with a calming influence is desperately needed. But with President Trump's most recent Cabinet appointments, his inner circle has become a ring of danger, rather than a reasoned counterbalance to Donald Trump's treacherous unraveling. Collectively, their authoritarian leanings, and in some instances, ethically-challenged or aggressive behavior patterns, may ultimately serve to enable and ignite an already volatile, ready-to-blow president.

While many past presidential administrations have struggled with their share of serious behavioral issues at varying degrees of severity, the stench of corruption in the current administration is at a concentrated level,[56] unlike any other administration in the history of our nation.[57] The advisors with a demonstrated history of crossing important boundaries in pursuit of their own goals present a real challenge for our nation. But the problem goes much deeper than the myriad ethics violations and the swamp culture associated with the Trump administration.[58] Many of the president's closest advisors also harbor retribution-oriented, authoritarian inclinations, further compromising their ability to competently guide the president regarding matters of war, while placing our nation at a new level of vulnerability.

With the president's pronounced instability and bellicose rhetoric on a sharp incline, his appointment of John Bolton as his national security advisor is tantamount to adding a boatload of gasoline to an already raging fire. In the entire eight years of the George W. Bush administration, while serving as undersecretary of state for arms control and international security and U.S. ambassador to the United

---

[56] Jonathan Chait, "Corruption, Not Russia, is Trump's Greatest Political Liability," New York Magazine, April 1, 2018, http://nymag.com/daily/intelligencer/2018/04/corruption-is-trumps-greatest-political-liability.html.

[57] Alexander Nazaryan, "Trump Administration: The Most Corrupt and Unethical in American History?" Newsweek, September 23, 2017, http://www.newsweek.com/trump-pruitt-price-devos-669853.

[58] McKay Coppins, "How the Swamp Drained Trump," The Atlantic, January 30, 2018, https://www.theatlantic.com/politics/archive/2018/01/swamp-trump/551807/.

Nations, John Bolton was the most dangerous member on the Bush team. He was part of a core group of neoconservatives on steroids that aggressively pushed the theory of weapons of mass destruction[59] because he wanted a war. Besides the betrayal of Trump's base in his hiring of the new national security advisor, Bolton's presence in the White House could very easily have a worldwide impact at a disastrous level. Bringing John Bolton into the Cabinet is an invitation to more wars and possibly a nuclear war. In our opinions, because of Trump's demonstrated history of extreme impulsivity, it will not take a lot of encouragement from his new national security advisor to push the president all the way over the edge.

Colin H. Kahl and Jon Wolfsthal, two of our nation's leading foreign policy experts, concur with our observations, asserting that John Bolton, serving as Trump's National Security Advisor, is a "national security threat."[60] In their 2018 *Foreign Policy* article, Kahl and Wolfsthal state: "Indeed, Bolton's ascendance increases the risk of not one but two wars—with North Korea and Iran."[61] In his 2018 *Wall Street Journal* op-ed, Bolton advocates for regime change in Iran, calling for "a new Iranian regime in 2019."[62] Bolton also states in a Fox News interview that "the only diplomatic option left is to end the North Korean regime,"[63] He expands on these views in the *WSJ*, laying out the "legal case for striking North Korea first."[64]

Bolton is unfit for Cabinet leadership because he is plagued by a well-documented history of problematic behavior patterns and aggressive posturing in service of authoritarian objectives.[65] He is oriented around American dominance over other countries and has not shied away from advocating manipulative and violent means to accomplish his goals: According to Kahl and Wolfsthal, Bolton has a "pattern of warping and misusing intelligence to build the case for war with rogue states."[66] Bolton "exaggerated what the U.S. government knew about weapons

---

[59] Greg Thielmann, "Bolton: A Prime Mover of the Iraq WMD Fiasco," Lobe Log, December 14, 2016, https://lobelog.com/bolton-a-prime-mover-of-the-iraq-wmd-fiasco/.

[60] Colin Kahl and Jon Wolfsthal, "John Bolton Is a National Security Threat," Foreign Policy, March 23, 2018, http://foreignpolicy.com/2018/03/23/john-bolton-is-a-national-security-threat/.

[61] Kahl, "John Bolton Is a National Security Threat."

[62] John Bolton, "Beyond the Iran Nuclear Deal," Wall Street Journal, January 15, 2018, https://www.wsj.com/articles/beyond-the-iran-nuclear-deal-1516044178.

[63] Gregory Krieg, "John Bolton on: bombing Iran, North Korea, Russia, and the Iraq War," CNN online, March 23, 2018, https://www.cnn.com/2018/03/23/politics/what-john-bolton-said-iraq-iran-north-korea/index.html.

[64] John Bolton, "The Legal Case for Striking North Korea First," Wall Street Journal, February 28, 2018, https://www.wsj.com/articles/the-legal-case-for-striking-north-korea-first-1519862374.

[65] Michael Meng, "On Authoritarianism: A Review Essay," Comparative Studies in Society and History 59, no. 4 (September 2017):1008-1020, https://doi.org/10.1017/S0010417517000354.

[66] Kahl, "John Bolton Is a National Security Threat."

programs in Iraq, Cuba, and Syria" when he served as a senior State Department official, according to Jonathan Landay and Warren Strobel, senior correspondents for national security, intelligence, and foreign policy at Reuters.[67]

Bolton also has a record of indirect hostility toward the Muslim community through his close association with two anti-Islam activists and conspiracy peddlers: Bolton wrote the foreword on Pamela Geller's book and has appeared on her radio program.[68] In 2016, Bolton "played a crucial role in Frank Gaffney's rehabilitation inside the conservative movement."[69] Even more disturbing, NBC News reports that between 2013 and March of 2018, John Bolton chaired the Gatestone Institute, "a nonprofit that has promoted misleading and false anti-Muslim news, some of which was amplified by a Russian troll factory."[70]

In 2014, Bolton hired Cambridge Analytica, a company that utilized improperly obtained Facebook data in order to exploit voters' psychological vulnerabilities,[71] raising the question regarding whether Bolton knowingly participated in the exploitation. Kahl and

Wolfsthal report that Bolton has a "tendency to see the ends as justifying the means, however horrific." Bolton uses revenge-seeking behavior with those who oppose him: Kahl and Wolfsthal state that he has a "long and documented history of stifling views that differ from his own and even punishing subordinates who disagree with him."[72]

Mike Pompeo, former director of the CIA and Trump's new secretary of state, is another questionable appointee with a behavioral history that suggests a willingness to use exaggeration and unsupported claims in pursuit of an authoritarian,[73] militaristic foreign policy. Pompeo presents in a much quieter, less bombastic fashion, compared to Bolton, but if one listens closely to his words, there

---

[67] Landay, "Clashes with Spy Agencies."

[68] Andrew Kaczynski, Nathan McDermott and Chris Massie, "John Bolton has a decade-long association with anti-Islam activist Pamela Geller," CNN online, March 23, 2018, https://www.cnn.com/2018/03/23/politics/kfile-john-bolton-pamela-geller/index.html.

[69] Peter Beinart, "John Bolton and the normalization of fringe conservatism," Atlantic, March 24, 2018, https://www.theatlantic.com/politics/archive/2018/03/john-bolton-anti-muslim-enabler/556442/.

[70] Heidi Przybyla, "John Bolton presided over anti-Muslim think tank," NBC New online, April 23, 2018, https://www.nbcnews.com/politics/white-house/john-bolton-chaired-anti-muslim-think-tank-n868171.

[71] Donie O'Sullivan, Drew Griffin and Patricia DiCarlo, "Ex-Cambridge Analytica Staff say Bolton super PAC used compromised Facebook data," CNN online, March 23, 2018, https://www.cnn.com/2018/03/23/politics/john-bolton-super-pac-cambridge-analytica/index.html.

[72] Kahl, "John Bolton Is a National Security Threat."

[73] Matthew Wills, "What Links Religion and Authoritarianism?" JSTOR, July 25, 2017, https://daily.jstor.org/what-links-religion-and-authoritarianism/.

is a pattern of ideas and actions that raise the likelihood that he will inflame rather than contain Trump's dangerousness.

According to the Paul R. Pillar, a retired CIA officer and senior fellow at the Center for Security Studies at Georgetown University, Pompeo is a "fierce ideologue" who "stepped out of the proper role of an intelligence director to be an advocate for hawkish policies." Pillar strongly asserts that "Mr. Pompeo would reinforce Mr. Trump's more destructive inclinations" in the role of secretary of state.[74]

Pillar reports that Pompeo made "imaginary" and groundless statements about "secret side deals" between Obama and the Iranians while he was in Congress, in an effort to "discredit and undermine" the 2015 nuclear accord with Iran.[75] According to Pillar, Pompeo, as CIA director, also made unsubstantiated claims in October of 2017, attempting to tie al-Qaeda to Iran,[76] just days after President Trump asserted that these two entities are linked.[77] Pillar is referring to a neocon think tank event,[78] where Pompeo alleged, "There have been times the Iranians have worked alongside al-Qaeda," describing their relationship as an "open secret."[79]

Ned Price, a former CIA counterterrorism analyst and special assistant to President Obama in national security affairs, adds to the narrative regarding Pompeo's tendency to twist intelligence, affirming that Pompeo has politicized his role as CIA director in relationship to evaluating Iran."[80] Price and Pillar both compare Pompeo's tactics to the neoconservative buildup to the Iraq invasion,[81] when unsupported charges were made attempting to link Iraq to al-Qaeda.[82] Pillar asserts that Pompeo stepped well outside of the bounds in promoting a "cherry-picked" report in an attempt to prove a relationship between these two entities.[83]

---

[74] Paul Pillar, "Where Does Mike Pompeo Stand on the Issues? Too Close to Trump," New York Times, March 13, 2018, https://www.nytimes.com/2018/03/13/opinion/mike-pompeo-issues-trump.html.

[75] Pillar, "Too Close to Trump."

[76] Pillar, "Too Close to Trump."

[77] Donald Trump, "Remarks by President Trump on Iran Strategy," White House online, October 13, 2017, https://www.whitehouse.gov/briefings-statements/remarks-president-trump-iran-strategy/.

[78] Pillar, "Too Close to Trump."

[79] Jenna Lifhits, "Pompeo: Al-Qaeda-Iran Connection an 'Open Secret,'" Weekly Standard, October 19, 2017, https://www.weeklystandard.com/pompeo-al-qaeda-iran-connection-an-open-secret/article/2010120.

[80] Ned Price, "Why Mike Pompeo Released More bin Laden Files," The Atlantic, November 8, 2017, https://www.theatlantic.com/international/archive/2017/11/iran-mike-pompeo-bin-laden-documents-cia/545093/.

[81] Pillar, "Too Close to Trump."

[82] Price, "Why Mike."

[83] Pillar, "Too Close to Trump."

Price states that Pompeo "wasn't about transparency" in his dealings with Iran, but rather, "Pompeo is playing politics with intelligence" in a "ploy to bolster the case against Iran." Price asserts that "Pompeo was only too happy to feed these hawks," which underscores "the danger." He expounds on the "danger," explaining that the "hawks" Pompeo is gratifying with his al-Qaeda-Iran claims are neoconservatives who "espouse nothing short of regime change, believing that an avowedly anti-Israel state sponsor of terrorism should not be countenanced. It's this latter crowd that has consistently pointed to Iran's ties with al-Qaeda as a prime exhibit in their case for regime change."

Jonathan Greenblatt, chief executive of the Anti-Defamation League, writes that Pompeo "has a long record of anti-Muslim statements."[84] Laurie Goodstein at the *New York Times* expounds on one of Pompeo's unsupported and misleading claims in 2013 about American Muslims.[85] In 2013, shortly after the Boston Marathon terrorist attack, Pompeo stated on the House floor that "silence has made these Islamic leaders across America potentially complicit in these acts,"[86] suggesting that American Muslims had not denounced the attacks and were therefore accomplices on some level. Goodstein reports that "in fact, more than a half dozen American Muslim organizations had issued statements condemning the bombing within hours of the attack."[87] While he was immediately corrected with these facts and more—that prayer vigils, blood drives, and news conferences had been organized by Muslim groups in the days that followed the bombing—Goodstein reports that Mike Pompeo refused to acknowledge that he was wrong or to apologize for his inflammatory remarks.[88]

Pompeo has close ties to anti-Islam groups and people. ACT for America, the largest "anti-Muslim group in the United States," promotes "hateful" conspiracy theories about Muslims and "stokes irrational fear of Muslims via a number of false claims," according to the Anti-Defamation League (ADL).[89] In 2016, Pompeo

---

[84] Jonathan Greenblatt, "Don't Overlook John Bolton and Mike Pompeo's Anti-Muslim Ties," Washington Post, April 12, 2018, https://www.washingtonpost.com/amphtml/opinions/dont-overlook-john-bolton-and-mike-pompeos-anti-muslim-ties/2018/04/12/6a4ce456-3dc3-11e8-a7d1-e4efec6389f0_story.html.

[85] Laurie Goodstein, "Pompeo and Bolton Appointments Raise Alarm Regarding Ties to Anti-Islam Groups," New York Times, April 6, 2018, https://www.nytimes.com/2018/04/06/us/pompeo-bolton-muslims.html.

[86] United Voices for America, "Congressman Mike Pompeo Anti-Muslim Bigotry from House Floor," Filmed [June 2013]. YouTube Video, 1:29. Posted [July 25, 2013], https://www.youtube.com/watch?v=PaEXDqtCV5w.

[87] Goodstein, "Pompeo and Bolton."

[88] Goodstein, "Pompeo and Bolton."

[89] Anti-Defamation League, "ACT for America," ADL online, https://www.adl.org/resources/profiles/act-for-america.

accepted ACT for America's highest honor—the National Security Eagle Award. Brigette Gabriel, the group's founder, has described Pompeo as "a steadfast ally."[90] Pompeo also has a close alliance with Frank Gaffney, a notorious Islamophobe.[91] Gaffney, founder of a neoconservative think tank, Center for Security Policy (CSP), has "promulgated a number of anti-Muslim conspiracy theories over the years," according to the ADL.[92] (Gaffney promotes the belief that the Muslim Brotherhood has a secret network infiltrating our government whose aim is to replace our nation's laws with Sharia law.[93]) Pompeo has made at least two dozen appearances on Frank Gaffney's radio show in recent years,[94] and in 2015, he participated in a roundtable discussion at CSP's *Defeat Jihad Summit*.[95]

As a Congress member, Pompeo co-sponsored a bill to ban the Muslim Brotherhood,[96] citing the belief that the group is a "terrorist organization."[97] When Trump tried to attach the same designation to the brotherhood more recently, CIA experts issued an internal memo with a strong warning, asserting that this approach will "fuel extremism" and drive a wedge between the United States and its American Muslim allies.[98] In the CIA's internally published document, they acknowledge that "a minority of MB (Muslim Brotherhood) members have engaged in violence," but go on to note that the MB, which has millions of followers around the world, has "rejected violence as a matter of official policy and opposed al-Qa'ida and ISIS."[99] The CIA understands nuance and the

[90] Peter Beinart "Mike Pompeo's Allies on the Anti-Muslim Right," Atlantic, March 15, 2018, https://www.theatlantic.com/international/archive/2018/03/pompeo-muslims/555680/.

[91] Philip Bump, "Meet Frank Gaffney, the anti-Muslim gadfly reportedly advising Trump's transition team," Chicago Tribune, November 15, 2016, http://www.chicagotribune.com/news/nationworld/politics/ct-anti-muslim-frank-gaffney-trump-transition-team-20161115-story.html.

[92] Anti-Defamation League, "Frank Gaffney Jr. and the Center for Security Policy," ADL online, https://www.adl.org/resources/profiles/frank-gaffney-jr-and-the-center-for-security-policy.

[93] Beinart, "Mike Pompeo's Allies."

[94] Beinart, "Mike Pompeo's Allies."

[95] Center for Security Policy, "Defeat Jihad Summit Challenges Islamic Supremacism," Center for Security Policy online, https://www.centerforsecuritypolicy.org/2015/02/10/watch-live-defeat-jihad-summit/.

[96] Beinart, "Mike Pompeo's Allies."

[97] Mario Diaz-Balart, "H.R.3892 – Muslim Brotherhood Terrorist Designation Act of 2015, 114th Congress (2015-2016)," Congress.gov online, https://www.congress.gov/bill/114th-congress/house-bill/3892/cosponsors.

[98] Blake Hounshell and Nahal Toosi, "CIA Memo Designating Muslim Brotherhood Could 'Fuel Extremism," Politico February 8, 2017, https://www.politico.com/magazine/story/2017/02/cia-memo-designating-muslim-brotherhood-could-fuel-extremism-214757.

[99] Hounshell, "CIA Memo."

polarizing danger of using rigid thinking when discussing complex dynamics within a huge organization. Unfortunately, Pompeo's authoritarian,[100] all-or-nothing thought process is the type of approach that will fuel extremism, rather than combating it.

Shaun Casey, former director of the State Department's office of religion and global affairs under the Obama administration, summarizes his reservations about Pompeo as the secretary of state: "My concern is that Mr. Pompeo has left a trail of horrific, inaccurate, bigoted statements and associations vis-à-vis Muslims around the world."[101]

Pompeo has also rattled the saber when discussing the future of North Korea's Kim Jong-un. As the CIA director, Pompeo made an aggressive statement in July of 2017 that was widely interpreted as a call for Kim's ouster, even though Pompeo denied that intent.[102] At the Aspen Security Forum, Pompeo asserted, "I'm hopeful that we will find a way to separate that regime (Kim Jong-un's government) from this system (weapons program)," adding that "The North Korean people, I'm sure, are lovely people and would love to see him go."[103] CIA officer Pillar reports that "Mr. Pompeo has consistently taken one of the most hawkish lines on dealing with Pyongyang."[104] During Senate confirmation hearings, however, Pompeo expressed a softening of his nondiplomatic position with North Korea, which was met with skepticism by certain senators,[105] concerned about the possibility of his duplicity. Between Pompeo's track record of making unreliable claims that appear to serve a hawkish agenda and his militaristic remarks, some wonder whether his meeting with Kim Jong-un, in preparation for the U.S.-North Korea denuclearization talks between the U.S. and North Korea has raised more skepticism—it is reasonable to wonder whether the U.S.-North Korea summit was more stagecraft than reflective of a genuine interest in diplomacy. In fact, strategists warn that "a failure to reach

---

[100] P. Wesley Schulz, William F. Stone and Richard Christie, "Authoritarianism and Mental Rigidity: The Einstellung Problem Revisited," Personality and Social Psychology Bulletin 23, No. 1 (January 1997): 3-9, http://journals.sagepub.com/doi/pdf/10.1177/0146167297231001.

[101] Goodstein, "Pompeo and Bolton."

[102] Alex Lockie, "The CIA director just dropped some heavy hints that the US is looking into regime change in North Korea," Business Insider, July 21, 2017, http://www.businessinsider.com/pompeo-us-north-korea-kim-jong-un-2017-7.

[103] Max Greenwood, "CIA chief hopeful for 'change' in North Korea," Hill, July 21, 2017, http://thehill.com/policy/national-security/343077-cia-chief-hopeful-that-us-will-separate-north-korean-regime-from.

[104] Pillar, "Too Close to Trump."

[105] Nick Wadhams and Laura Litvan, "Pompeo Says Softer U.S. Policy Toward Russia Is Now Over," Bloomberg, April 11, 2018, https://www.bloomberg.com/news/articles/2018-04-12/pompeo-will-say-softer-u-s-policy-toward-russia-is-now-over.

an agreement could "bolster Washington's appetite for military action." CNBC reports that Georgetown University professor and senior advisor at the Center for Strategic and International Studies contends that "should the summit fail, it may actually bring us closer to war as we will have exhausted all diplomatic options."[106] Other foreign policy experts argue that even if an "agreement" of some kind is reached, it will not be substantive in nature and ultimately will not advance the peace process. Yukari Easton, a researcher and an ACE-Nikaido fellow at the East Asian Studies Center at University of Southern California, speculates, "The most likely outcome is that we will essentially end up where we began."[107]

Mike Pompeo's record of exaggerated or groundless assertions extends beyond his tendency toward militarism. Pompeo made an untrue statement to the public when he asserted, as CIA director, that "U.S. intelligence agencies had concluded that Russian interference did not affect the outcome of the 2016 U.S. presidential election."[108] In reality, no one within the intelligence community has issued an official statement regarding the impact of Russian meddling on the election, nor would they. Analyzing the brunt of Russian interference on voters' decisions during an election period is well outside the scope of what U.S. intelligence agencies, such as the CIA, can do. The CIA is not a polling company.

The Gospel of War

Unbeknownst to many Americans, there is another powerful, hawkish influence within the Trump Cabinet who brings vengeance-oriented, authoritarian leadership to the president's inner circle on a weekly basis. Rev. Ralph Drollinger, a former National Basketball Association player and president of Capitol Ministries,[109] wields a tremendous amount of authority and sway with as many as eight of Trump's Cabinet members who attend his weekly prayer and Bible study meetings in the White House's West Wing.[110] (The meetings were recently moved to this new

---

[106] Nyshka Chandran, "A failed US-North Korea summit could increase the risk of armed conflict," CNBC online, April 25, 2018, https://www.cnbc.com/2018/04/25/a-failed-us-north-korea-summit-could-increase-the-risk-of-armed-conflict.html.

[107] Yukari Easton, "Why US-North Korea Talks Will Fail," The Diplomat May 1, 2018, https://the-diplomat.com/2018/05/why-us-north-korea-talks-will-fail/.

[108] Warren Strobel, "CIA's Pompeo asserts Russian meddling did not sway U.S. election result," Reuters, October 19, 2017, https://uk.reuters.com/article/uk-usa-trump-russia/cias-pompeo-asserts-russian-meddling-did-not-sway-u-s-election-result-idUKKBN1CP02C.

[109] "Capitol Ministries Administration," Capitol Ministries website, accessed April 30, 2018, https://capmin.org/about/administration/.

[110] Nina Burleigh, "Trump Cabinet Spiritual Adviser Shares his Views, and Some Find Them Spooky," Newsweek, October 31, 2017, http://www.newsweek.com/trump-cabinet-spiritual-adviser-views-697479.

location to accommodate Vice President Mike Pence's security needs.[111]) In addition to Pence, the BBC reports that Jeff Sessions (Attorney General), Mike Pompeo (Secretary of State), Rick Perry (Secretary of Energy), and Betsy DeVos (Secretary of Education) attend the meetings.[112] *Newsweek* adds Ben Carson (housing and urban development) and Sonny Perdue (agriculture) to the list of Cabinet members attending the meeting.[113] Scott Pruitt (Environmental Protection Agency) is also a participant in the meetings, according to CBN.[114] Other senior officials in the Trump administration also attend Drollinger's West Wing meetings, according to *The New York Times*.[115]

Drollinger, who describes himself as a "prophetic voice," told German newspaper *Welt Am Sonntag* that he believes the government's "God-given responsibility" and "primary calling is to moralize a fallen world through the use of force." Drollinger added: "I think the best president is the one who is best going to use government as an adjudicator of wrongdoing. And I always thought that Trump would be the best at that."[116]

Drollinger's teachings on his website include the belief that the U.S. government (and President Trump) have a God-given duty to expand outside its borders, "bearing the sword," and serving as an "avenger who brings on wrath" on any nation who "practices evil."[117] Drollinger is especially vigilant regarding Islam, listing it as a "false religion" and asserting that it "has historically spread through the sword and seeks nothing less than world conquest for Allah."[118] Ironically, Drollinger's avenging angel theology sounds more like a call to jihad, than traditional Christianity doctrine.

---

[111] Burleigh, "Trump Cabinet."

[112] Owen Amos, "Inside the White House Bible Study group," BBC News online, April 8, 2018, http://www.bbc.com/news/world-us-canada-43534724.

[113] Burleigh, "Trump Cabinet."

[114] CBN News, "Trump Cabinet Members Praying, Studying the Bible together," CBN online, April 24, 2017, http://www1.cbn.com/beltwaybuzz/archive/2017/04/24/trump-cabinet-members-praying-studying-the-bible-together.

[115] Katherine Stewart, "The Museum of the Bible Is a Safe Space for Christian Nationalists," New York Times, January 6, 2018, https://www.nytimes.com/2018/01/06/opinion/sunday/the-museum-of-the-bible-is-a-safe-space-for-christian-nationalists.html.

[116] Von Lucas Wiegelmann, "Meet the preacher who teaches the Bible to the U.S. Cabinet," Welt Am Sonntag, October 29, 2017, https://www.welt.de/kultur/article170140247/Meet-the-preacher-who-teaches-the-Bible-to-the-US-Cabinet.html.

[117] Ralph Drollinger, "The ISIS Threat: The Bible on When War is Justifiable," Capitol Ministries (blog), July 6, 2015, https://capmin.org/the-isis-threat-the-bible-on-when-war-is-justifiable/.

[118] Ralph Drollinger, "How Would Your Rate Level of Spiritual Discernment?" Capitol Ministries (blog), March 24, 2014, https://capmin.org/how-would-you-rate-your-level-of-spiritual-discernment/.

During the weekly meetings, Drollinger lobbies Trump's inner circle with autocratic tenets rooted in a retribution-oriented worldview.[119] Drollinger believes in the Bible's "inerrancy," interpreting its words as "literal,"[120] an approach to scripture that has been linked in several important studies to authoritarianism. Marc Hetherington and Jonathan Weiler's robust research found a highly significant relationship between authoritarianism and those who use a "literal" interpretation of the Bible, consistent with the authoritarian's "aversion to ambiguity."[121] Wink, Dillon and Prettyman found in their longitudinal study a strong tie between authoritarianism and those who believe that there is only one "inerrant set of religious teachings," an approach to understanding that is "associated with rigidity in the processing of information" and "low cognitive complexity."[122]

Drollinger teaches that "violence does not necessarily lead to more violence," insisting that "God specifically ordains the use of corporate force against evil."[123] Drollinger expands on his war doctrine on his website: "When war is justified and righteous, a country's leadership should never enter into it with 'Low Testosterone.' It is an all or nothing commitment of the totality of the nation in its decisive quest for all out victory as quickly as possible!"[124]

Drollinger's extreme authoritarian ideology does not represent mainstream Christianity or all evangelical Christians. His intolerant views have led to multiple fallouts;[125] for example, he considers "women's liberation" to be a tool of "Satan"[126] and has called mothers, who work outside of the home, "sinners."[127] Drollinger has also alienated many members of the evangelical community. Drollinger's home

---

[119] Ralph Drollinger, "Institutions: Are You a Tritutionalist or a Pentetutionalist?" Capitol Ministries (blog), October 30, 2017, https://capmin.org/are-you-a-tritutionalist-or-a-pentetutionalist/.

[120] "Capitol Ministries Responds to Fake News from The L.A. Times and Others," Capitol Ministries online, accessed April 30, 2018. https://capmin.org/resources/ministry-updates/capitol-ministries-responds-fake-news-la-times-others/.

[121] Marc Hetherington and Jonathan Weiler, Authoritarianism and Polarization in American Politics (New York: Cambridge University Press, 2009), 59-60.

[122] Paul Wink, Michele Dillon and Adrienne Prettyman, . "Religiousness, Spiritual Seeking, and Authoritarianism: Findings from a Longitudinal Study," Journal for the Scientific Study of Religion 46, no. 3 (September 2007): 321-335, https://www.jstor.org/stable/4621983?mag=what-links-religion-and-authoritarianism&seq=3#page_scan_tab_contents.

[123] Ralph Drollinger, "The ISIS Threat: The Bible on When War is Justifiable—Part 2," Capitol Ministries (blog), July 13, 2015, https://capmin.org/the-isis-threat-the-bible-on-when-war-is-justifiable-part-2/.

[124] Drollinger, "The ISIS Thread."

[125] Evan Halper, "He once said mothers do not belong in state office. Now he leads the Trump Cabinet in Bible study," Los Angeles Times, August 3, 2017, http://www.latimes.com/politics/la-na-la-pol-trump-cabinet-pastor-20170803-story.html.

[126] Ralph Drollinger, "Spiritual Discernment."

[127] Halper, "Bible Study."

congregation, Grace Church, severed ties with him in 2009; Grace Church officials gave a statement in that year, asserting that "Ralph Drollinger is not biblically qualified for spiritual leadership."[128] Earlier in 2009, Frank Erb, the California state director for Capitol Ministries resigned, along with "nearly all state directors, board members and staff," over "concerns" regarding Drollinger's "leadership."[129]

According to *Newsweek*, Drollinger first "endeared himself to Trump" in 2016 "when he called on him to create a 'benevolent dictatorship.'"[130] (Drollinger's website minimizes his use of this phrase, insisting that it was a comment made only "in passing,"[131] failing to recognize how Drollinger's reflexive speech patterns have an authoritarian tone, whether intended or not.) In a BBC interview, Drollinger boasts that "of all the Bible studies I've written on policy, Trump's enacting everything I've written," asserting that he and the president share the same world view.[132] Drollinger also reports in the *Welt Am Sonntag* interview that he has a "pen pal relationship" with Donald Trump who receives his notes after each meeting and "has been writing notes back" to him. Drollinger observes: "He (Trump) likes loyalty. I supported him from very early on in the campaign and Jeff Sessions would tell you I influenced him to do the same in the Bible study."[133]

We believe it is reasonable to conclude that as many as eight of Donald Trump's Cabinet secretaries are probably on board with Drollinger's authoritarian ideology. Because Drollinger's "high testosterone" model of leadership includes the belief that President Trump has the "God-given" right to punish nations that "practice evil" and to "moralize a fallen world through the use of force," we also have deep concern that the president's Cabinet may not encourage him to use restraint as he considers war with North Korea and Iran.

Mike Pompeo directly credits Drollinger as an important influence in his life during a July 2015 speech at Summit Church in Wichita, Kansas. Pompeo expresses pleasure that he and many other Congress members who share his belief system, are "taking our guidance from the same place." (It appears that Drollinger is a contributor to this "guidance," since he runs meetings for many Congress members

[128] Capitol Weekly staff, "Capitol Ministries state director leaves, joins new Christian group," Capitol Weekly online, November 12, 2009, http://capitolweekly.net/capitol-ministries-replaced-by-new-nationwide-christian-group/.

[129] Capitol Weekly staff, "Capitol Ministries."

[130] Nina Burleigh, "Does God Believe in Trump? White Evangelicals are Sticking with Their 'Prince of Lies," Newsweek, October 5, 2017, http://www.newsweek.com/2017/10/13/donald-trump-white-evangelicals-support-god-677587.html.

[131] "Capitol Ministries Responds to False and Misleading Newsweek Story," Capitol Ministries online, accessed on April 30, 2018, https://capmin.org/capitol-ministries-responds-to-newsweek/.

[132] Amos, "Inside the White House."

[133] Wiegelmann, "Meet the Preacher."

as well.[134]) Pompeo asserts that he has "firm convictions about the direction America needs to go." In keeping with Drollinger's emphasis on retribution, Pompeo's presentation focuses on punishment for the "wicked" in response to the fact that "this evil is all around us." He repeatedly underscores that "we are engaged in a struggle against radical Islam" and warns, "Woe to those who call evil good." In his speech, Pompeo praises our military and its commitment to "making sure America remains the most exceptional nation in the world." And Pompeo quotes from Jeremiah 8:12 with an authoritarian, vengeance-filled flair: "Are they ashamed of their detestable conduct? No, they have no shame at all, so they will fall among the fallen, they will be brought down when they are punished."[135]

Vice President Mike Pence has also utilized saber-rattling words, suggestive of Drollinger's impact, while referencing North Korea: In April of 2017, he tweeted: "Strategic patience has been the approach of last admin & beyond. That approach has failed. The era of strategic patience is over."[136] And just a few days later, Pence used Drollinger-esque, war-oriented language, referencing biblical weaponry in relation to North Korea; on April 19, 2017, he told 2,500 American sailors stationed in Asia that "under President Trump … the sword stands ready."[137]

Mike Pence's war-prone eschatology moves beyond his close association with Ralph Drollinger. The vice president's "steady role in pushing" for the movement of the American Embassy from Tel Aviv to Jerusalem provides an important glimpse into Pence's apocalyptic ideology.[138] His alliance with megachurch pastor and evangelical extremist[139] John Hagee[140] provides an even deeper look into the

---

134 "Congressional Sponsors," Capitol Ministries website, accessed May 7, 2018, https://capmin.org/ministries/washington-dc/congressional-sponsors/.

135 Summit Church, "Summit Church God and Country Rally 2015," Filmed [June 28, 2015]. YouTube Video, 42.37. Posted [July 8, 2015], https://www.youtube.com/watch?time_continue=13&v=sO0opXYM52w.

136 Mike Pence (@VP), "Strategic patience has been the approach of last admin & beyond. That approach has failed. The era of strategic patience is over. #VPinAsia," Twitter, April 16, 2017, 11:53 p.m., https://twitter.com/vp/status/853863868212289537.

137 Associated Press, "Mike Pence's warning to North Korea: 'The sword stands ready,'" Los Angeles Times, April 19, 2017, http://www.latimes.com/politics/washington/la-na-essential-washington-updates-mike-pence-s-warning-to-north-korea-1492605388-htmlstory.html.

138 COG writer, "Mike Pence, Jerusalem, Evangelicals and the 'End of the World,'" Church of God News online, January 19, 2018, http://www.cogwriter.com/news/prophecy/mike-pence-jerusalem-evangelicals-and-the-end-of-the-world/.

139 Noah Bierman, "Who really wants Trump to recognize Jerusalem? His evangelical supporters back home," Los Angeles Times, December 6, 2017, http://www.latimes.com/politics/la-na-pol-trump-israel-politics-20171206-story.html.

140 Ben Mathis-Lilley, "Critics Question Whether Pastor Who Said Hitler Was Sent by God Was Good Choice to Speak at U.S. Embassy in Israel," Slate, May 14, 2018, https://slate.com/news-and-politics/2018/05/israel-embassy-pastor-said-hitler-was-sent-by-god.html.

beliefs that guide the vice president's position on Jerusalem, evidenced in "his long public record of Christian Zionism,"[141] according to Dan Hummel, a historian and fellow at the Harvard Kennedy School. Hagee is the nation's most outspoken leader in the Christian Zionism movement. Not to be confused with Zionism, *Christian Zionism*, possesses an "absolutist war script for the Middle East and for the end of the world," according to Barbara Rossing, a Harvard-trained professor of New Testament at the Lutheran School of Theology at Chicago.[142] Hagee also actively promotes a geopolitical ideology known as "dispensational premillennialism," a theological system that posits that when Jerusalem is recognized as the capital of Israel, an important biblical prophecy will be fulfilled, ushering in the next phase in God's plan—an apocalyptic era in which God will wage war against Israel's enemies.[143] Also known as the "Battle of Armageddon," Hagee describes this "third world war" in graphic terms, asserting that Israel will be covered in "a sea of human blood" during this period,[144] culminating in God's destruction of all of Israel's enemies, including Iran.[145] Hagee predicts in his book *Jerusalem Countdown:* "We are on a countdown to crisis. The coming nuclear showdown with Iran is a certainty. The battle for Jerusalem has already begun. That war will affect every nation on Earth, including America, and will affect every person on Planet Earth."[146]

Hagee's views on Islam add more insight into the way he thinks and the beliefs that drive his agenda within the White House. In a 2016 sermon, Hagee predicted that before the last battle of humanity occurs, Islam will have become the "world's religion."[147] And he makes militaristic and paranoia-tinged claims regarding "radical Islamic extremists," asserting that "America has been invaded by an invisible army of millions who intend to destroy this nation," insisting that "it is time to identify

---

[141] Dan Hummel, "What you need to know about Mike Pence's speech to Christians United for Israel," Washington Post, July 17, 2017, https://www.washingtonpost.com/news/made-by-history/wp/2017/07/17/what-you-need-to-know-about-mike-pences-speech-to-christians-united-for-israel/?utm_term=.3a0cd033d915.

[142] Barbara Rossing, The Rapture Exposed: The Message of Hope in the Book of Revelation (New York: Basic Books, 2004).

[143] Tara Burton, "Pastor at US Embassy opening in Jerusalem says Trump is 'on the right side' of God," Vox, May 14, 2018, https://www.vox.com/2018/5/14/17352676/robert-jeffress-jerusalem-embassy-israel-prayer.

[144] John Hagee, Earth's Final Moments: Powerful Insight and Understanding of the Prophetic Signs that Surround Us (Lake Mary Florida: Charisma House, 2011),110.

[145] Ben Akhtar, "John Hagee 2016, The King of the West: The Final Game of Thrones," YouTube Video, Posted [May 20, 2016], https://www.youtube.com/watch?v=Y-L9h0Rqz6M.

[146] John Hagee, Jerusalem Countdown. (Lake Mary, FL: Frontline, 2007).

[147] Ben Akhtar, "John Hagee 2016."

our enemies and wipe them off the face of the earth before they destroy us from within."[148]

John Hagee, like Drollinger, is a powerful influence inside Washington. He and his Christian Zionist organization are credited with "getting their man in the White House" with Mike Pence as vice president, and many wonder if Hagee played a role in Trump's abandonment of the two-state solution in Israel.[149] In 2017, Hagee appealed to Trump's fragile ego, predicting that "if President Trump moves the embassy into Jerusalem, he will historically step into immortality."[150] (This view dovetails nicely with the belief, held by many conservative evangelicals, that Trump is the strong man who will "make the world ready for a final battle between good and evil.")[151] Hagee invited Vice President Pence to be the keynote speaker at Hagee's Christians United for Israel rally for Christian Zionists in 2017, which, according to Dr. Hummel, "signals a new era of Christian Zionist influence in the White House".[152] At the summit, Pence, described by Hummel as an "ardent Christian Zionist,"[153] discussed the fulfillment of biblical prophecy with the creation of the state of Israel.[154] Hagee's involvement in this significant geopolitical event was capped off when he led the benediction prayer at the opening of the U.S. Embassy in Jerusalem in May of 2018.[155]

Regardless of whether Donald Trump subscribes to Christian Zionism or dispensational millennialism, Hagee's belief that Trump has earned political immortality may serve to strengthen Trump's grandiosity, emboldening him to act out as he struggles through an unprecedented level of personal crisis. It is also conceivable that Hagee's deeply held suspicions about Iran and Islam may be

---

[148] John Hagee, "The Coming Fourth Reich," John Hagee Ministries, Accessed May 21, 2018, https://www.jhm.org/Articles/2016-09-01-the-coming-fourth-reich.

[149] "How Christian Zionists Got Their Man into the White House," Middle East Eye, Accessed May 21, 2018, http://www.middleeasteye.net/essays/battle-armageddon-776157873.

[150] Kaitlyn Schallhorn, "Why Trump's Promise to Move US Embassy to Jerusalem Is so Controversial," Fox News, May 14, 2018, Accessed May 21, 2018, http://www.foxnews.com/politics/2018/05/14/why-trumps-promise-to-move-us-embassy-to-jerusalem-is-so-controversial.html.

[151] Matthew Gabriele, "Trump's Recognition of Jerusalem Excites Apocalyptic Fervor," Religion News Service, December 11, 2017, Accessed May 21, 2018, https://religionnews.com/2017/12/11/trumps-recognition-of-jerusalem-excites-apocalyptic-fervor/.

[152] Hummel, "What you need to know."

[153] Hummel, "What you need to know."

[154] Lauren Markoe, "Pence roots administration's support for Israel in faith," Baptist Standard, July 19, 2017, https://www.baptiststandard.com/news/nation/pence-roots-administration-s-support-for-israel-in-faith/.

[155] Kevin Bohn and Daniel Burke, "Controversial US pastors to take part in Jerusalem embassy opening," CNN, May 14, 2018, Accessed May 20th, 2018, https://www.cnn.com/2018/05/13/politics/hagee-jeffress-us-embassy-jerusalem/index.html.

serving an insidious role inside the president's head, granting him a "theological" justification for using Iran as the ultimate "poison container" as he seeks to externalize his internal agony. And regardless of whether the Cabinet overtly supports a pre-emptive war with Iran or North Korea, Drollinger's endorsement of using "force" against the "wicked" and his confidence in Trump—that he is "the one who is best going to use government as an adjudicator of wrongdoing"— adds to the danger.[156]

Given the president's well-documented pattern of disturbing conduct and the profound level of psychological distress he is experiencing, it is quite possible that Trump could use Drollinger's words as a formal blessing to act out in a cataclysmic fashion. By twisting Drollinger's authoritarian license to wage war with a bad guy into an invitation to initiate a first strike, Trump may find the ultimate distraction from the pain of the Mueller probe that could lead to catastrophic results. As we wrote in our 2017 article, leaders with Cluster B behaviors may "take drastic measures to avoid humiliation. Extreme examples of this dynamic include cult leaders like David Koresh and Jim Jones, who chose mass suicide over allowing themselves to be arrested in front of their supporters."[157] And because Trump has the blessing of many conservative evangelicals who believe he has been chosen to hasten the "end times," this potentially cataclysmic event may be welcomed by up to one-third of our nation, bringing new meaning to the phrase, "self-fulfilling prophesy."[158]

Conclusion

As the balance of power shifts to the top of the executive branch, with few to no checks coming from Congress or, likely, from the Trump Cabinet, we believe that the United States is on a path to war that goes beyond occasional strikes in Syria. When presidents decide whether to go to war, the number of people they consult is limited—usually just a few—including the secretary of state and national security advisor. As Donald Trump continues to psychologically devolve, besieged by unbearable stress and humiliation, it is essential that his inner circle provides a steady and containing environment for the president. By elevating Bolton and Pompeo into his cadre of confidants, we are concerned that Trump is courting disaster, drawing men who exacerbate the darkest elements in his character, rather than containing them.

---

[156] Wiegelmann, "Meet the Preacher."

[157] Painter and Watt, "Mental Health Matters."

[158] Matthew Avery Sutton, "Donald Trump, the herald of evangelicals' end times," Seattle Times, September 30, 2016, https://www.seattletimes.com/opinion/donald-trump-the-herald-of-evangelicals-end-times/.

Even if Trump and his team are not sincere in their threats to engage militarily, their bellicose challenges may accidentally provoke a reactive first strike from the impulsive leaders in Iran or North Korea. When you combine this reality with the rest of his Cabinet's seemingly quiet alignment with a radical, militaristic authoritarian leader who believes that Trump possesses the authority to wage war with any nation that is considered "evil," we believe the United States is facing a real danger. The palpable possibility exists that the president will take advantage of the encouragement and belligerent support that he receives from his Cabinet members, in pursuit of his own distracting and destructive agenda. The prospects of this agenda being put into practice are most frightening.

Richard Painter has been the S. Walter Richey Professor of Corporate Law at the University of Minnesota Law School since 2007. From February 2005 to July 2007, he was associate counsel to the president in the White House Counsel's office, serving as the chief ethics lawyer for President George W. Bush. Currently, he's a candidate for U.S. Senate in Minnesota.

Leanne Watt, Ph.D., M.A. is a clinical psychologist working in private practice for the last 25 years. She is a graduate of UCLA School of Medicine's post-doctoral fellowship program in clinical psychology. Dr. Watt completed an NIH post-doctoral research fellowship in neuropsychology at Keck School of Medicine of USC. She received her Ph.D. in clinical psychology from The School of Psychology at Fuller Theological Seminary (FTS) and completed a masters degree in theology from FTS.

Bibliography

Akhtar, Ben. "John Hagee 2016, The King of the West: The Final Game of Thrones." *YouTube Video*, Posted [May 20, 2016]. https://www.youtube.com/watch?v=Y-L9h0Rqz6M.

Amos, Owen. "Inside the White House Bible Study group." *BBC News* online, April 8, 2018. http://www.bbc.com/news/world-us-canada-43534724.

Anti-Defamation League. "ACT for America." ADL online. https://www.adl.org/resources/profiles/act-for-america.

Anti-Defamation League. "Frank Gaffney Jr. and the Center for Security Policy." ADL online. https://www.adl.org/resources/profiles/frank-gaffney-jr-and-the-center-for-security-policy.

Associated Press. "Mike Pence's warning to North Korea: 'The sword stands ready.'" *Los Angeles Times*, April 19, 2017. http://www.latimes.com/politics/washington/la-na-essential-washington-updates-mike-pence-s-warning-to-north-korea-1492605388-htmlstory.html.

Barclay, Eliza. "The psychiatrist who briefed Congress on Trump's mental state: 'this is an emergency.'" *Vox,* updated January 6, 2018. https://www.vox.com/science-and-health/2018/1/5/16770060/trump-mental-health-psychiatrist-25th-amendment.

Beinart, Peter. "John Bolton and the normalization of fringe conservatism." *Atlantic*, March 24, 2018. https://www.theatlantic.com/politics/archive/2018/03/john-bolton-anti-muslim-enabler/556442/.

Beinart, Peter. "Mike Pompeo's Allies on the Anti-Muslim Right." *Atlantic*, March 15, 2018. https://www.theatlantic.com/international/archive/2018/03/pompeo-muslims/555680/.

Benen, Steve. "Trump's first cabinet meeting was surprisingly creepy." *MSNBC* online, June 12, 2017. http://www.msnbc.com/rachel-maddow-show/trumps-first-full-cabinet-meeting-was-surprisingly-creepy.

Bierman, Noah. "Who really wants Trump to recognize Jerusalem? His evangelical supporters back home." *Los Angeles Times*, December 6, 2017. http://www.latimes.com/politics/la-na-pol-trump-israel-politics-20171206-story.html.

Bohn, Kevin and Daniel Burke. "Controversial US pastors to take part in Jerusalem embassy opening." CNN, May 14, 2018, Accessed May 20th, 2018. https://www.cnn.com/2018/05/13/politics/hagee-jeffress-us-embassy-jerusalem/index.html.

Bolton, John. "Beyond the Iran Nuclear Deal." *Wall Street Journal*, January 15, 2018. https://www.wsj.com/articles/beyond-the-iran-nuclear-deal-1516044178.

Bolton, John. "How to get out of the Iran Nuclear Deal." *National Review,* August 28, 2017. https://www.nationalreview.com/2017/08/iran-nuclear-deal-exit-strategy-john-bolton-memo-trump/.

Bolton, John. "The Legal Case for Striking North Korea First." *Wall Street Journal*, February 28, 2018. https://www.wsj.com/articles/the-legal-case-for-striking-north-korea-first-1519862374.

Bump, Philip. "Meet Frank Gaffney, the anti-Muslim gadfly reportedly advising Trump's transition team." *Chicago Tribune*, November 15, 2016. http://www.chicagotribune.com/news/nationworld/politics/ct-anti-muslim-frank-gaffney-trump-transition-team-20161115-story.html.

Burleigh, Nina. "Does God Believe in Trump? White Evangelicals are Sticking with Their 'Prince of Lies.'" *Newsweek*, October 5, 2017. http://www.newsweek.com/2017/10/13/donald-trump-white-evangelicals-support-god-677587.html.

Burleigh, Nina. "Trump Cabinet Spiritual Adviser Shares his Views, and Some Find Them Spooky." *Newsweek*, October 31, 2017. http://www.newsweek.com/trump-cabinet-spiritual-adviser-views-697479.

Burton, Tara. "Pastor at US Embassy opening in Jerusalem says Trump is 'on the right side' of God." *Vox*, May 14, 2018. https://www.vox.com/2018/5/14/17352676/robert-jeffress-jerusalem-embassy-israel-prayer.

Cameron, James. "The high price of Trump's nuclear saber-rattling." *Washington Post*, December 7, 2017. https://www.washingtonpost.com/news/made-by-history/wp/2017/12/07/the-high-price-of-trumps-nuclear-saber-rattling/?utm_term=.ff9c11cb075f.

"Capitol Ministries Administration." Capitol Ministries online, accessed April 30, 2018. https://capmin.org/about/administration/.

"Capitol Ministries Responds to Fake News from The L.A. Times and Others." Capitol Ministries online, accessed April 30, 2018. https://capmin.org/resources/ministry-updates/capitol-ministries-responds-fake-news-la-times-others/.

"Capitol Ministries Responds to False and Misleading Newsweek Story." Capitol Ministries online, accessed on April 30, 2018. https://capmin.org/capitol-ministries-responds-to-newsweek/.

"Congressional Sponsors." Capitol Ministries online, accessed May 7, 2018. https://capmin.org/ministries/washington-dc/congressional-sponsors/.

Capitol Weekly staff. "Capitol Ministries state director leaves, joins new Christian group." *Capitol Weekly* online, November 12, 2009. http://capitolweekly.net/capitol-ministries-replaced-by-new-nationwide-christian-group/.

CBN News staff. "Trump Cabinet Members Praying, Studying the Bible Together." *CBN online*, April 24, 2017.http://www1.cbn.com/beltwaybuzz/archive/2017/04/24/trump-cabinet-members-praying-studying-the-bible-together.

Center for Security Policy. "Defeat Jihad Summit Challenges Islamic Supremacism." Center for Security Policy online, February 10, 2015. https://www.centerforsecuritypolicy.org/2015/02/10/watch-live-defeat-jihad-summit/.

Chait, Jonathan. "Corruption, Not Russia, is Trump's Greatest Political Liability." *New York Magazine*, April 1, 2018. http://nymag.com/daily/intelligencer/2018/04/corruption-is-trumps-greatest-political-liability.html.

Chandran, Nyshka. "A failed US-North Korea summit could increase the risk of armed conflict." CNBC online, April 25, 2018. https://www.cnbc.com/2018/04/25/a-failed-us-north-korea-summit-could-increase-the-risk-of-armed-conflict.html.

COG writer. "Mike Pence, Jerusalem, Evangelicals and the 'End of the World.'" Church of God News online, January 19, 2018. http://www.cogwriter.com/news/prophecy/mike-pence-jerusalem-evangelicals-and-the-end-of-the-world/.

Coppins, McKay. "How the Swamp Drained Trump." *The Atlantic*, January 30, 2018. https://www.theatlantic.com/politics/archive/2018/01/swamp-trump/551807/.

Diaz-Balart, Mario. "H.R.3892 – Muslim Brotherhood Terrorist Designation Act of 2015, 114th Congress (2015-2016)." Congress online. https://www.congress.gov/bill/114th-congress/house-bill/3892/cosponsors.

Drollinger, Ralph. "How Would Your Rate Level of Spiritual Discernment?" Capitol Ministries (blog), March 24, 2014. https://capmin.org/how-would-you-rate-your-level-of-spiritual-discernment/.

Drollinger, Ralph. "Institutions: Are You a Tritutionalist or a Pentetutionalist?" Capitol Ministries (blog), October 30, 2017. https://capmin.org/are-you-a-tritutionalist-or-a-pentetutionalist/.

Drollinger, Ralph. "The ISIS Thread: The Bible on When War is Justifiable." Capitol Ministries (blog). https://capmin.org/the-isis-threat-the-bible-on-when-war-is-justifiable//.

Drollinger, Ralph. "The ISIS Threat: The Bible on When War is Justifiable—Part 2." Capitol Ministries (blog), July 13, 2015. https://capmin.org/the-isis-threat-the-bible-on-when-war-is-justifiable-part-2/.

Easton, Yukari. "Why US-North Korea Talks Will Fail." The Diplomat, May 1, 2018. https://thediplomat.com/2018/05/why-us-north-korea-talks-will-fail/.

Entous, Adam. "House majority leader in 2016: 'I Think Putin Pays' Trump." Washington Post, May 17, 2017. https://www.washingtonpost.com/world/national-security/house-majority-leader-to-colleagues-in-2016-i-think-putin-pays-trump/2017/05/17/515f6f8a-3aff-11e7-8854-21f359183e8c_story.html?utm_term=.30093cea1ed5.

Gabriele, Matthew. "Trump's Recognition of Jerusalem Excites Apocalyptic Fervor." Religion News Service, December 11, 2017, Accessed May 21, 2018. https://religionnews.com/2017/12/11/trumps-recognition-of-jerusalem-excites-apocalyptic-fervor/.

Gaouette, Nicole. "U.S. and Israeli officials intensify the drumbeat against Iran." CNN online, April 27, 2018. https://www.cnn.com/2018/04/27/politics/us-israel-iran-dangers/index.html.

Glass, Andrew. "The 25th Amendment was ratified Feb. 10, 1967." Politico, February 10, 2012. https://www.politico.com/story/2012/02/nevada-puts-25th-amendment-over-the-top-072700.

Goodstein, Laurie. "Pompeo and Bolton Appointments Raise Alarm Regarding Ties to Anti-Islam Groups." New York Times, April 6, 2018. https://www.nytimes.com/2018/04/06/us/pompeo-bolton-muslims.html.

Greenblatt, Jonathan. "Don't Overlook John Bolton and Mike Pompeo's Anti-Muslim Ties." Washington Post, April 12, 2018. https://www.washingtonpost.com/amphtml/opinions/dont-overlook-john-bolton-and-mike-pompeos-anti-muslim-ties/2018/04/12/6a4ce456-3dc3-11e8-a7d1-e4efec6389f0_story.html.

Greenwood, Max. "CIA chief hopeful for 'change' in North Korea." Hill, July 21, 2017. http://thehill.com/policy/national-security/343077-cia-chief-hopeful-that-us-will-separate-north-korean-regime-from.

Hagee, John. Earth's Final Moments: Powerful Insight and Understanding of the Prophetic Signs that Surround Us. (Lake Mary Florida: Charisma House, 2011),110.

Hagee, John. Jerusalem Countdown. (Lake Mary, FL: Frontline, 2007).

Hagee, John. "The Coming Fourth Reich." John Hagee Ministries, Accessed May 21, 2018. https://www.jhm.org/Articles/2016-09-01-the-coming-fourth-reich.

Halper, Evan. "He once said mothers do not belong in state office. Now he leads the Trump Cabinet in Bible study." *Los Angeles Times*, August 3, 2017. http://www.latimes.com/politics/la-na-la-pol-trump-cabinet-pastor-20170803-story.html.

Hetherington, Marc and Jonathan Weiler. *Authoritarianism and Polarization in American Politics*. New York: Cambridge University Press, 2009.

Hounshell, Blake and Nahal Toosi. "CIA Memo Designating Muslim Brotherhood Could 'Fuel Extremism." *Politico* February 8, 2017. https://www.politico.com/magazine/story/2017/02/cia-memo-designating-muslim-brotherhood-could-fuel-extremism-214757.

Hummel, Dan. "What you need to know about Mike Pence's speech to Christians United for Israel." *Washington Post*, July 17, 2017. https://www.washingtonpost.com/news/made-by-history/wp/2017/07/17/what-you-need-to-know-about-mike-pences-speech-to-christians-united-for-israel/?utm_term=.3a0cd033d915.

Kaczynski, Andrew, Nathan McDermott and Chris Massie. "John Bolton has a decade-long association with anti-Islam activist Pamela Geller." *CNN* online, March 23, 2018. https://www.cnn.com/2018/03/23/politics/kfile-john-bolton-pamela-geller/index.html.

Kahl, Colin and Jon Wolfsthal. "John Bolton Is a National Security Threat." *Foreign Policy*, March 23, 2018. http://foreignpolicy.com/2018/03/23/john-bolton-is-a-national-security-threat/.

Kakkar, Hemant and Niro Sivanathan. "When the appeal of a dominant leader is greater than a prestige leader." *PNAS* 114, no.26 (June 2017): 6734-6739. https://doi.org/10.1073/pnas.1617711114.

Krieg, Gregory. "John Bolton on: bombing Iran, North Korea, Russia, and the Iraq War." *CNN* online, March 23, 2018. https://www.cnn.com/2018/03/23/politics/what-john-bolton-said-iraq-iran-north-korea/index.html.

Landay, Jonathan and Warren Strobel. "Trump's new security advisor known for clashes with spy agencies." Reuters, March 23, 2018. https://www.reuters.com/article/us-usa-trump-bolton-intelligence/trumps-new-security-adviser-known-for-clashes-with-spy-agencies-idUSKBN1GZ37N.

Lifhits, Jenna. "Pompeo: Al-Qaeda-Iran Connection an 'Open Secret." *Weekly Standard*, October 19, 2017. https://www.weeklystandard.com/pompeo-al-qaeda-iran-connection-an-open-secret/article/2010120.

Lockie, Alex. "The CIA director just dropped some heavy hints that the US is looking into regime change in North Korea." Business Insider online, July 21, 2017. http://www.businessinsider.com/pompeo-us-north-korea-kim-jong-un-2017-7.

Lynch, Colum and Elias Groll. "Trump Taps Uber-Hawk Bolton as National Security Advisor." *Foreign Policy*, March 22, 2018. http://foreignpolicy.com/2018/03/22/trump-taps-uber-hawk-bolton-as-national-security-adviser/.

Markoe, Lauren. "Pence roots administration's support for Israel in faith." Baptist Standard, July 19, 2017. https://www.baptiststandard.com/news/nation/pence-roots-administration-s-support-for-israel-in-faith/.

Mathis-Lilley, Ben. "Critics Question Whether Pastor Who Said Hitler Was Sent by God Was Good Choice to Speak at U.S. Embassy in Israel." *Slate*, May 14, 2018. https://slate.com/news-and-politics/2018/05/israel-embassy-pastor-said-hitler-was-sent-by-god.html.

Mayo Clinic staff. "Antisocial Personality Disorder." Mayo Clinic online, last modified August 4, 2017. https://www.mayoclinic.org/diseases-conditions/antisocial-personality-disorder/symptoms-causes/syc-20353928.

Mayo Clinic staff. "Narcissistic Personality Disorder." Mayo Clinic online, last modified November 18, 2017. https://www.mayoclinic.org/diseases-conditions/narcissistic-person-ality-disorder/symptoms-causes/syc-20366662.

Mayo Clinic staff. "Personality Disorders: Symptoms and Causes." Mayo Clinic online, last modified September 23, 2016. https://www.mayoclinic.org/diseases-conditions/personality-disorders/symptoms-causes/syc-20354463.

Meng, Michael. "On Authoritarianism: A Review Essay." *Comparative Studies in Society and History* 59, no. 4 (September 2017):1008-1020. https://doi.org/10.1017/S0010417517000354.

Nazaryan, Alexander. "Trump Administration: The Most Corrupt and Unethical in American History?" *Newsweek,* September 23, 2017. http://www.newsweek.com/trump-pruitt-price-devos-669853.

O'Sullivan, Donie, Drew Griffin and Patricia DiCarlo. "Ex-Cambridge Analytica Staff say Bolton super PAC used compromised Facebook data." *CNN* online, March 23, 2018. https://www.cnn.com/2018/03/23/politics/john-bolton-super-pac-cambridge-analytica/index.html.

Painter, Richard and Leanne E. Watt. "The 25th Amendment Proves Why Donald Trump's Mental Health Matters." *NBC News* Think online, October 18, 2017. https://www.nbcnews.com/think/opinion/25th-amendment-proves-why-trump-s-mental-health-matters-ncna801666.

Pence, Mike (@VP). "Strategic patience has been the approach of last admin & beyond. That approach has failed. The era of strategic patience is over. #VPinAsia." Twitter, April 16, 2017, 11:53 p.m. https://twitter.com/vp/status/853863868212289537.

Pillar, Paul. "Where Does Mike Pompeo Stand on the Issues? Too Close to Trump." *New York Times*, March 13, 2018. https://www.nytimes.com/2018/03/13/opinion/mike-pompeo-issues-trump.html.

Price, Ned. "Why Mike Pompeo Released More bin Laden Files." *The Atlantic*, November 8, 2017. https://www.theatlantic.com/international/archive/2017/11/iran-mike-pompeo-bin-laden-documents-cia/545093/.

Przybyla, Heidi. "John Bolton presided over anti-Muslim think tank." *NBC New* online, April 23, 2018. https://www.nbcnews.com/politics/white-house/john-bolton-chaired-anti-muslim-think-tank-n868171.

Rossing, Barbara. *The Rapture Exposed: The Message of Hope in the Book of Revelation* (New York: Basic Books, 2004).

Schallhorn, Kaitlyn. "Why Trump's Promise to Move US Embassy to Jerusalem Is So Contro-versial." Fox News, May 14, 2018, Accessed May 21, 2018. http://www.foxnews.com/politics/2018/05/14/why-trumps-promise-to-move-us-embassy-to-jerusalem-is-so-controversial.html.

Schulz, P. Wesley, William F. Stone and Richard Christie. "Authoritarianism and Mental Rigidity: The Einstellung Problem Revisited." *Personality and Social Psychology Bulletin* 23, No. 1 (January 1997): 3-9. http://journals.sagepub.com/doi/pdf/10.1177/0146167297231001.

Sinclair, Harriet. "Most Americans Fear Major War Under Trump, Polls Show." *Newsweek*, October 19, 2017. http://www.newsweek.com/most-americans-fear-major-war-under-trump-poll-shows-688214.

Stewart, Katherine. "The Museum of the Bible Is a Safe Space for Christian Nationalists." *New York Times*, January 6, 2018. https://www.nytimes.com/2018/01/06/opinion/sunday/the-museum-of-the-bible-is-a-safe-space-for-christian-nationalists.html.

Strobel, Warren. "CIA's Pompeo asserts Russian meddling did not sway U.S. election result." Reuters, October 19, 2017. https://uk.reuters.com/article/uk-usa-trump-russia/cias-pompeo-asserts-russian-meddling-did-not-sway-u-s-election-result-idUKKBN1CP02C.

Strong, Morgan. "How Christian Zionists Got Their Man into the White House." Middle East Eye, January 8, 2018. Accessed May 21, 2018. http://www.middleeasteye.net/essays/battle-armageddon-776157873.

Summit Church. "Summit Church God and Country Rally 2015." Filmed [June 28, 2015]. YouTube Video, 42.37. Posted [July 8, 2015]. https://www.youtube.com/watch?time_continue=13&v=sO0opXYM52w.

Sutton, Matthew Avery. "Donald Trump, the herald of evangelicals' end times." *Seattle Times*, September 30, 2016. https://www.seattletimes.com/opinion/donald-trump-the-herald-of-evangelicals-end-times/.

Thielmann, Greg. "Bolton: A Prime Mover of the Iraq WMD Fiasco." *Lobe Log*, December 14, 2016. https://lobelog.com/bolton-a-prime-mover-of-the-iraq-wmd-fiasco/.

Trump, Donald. "Remarks by President Trump on Iran Strategy." White House online, October 13, 2017. https://www.whitehouse.gov/briefings-statements/remarks-president-trump-iran-strategy/.

United Voices for America. "Congressman Mike Pompeo Anti-Muslim Bigotry from House Floor." Filmed [June 2013]. YouTube Video, 1:29. Posted [July 25, 2013]. https://www.youtube.com/watch?v=PaEXDqtCV5w.

Wadhams, Nick and Laura Litvan. "Pompeo Says Softer U.S. Policy Toward Russia Is Now Over." Bloomberg, April 11, 2018. https://www.bloomberg.com/news/articles/2018-04-12/pompeo-will-say-softer-u-s-policy-toward-russia-is-now-over.

Wiegelmann, Von Lucas. "Meet the preacher who teaches the Bible to the U.S. Cabinet." *Welt Am Sonntag*, October 29, 2017. https://www.welt.de/kultur/article170140247/Meet-the-preacher-who-teaches-the-Bible-to-the-US-Cabinet.html.

Wills, Matthew. "What Links Religion and Authoritarianism?" JSTOR, July 25, 2017. https://daily.jstor.org/what-links-religion-and-authoritarianism/.

Wink, Paul, Michele Dillon and Adrienne Prettyman. "Religiousness, Spiritual Seeking, and Authoritarianism: Findings from a Longitudinal Study," *Journal for the Scientific Study of Religion* 46, no. 3 (September 2007): 321-335. https://www.jstor.org/stable/4621983?mag=what-links-religion-and-authoritarianism&seq=3#page_scan_tab_contents.

Atomic bomb explosion on the Bikini Atoll test site. View is at sea level. *Harry S. Truman Library & Museum*

Chapter 11

The Greatest Danger to America is Her Commander in Chief

By Joe Cirincione

The greatest nuclear danger to America does not come from a foreign threat or a terrorist group but from our own president.[159] Donald Trump presents three unique nuclear risks to the nation.

The first is the power that Trump, or any president, has to launch nuclear weapons whenever he wants for whatever reason he wants. The serious questions about the president's mental stability presented in this volume should make every American reconsider this system. Trump's inexperience and impulsiveness also gravely increase the risk of his starting new wars that could escalate into nuclear conflicts. Finally, his temperament, policies, and choice of advisors risk collapsing the intricate system of global alliances and restraints that presidents of both parties erected to stop the spread of the deadliest weapons ever invented.

Trump's firing of more moderate officials and his choice of noted hawks as their replacements have exacerbated all these risks, most notably his choice of John Bolton as his third national security advisor in fourteen months and nomination of Michael Pompeo as his second secretary of state. Both add to the *war cabinet* that Trump is assembling, as *Washington Post* columnist David Ignatius warned.[160] "A bellicose president now has a person with similar traits as his chief White House foreign policy adviser, he says, "That scares people, at home and abroad."

Many hold similar fears about Trump's choice to lead the State Department. "Mike Pompeo stands out for both criticizing the [Iran nuclear] deal and painting an unrealistic scenario about the relative ease of destroying Iran's nuclear capacity through a bombing campaign," said Senator Tim Kaine of Virginia this April, announcing his opposition to the nomination. "I believe that Mike Pompeo would exacerbate President Trump's weaknesses rather than uphold our diplomatic legacy."

---

[159] Joe Cirincione, "Last Year's Top 5 Worst Nuclear Nightmares (That Aren't Going Away)" Defense One, December 27, 2017, https://www.defenseone.com/ideas/2017/12/last-years-top-5-worst-nuclear-nightmares-arent-going-away/144845/

[160] David Ignatius, "The enfant terrible enters the White House," The Washington Post, March 27, 2018, https://www.washingtonpost.com/opinions/trumps-war-cabinet-is-now-complete/2018/03/27/3a25b1cc-3201-11e8-8abc-22a366b72f2d_story.html?utm_term=.99c558ae84e1&noredirect=on

Some of the president's ardent supporters share these concerns. A close Trump confidant told journalists that Trump is now "a president who is being encouraged and goaded on by people around him. It really is a president unhinged."[161]

Even before the latest cabinet turmoil, Americans worried about Trump's grip on national security policy. According to a *Washington Post* poll, over 60 percent of the American public does not trust Donald Trump to make wise decisions on nuclear weapons.[162] About half fear that he will launch a nuclear attack without justification. Tom Collina details the dangers of Trump's nuclear launch authority in his chapter in this book.

A new nuclear weapons plan from the Pentagon will give the public more reason to worry. The "Nuclear Posture Review" released in February 2018 operationalizes Trump's worst impulses. It adds new weapons and new missions and breaks with decades of bipartisan strategy that sought to reduce nuclear arsenals. It puts real weapons behind Trump's views, revealed in his boast to MSNBC host Mika Brzezinski after his election, "Let it be an arms race." This has become a theme of his presidency, with repeated claims that the U.S. should be "top of the pack" and most recently threatening this March, in a phone call with Russian President Vladimir Putin, "If you want to have an arms race, we can do that, but I'll win."[163]

This fascination with the size and power of nuclear weapons may have led to the firing of Secretary of State Rex Tillerson. Trump, at a July 2017 Pentagon nuclear policy briefing, reportedly said he wanted a massive increase in the nuclear arsenal. He was being shown a chart depicting the rise and fall of global nuclear arsenals over the decades when he suddenly pointed to the 32,000-weapon high point of the U.S. stockpile in the 1960's and said, "I want that many," according to NBC News reporters.[164] That would require an eight-fold increase in the roughly 4,000

[161] Philip Rucker and Robert Costa, "'Tired of the wait game': White House stabilizers gone, Trump calling his own shots," The Washington Post, March 31, 2018, https://www.washington-post.com/politics/unhinged-or-unleashed-white-house-stabilizers-gone-trump-calling-his-own-shots/2018/03/31/19447ae2-343b-11e8-8bdd-cdb33a5eef83_story.html?utm_term=.8810f3b3471d

[162] Emily Guskin, "Most Americans don't trust President Trump with the 'nuclear button,'" The Washington Post, January 23, 2018, https://www.washingtonpost.com/news/the-fix/wp/2018/01/23/most-americans-dont-trust-president-trump-with-the-nuclear-button/?utm_term=.e9ee55a745b1

[163] Rosa Brooks, "Donald Trump Is America's Experiment in Having No Government," Foreign Policy, April 28, 2017, http://foreignpolicy.com/2017/04/28/donald-trump-is-americas-experiment-in-having-no-government/

[164] Courtney Kube, Kristen Walker, Carol E. Lee and Savannah Guthrie, "Trump Wanted Tenfold Increase in Nuclear Arsenal, Surprising Military," NBC News Online, avannah Guthrie, NBCnews.com,

operational nuclear weapons now in the U.S. arsenal.[165] Fuming afterward, Tillerson called Trump "a f***ing moron." Tillerson never denied making the remark. Their relationship soon soured.

Tillerson is gone, and the man he judged a moron still runs America's nuclear policy. It is not just a return to the arms race that worries experts. Trump has threatened other nations with "fire and fury" and asked, "If we have [nuclear weapons] why can't we use them?" The new Pentagon nuclear posture review not only gives him a $1.7 trillion rebuild of the Cold War arsenal, it adds so-called "low-yield" nuclear weapons that the president might be more willing to use, and then expands the contingencies in which the president could use them, adding more types of targets, for more reasons.

Thanks to this plan, Trump might be more likely to order the use of nuclear weapons in Korea, Iran, or anywhere else he feels threatened. "The use of just one small nuclear weapon would almost certainly trigger a like-for-like retaliation, followed by a similar or stronger response from the original aggressor and progression toward a nuclear apocalypse," nuclear experts Phil Coyle and James McKeon warn.[166] "The assumption that crossing the nuclear threshold can lead to anything other than colossal destruction puts hundreds of millions of lives at risk."

In a dangerous feedback loop, Trump's policies are increasing the threats to America, creating the very crises that could escalate into conventional military conflict and then nuclear war. This is not hyperbole; this is a very real fear shared by a broad range of bipartisan national security experts.

One of the most urgent involves Iran, a potential nuclear threat that most experts believed we had bottled up with a historic agreement in 2015 that slashed Iran's nuclear program, froze it, and put it under an airtight verification regime.[167] Trump's repeated pledges to tear up the agreement negotiated by the United States, our allies, and partners risks destroying this wall of restraint. Bolton and Pompeo are fierce critics of the agreement, raising fears of its imminent demise. If it goes, sanctions on Iran would end, Iran would be free to restart its program,

October 11, 2017, https://www.nbcnews.com/news/all/trump-wanted-dramatic-increase-nuclear-arsenal-meeting-military-leaders-n809701

[165] Hans M. Christensen and Robert S. Norris, "United States nuclear forces, 2018," March 5, 2018, Taylor & Francis Online, https://www.tandfonline.com/doi/full/10.1080/00963402.2018.1438219

[166] Philip E. Coyle and James McKeon, "The Huge Risk of Small Nukes," Politico, March 10, 2017, https://www.politico.com/agenda/story/2017/03/huge-risk-small-nuclear-weapons-000350

[167] "Iran Nuclear Agreement," Ploughshares Fund, https://www.ploughshares.org/topic/iran-nuclear-agreement

raising the risks of a regional nuclear arms race, or, worse, a new war in the Middle East apparently favored by Bolton[168] and Pompeo.[169]

In response, in mid-March almost 120 former military leaders and diplomats, including 50 retired flag officers and at least four former American ambassadors to Israel, wrote[170] the president urging him to keep the deal. "Ditching it would serve no national security purpose," they warned. Similarly, the Israeli national security establishment is nearly united in its desire to keep the deal that solved one of Israel's greatest threats. "Without a doubt, the nuclear deal between Iran and the West is an historic turning point," said Israel's military chief of staff General Gadi Eizenkot.[171] "This is a real change. This is a strategic turning point." Rather than rip up the deal, Uzi Arad, former national security to Prime Minister Benjamin Netanyahu says, "The less risky approach is to build in the existing agreement. ... It imposes ceilings and benchmarks and verifications that you do not want to lose. Why lose it."[172]

Why indeed? Why is Trump so determined to kill the deal? If the deal dies, it could be more the result of the president's psychology than a rational national security strategy.

Trump appears to be on a mission to raze to the ground all of President Barack Obama's achievements. He has pulled out of Obama's greatest environmental victory, the Paris climate accord. He has ended Obama's signature immigration move, the so-called Dreamers' Act. He has scuttled Obama's major trade pacts, sabotaged his health care act, repealed his consumer protections, and now aims to destroy, for no feasible gain, Obama's major national security achievement, the solution to the Iranian nuclear crisis. Trump acts as if he is Rome and Obama, Carthage. He is determined to plow over Obama's legacy and sow the ground with salt.

If killing the Iran deal out of revenge could allow Iran to restart its nuclear program and raise again the risk of U.S. or Israel attacks, the crisis with North Korea

---

[168] Julian Borger, "John Bolton: foreign policy radical who backs war with Iran and North Korea," The Guardian, March 23, 2018, https://www.theguardian.com/us-news/2018/mar/23/john-bolton-foreign-policy-radical-who-backs-war-with-iran-and-north-korea

[169] Robin Wright, "With Mike Pompeo at the State Department, Are the Uber-Hawks Winning?" The New Yorker, March 13, 2018, https://www.newyorker.com/news/news-desk/with-mike-pompeo-at-the-state-department-are-the-uber-hawks-winning

[170] Rick Gladstone, "U.S. Experts Say Why Trump Should Support Iran Deal," The New York Times, March 26, 2018, https://www.nytimes.com/2018/03/26/world/middleeast/iran-nuclear-letter.html

[171] J.J. Goldberg, "Israel's Top General Praises Iran Deal as 'Strategic Turning Point' in Slap at Bibi," Forward, January 26, 2016, https://forward.com/opinion/331714/israels-top-general-praises-iran-deal-as-strategic-turning-point-in-slap-at/

[172] "Israel Defense Experts Warn Against Dropping Iran Nuclear Deal," EP Today, October 13, 2017, http://eptoday.com/israeli-defense-experts-warn-against-dropping-iran-nuclear-deal/

could be even more urgent. Spring 2018 brings a moment of hope for resolving this crisis—a moment when diplomacy seems to have stayed the drive to war that terrorized Americans and our Asian allies repeatedly in a 2017 characterized by North Korean tests and bizarre claims by Trump, such as the one about a phantom "armada" streaming to the peninsula in April.[173]

This hope could be short-lived. If the summit goes poorly, Trump could swing back to his threats of war and nuclear buttons that infamously began this year.[174] Trump's sudden acceptance of North Korean leader Kim Jong-un's invitation to meet, startling his aides and the South Korean officials briefing him, may have been because Trump "thought that Kim would meet to give up his nuclear weapons," warns nuclear expert Jeffrey Lewis.[175] "But for Kim the meeting is about being treated as an equal because of his nuclear and missile programs." Darkly, Lewis fears that the president's staff may have not told Trump the truth about the limited nature of this summit, where some steps could be taken to reduce the nuclear risks, because they are genuinely "afraid that Trump is going to do something insane on North Korea and latched on to this opportunity to shift the president's focus from fire and fury to cheeseburger summits."

Now, however, this inflated expectation is being pumped up[176] by John Bolton who writes that we should bomb North Korea.[177] Bolton has a history of sabotaging previous agreements that restrained that nation's programs. "With the appointment of Bolton, the chances of a diplomatic blow-up are higher than before," notes former State Department official Alexandra Bell and her co-author James McKeon.[178] "Bolton played an instrumental role in the destruction of the 1994 Agreed Framework between the United States and North Korea. That

---

[173] Simon Denyer and Emily Rauhala, "Despite Talk of a Military Strike, Trump's 'Armada' Actually Sailed Away from Korea," The Washington Post, April 18, 2017, https://www.washingtonpost.com/world/despite-talk-of-a-military-strike-trumps-armada-was-a-long-way-from-korea/2017/04/18/e8ef4237-e26a-4cfc-b5e9-526c3a17bd41_story.html?nid&utm_term=.f6a560a7cc55

[174] Eli Watkins, "Trump Taunts North Korea: My Nuclear Button Is 'Much Bigger,' 'More Powerful,'" CNN, January 3, 2018, https://www.cnn.com/2018/01/02/politics/donald-trump-north-korea-nuclear/index.html

[175] Jeffrey Lewis, "The Trump-Kim Summit Won't End Well," Foreign Policy, March 9, 2018, http://foreignpolicy.com/2018/03/09/nixon-goes-to-mcdonaldland/

[176] Uri Friedman, "John Bolton's Radical Views on North Korea," The Atlantic, March 23, 2018, https://www.theatlantic.com/international/archive/2018/03/john-bolton-north-korea/556370/

[177] John Bolton, "The Military Options for North Korea," The Wall Street Journal, August 2, 2017, https://www.wsj.com/articles/the-military-options-for-north-korea-1501718189

[178] Alexandra Bell and James McKeon, "Three Strikes Means Bolton Should Be Out," Bulletin of the Atomic Scientists, March 30, 2018, https://thebulletin.org/three-strikes-means-bolton-should-be-out11648

agreement, while not perfect, successfully limited North Korea's production of plutonium for about eight years."[179]

The damage to America's security goes beyond Iran and North Korea. Trump's tweets and erratic behavior have gravely shaken allied confidence in his leadership and America's reliability.[180] Council on Foreign Relations President Richard Haass says that they have "accelerated a move by others to carry out a more independent foreign policy that doesn't defer as much to the United States."[181] The results? America is separating from her allies, squandering our global leadership, promoting incoherent foreign policies, and, as a result, is more isolated than any time in recent memory.

This is the final danger from Trump's instability: the destruction of the global system of treaties, laws, institutions, alliances, and security agreements that, while not perfect, have been the major reason that great powers have not gone to war in over seventy years. It is not the fear of the nuclear bomb that stops these wars (though that plays a role); it is the confidence that disputes can be resolved, economic benefits preserved, and a rough form of justice achieved through this liberal global order.

Trump threatens all that. He is the first president of the United States since World War II who does not see himself as the leader of the West, the leader of the liberal order. Instead, he sees our European and Asian allies as economic rivals. He praises autocrats; slams democratic leaders; abandons treaties and accords painstakingly negotiated; and encourages conflict in some of the most volatile regions on Earth.

A prime example is Trump's silence[182] when the heir apparent to the kingdom of Saudi Arabia announced his nuclear plans on American television.[183] "Without a doubt," Crown Prince Mohammad bin Salman told CBS host Norah O'Donnell, "if Iran developed a nuclear bomb, we will follow suit as soon as possible." Not a single

[179] Jeffrey Lewis, "Revisiting the Agreed Framework," 38 North, May 15, 2015, https://www. 38north.org/2015/05/jlewis051415/

[180] Joe Cirincione, "Just Why Trump's North Korea Tweet Is So Dangerously Destabilizing," Daily News, http://beta.nydailynews.com/opinion/trump-north-korea-tweet-dangerously-destabilizing-article-1.3737572

[181] Anderson Cooper, "Council of Foreign Relations President Richard Haass: The Trump administration has "accelerated a move by others to carry out a more independent foreign policy that doesn't defer as much to the United States," CNN, January 2, 2018, https://twitter. com/ac360/status/948374694729629696?lang=en

[182] Joe Cirincione, "Trump's Silence on a Saudi Nuclear Bomb," Lobe Log, March 30, 2018, https://lobelog.com/trumps-silence-on-a-saudi-nuclear-bomb/

[183] "Saudi Crown Prince: If Iran Develops Nuclear Bomb, So Will We," CBS News, March 15, 2018, https://www.cbsnews.com/news/saudi-crown-prince-mohammed-bin-salman-iran-nuclear-bomb-saudi-arabia/

voice of protest was heard from the Trump administration. This is another shocking break with the policies Democratic and Republican presidents have followed since President Harry Truman told the United Kingdom that despite that nation's key role in developing the bomb with us, we would oppose Britain building its own nuclear arsenal.

The United States has never encouraged any nation, friend or foe, to get the bomb. Through diplomacy, treaties, security agreements, and strong-arming, American leaders have stopped scores of nations from going nuclear over the decades. Even when such efforts failed, as with, for example, Israel, India, and Pakistan, officials tried.[184] That policy appears to be at an end, due to Donald Trump's bizarre views.

As a presidential candidate Trump told CNN's Anderson Cooper that it was "only a matter of time before other countries get nuclear weapons."[185] He talked favorably about Japan and South Korea having their own weapons. Most pointedly, when Cooper asked if Saudi Arabia should get nuclear weapons, he responded: "Saudi Arabia, absolutely." In a rambling discourse that referenced Trump's uncle being a professor at MIT, Trump said, "At some point we have to say, you know what, we're better off if Japan protects itself against this maniac in North Korea, we're better off, frankly, if South Korea is going to start to protect itself."

Trump is turning U.S. nuclear policy into a dangerous game of nuclear roulette. American presidents have an outsized role in setting national security strategy. Nowhere is that more so than with nuclear policy. Nuclear weapons are often called "the president's weapons," reflecting the relative lack of influence that Congress, the courts, and the public have in setting nuclear plans.

It is thus uniquely dangerous when the nation has a president who does not know from one day to the next what he will do. *New York Times* reporters Julie Hirschfeld Davis and Mark Lander detailed, "after another week of chaos" this March, "no one knows what comes next." They wrote, "Aides said there was no grand strategy to the president's actions, and that he got up each morning this week not knowing what he would do."[186] Each day brings a new spin of the wheel. No one can predict where it will stop.

---

[184] Joe Cirincione, "Trump's Silence on a Saudi Nuclear Bomb," Lobe Log, March 30, 2018, https://lobelog.com/trumps-silence-on-a-saudi-nuclear-bomb/

[185] "Full Rush Transcript: Donald Trump, CNN Milwaukee Republican Presidential Town Hall," CNN Press Room, March 29, 2016, http://cnnpressroom.blogs.cnn.com/2016/03/29/full-rush-transcript-donald-trump-cnn-milwaukee-republican-presidential-town-hall/

[186] Mark Landler and Julie Hirschfeld Davis, "After Another Week of Chaos, Trump Repairs to Palm Beach. No One Knows What Comes Next," The New York Times, March 23, 2018, https://www.nytimes.com/2018/03/23/us/politics/trump-chaos-trade-russia-national-security.html?smid=tw-share

Such a temperament, such a mental state in a president is enormously dangerous on many fronts. When it comes to nuclear weapons, it is horrifying. An irrational, impulsive decision by Donald Trump taken in a matter of minutes could threaten the survival of all humanity has constructed over the millennia.

This cannot stand.

Joe Cirincione is president of Ploughshares Fund, a global security foundation. He has worked on nuclear weapons policy in Washington for over 35 years, including for nine years as professional staff on the U.S. House of Representatives Committees on Armed Services and Government Operations. He is a former member of the International Security Advisory Board for Secretaries of State John Kerry and Hillary Clinton. He teaches at Georgetown University and is a member of the Council on Foreign Relations.

Chapter 12

Bluffing Us Into the Nuclear Abyss?
What October 1962 Teaches Us About
Nuclear Risks Under Trump

by James G. Blight and Janet M. Lang

The Senator: This is an abyss into which it is better not to look.
The Count: My friend, we are not free not to look.
Joseph de Maistre[187]

Trump firmly believes (it is difficult to complete a sentence that starts with these words) in the value of bluffing. … It is all too obvious that Trump is not only bluffing, but is doing so incompetently.
Amitai Etzioni[188]

Never, Ever, Bluff With Nukes: A Key Lesson From October 1962

The world came closer to being blown up in the Cuban Missile Crisis of October 1962 than at any moment before or since. On what is now called *Black Saturday*, October 27, 1962, the U.S., Soviet Union, and Cuba hovered precariously, like the spiders in Jonathan Edwards' hellfire and brimstone sermon, over an abyss of annihilation, an abyss to which they had arrived inadvertently, blinded by fears and misperceptions.[189] The project of avoiding nuclear war in the age of Donald

---

[187] Joseph de Maistre, St. Petersburg Dialogues, or Conversations on the Temporal Government of Providence, trans. by Richard A. LeBrun (Montreal and Kingston: McGill and Queens University Press, 1993, p. 145). Cited in John Gray, Black Mass: Apocalyptic Religion and the Death of Utopia (New York: Farrar, Straus & Giroux, 2007), p. v.

[188] Amitai Etzioni, "Donald Trump and the Art of Foreign Policy Bluffing." Huffington Post, September 12, 2017.

[189] Jonathan Edwards, "Sinners in the Hands of an Angry God," a sermon delivered in Enfield, Connecticut, July 8, 1741. It is widely available on the web and in many editions of Edwards' works. The sermon is the gold standard for arousing in Edwards' listeners, and readers ever since, a palpable fear of imminent, total annihilation. Edwards was a virtuoso of the use of frightening images, mostly of the fire and brimstone variety, consistent with the Calvinism in which Edwards and his listeners were immersed. Have a look. Keep the imagery and jettison theology, and what is left is not a bad description of what we face in trying to live with nuclear weapons into the indefinite future. Consider, for example, the implications for nuclear danger in the age of Trump of Edwards' biblical epigraph for his sermon, from Deuteronomy, chapter 32, verse 35: "Thy foot shall slide in due time." One way to put the premise of this book is that, since the inauguration of Trump, the sense of sliding

Trump must begin with an understanding of our closest call, what made it so dangerous, and what we need to worry about with the current White House occupant in command of the U.S. nuclear arsenal.

The Cuban Missile Crisis spun out of control because the leaders of the superpowers were bluffing each other, while the leaders of Cuba were in deadly earnest about fighting a war to its bloody conclusion. Nikita Khrushchev's bold gamble to deploy weapons in Cuba, a mere 90 miles from Florida, was meant to support Cuba and help correct the nuclear balance of power, not to threaten the U.S. with imminent nuclear annihilation. And Kennedy's ramping up of military pressure on the Russians to remove the weapons was also a bluff, meant only to achieve their removal, not the destruction of Cuba. But the superpower bluffing and bargaining match had no traction with Fidel Castro and his Cuban constituents, who were unfamiliar with the bluffing tactics of the superpowers. They were prepared instead for all-out war with the U.S. and their eventual martyrdom, and in so doing brought the world to the brink of Armageddon.[190]

The bottom line, based on what happened in October 1962 and on what almost happened: never bluff with nuclear weapons, because you never know when your bluff will be called, the war begins, and the world is destroyed.

Black Saturday, October 27, 1962:
How the End of Everything Might Have Begun

We have investigated the October 1962 Cuban Missile Crisis for more than thirty years. We have reported our results in books, movies, articles, and

---

toward the nuclear abyss has become palpable to anyone who has been paying attention to his inflammatory remarks, which are seldom constrained by any connection to the world beyond the fantasies broadcast by Fox News.

[190] In the more than half century since the Cuban Missile Crisis, the event has usually been portrayed in the West as an almost exclusively U.S.-Soviet confrontation, with the Cubans relegated to the status of bit players, or less. This mythology has been blown up by our research, and research of others on our team, over the past three decades. We have focused on Cuba—what was happening and what was expected to happen in the theater of operations—where the war would likely have started, and where the Cubans and Russians stationed on the island were preparing for Armageddon and martyrdom. See James G. Blight, Bruce J. Allyn and David A. Welch, Cuba on the Brink: Castro, The Missile Crisis and the Soviet Collapse, 2nd paperback ed. (Lanham, MD: Rowman & Littlefield, 2002); James G. Blight and Janet M. Lang, The Armageddon Letters: Kennedy, Khrushchev and Castro in the Cuban Missile Crisis (Lanham, MD: Rowman & Littlefield, 2012); and especially James G. Blight and Janet M. Lang, Dark Beyond Darkness: The Cuban Missile Crisis as History, Warning and Catalyst (Lanham, MD: Rowman & Littlefield, 2018). In addition, our focus on Cuba in the crisis informed the views expressed by former U.S. Defense Secretary Robert S. McNamara, in the 2004 Academy Award-winning film, "The Fog of War," on which we served as principal substantive advisors to both Morris and McNamara.

presentations all over the world. We have learned a lot about nuclear danger in what has become the great nuclear laboratory of the Cuban Missile Crisis. The crisis has been figuratively peeled, layer-by-layer like an onion, by hundreds of investigators all over the world until its hard core of undeniable reality is visible to anyone who cares to look. The documentation—including declassified written material, authoritative oral testimony, and scholarly commentary—is immense. We have been involved in this research process continuously since its origins in the mid-1980s. This is what it all adds up to:

- If history were a game of roulette;
- And if exactly those conditions present by Black Saturday, October 27, 1962, could be reinstituted by some process of black magic;
- And if we were to spin the roulette wheel of history 100 times;
- In our estimation, we will get Armageddon on at least 95 of those spins.

We now know for certain how supremely lucky we were that the Cuban Missile Crisis did not explode into Armageddon. However you define *lucky*, most of us would agree that we would be fools to expect to be that lucky the next time the possible use of nuclear weapons comes into play in some deep crisis.

What our research proves beyond a doubt is that civilization-destroying Armageddon is possible, that it is possible even if none of the relevant leaders and governments are seeking a nuclear war.[191]

When Castro Called Kennedy's and Khrushchev's Bluffs

We need to understand Donald Trump's nuclear bluffing in the context of what happened in the Cuban Missile Crisis. It was so dangerous because one of the actors, Cuba, believed it was doomed, that nothing it could do short of preemptive, unconditional surrender would permit it to survive. The Cubans were mistaken in the belief that they were doomed, but they had good reasons for believing they were right. In a now famous letter, Fidel Castro, on October 27, 1962, asked his Russian ally to take revenge on the U.S. in the event of an attack, which they regarded as inevitable and imminent. Khrushchev was shocked and horrified when an aide read Castro's request to him to nuke the United States the moment the U.S. invasion began.[192]

---

[191] This section draws on Blight and Lang, Dark Beyond Darkness, chapter 12.

[192] This letter is our candidate for the most stunning single document of the nuclear age: a request, however contingent, from the leader of a sovereign nation to another such leader to order the annihilation of roughly 180 million people. To what end? They sought what was to them their best option: to become martyrs for the global victory of socialism in that moment when the Cuban Missile Crisis became a nuclear war, a moment when Cuba became the hinge of the world. In our

But the U.S. did not invade. Instead, it agreed never to invade Cuba, and the Russians agreed to remove the nukes. From the Cuban perspective, Khrushchev was a spineless bluffer. He was not prepared to go *all the way* to nuclear war, as Che Guevara put it mockingly to Soviet negotiator Anastas Mikoyan in November 1962.[193] Kennedy, too, was bluffing. His threats to Cuba were, in his mind, designed only to make the Russians remove the missiles, not to threaten the viability of the Cuban regime. But the Cubans were *not* bluffing. Small, independent countries that feel cornered by big powers cannot afford to bluff. We now know that if the Cubans had possessed the ability to use the nuclear weapons stationed on their island by the Russians, they would have used them in the manner they were requesting of the Russians.

The Bluffer-in-Chief:
Nuclear Danger in the Trump Era
In addition to the hellish mixture of historical enmity, mistrust, and nuclear capability that threaten nuclear war around the world, we must now worry about a perverse circumstance that is unique in the history of the nuclear age. Since January 20, 2017, a superpower has been led by someone whose uninformed, unhinged riffs not only contain nonsense about his crowd size, his hand size, or the size of his other bodily parts, but also contain frequent threats or bluffs involving nuclear weapons.

Here is what Donald Trump, wheeler-dealer, real estate tycoon, four-Pinocchio-level liar, and addicted bluffer had to say on March 30, 2016, about nuclear weapons during his presidential campaign, in a forum with MSNBC host, Chris Matthews:

Matthews: Can you tell the Middle East we're not using a nuclear weapon on anybody?

Trump: I would never say that. I would never take any of my cards off the table.

Matthews: How about Europe? We won't use it in Europe?

Trump: I—I'm not going to take it off the table.

Matthews: You might use it in Europe?

---

view, this represents not the insanity of the Cubans, but the insanity of the situation in which the Cubans found themselves, thanks to their own missteps and the arrogant gamesmanship of the superpowers. The full text of the letter from Castro to Khrushchev, with some commentary by us, may be found in Blight and Lang, Armageddon Letters, pp. 112-118, and Blight and Lang, Dark Beyond Darkness, pp. 31-44.

[193] See Blight and Lang, Armageddon Letters, pp. 186-192, for the on the ground context of Mikoyan's discussions in Havana.

[LAUGHTER]

Trump: No, I don't think so. But I'm not taking …

Matthews: Well, *just say it. "I will never use a nuclear weapon in Europe."*

Trump: I am not—I am not taking cards off the table.

Matthews: OK.

Trump: I am not going to use nuclear, but I'm not taking any cards off the table.[194]

In his new book, *The Doomsday Machine,* Daniel Ellsberg points out that Trump is bluffing in an especially dangerous way in statements such as he made to Chris Matthews. Trump, according to Ellsberg, indicates that as president he will be bluffing in his nuclear threats "most, if not all, of the time" combining his bluffs about nuclear attacks with, as Ellsberg emphasizes, "advertising and exploiting his own unpredictability, deliberately creating uncertainty in an adversary by demonstrating impulsive, erratic, vindictive behavior—reminiscent to many observers of Nixon's madman theory."[195]

As president, Trump has moved to try to provide his nuclear bluffs with a thin veneer of credibility. In July 2017, Trump told his advisors he wanted a tenfold increase in U.S. nukes. That's roughly equal to the size of the U.S. and Soviet arsenals *combined* during the Cold War. In August 2017, he announced that if North Korea continued to threaten the U.S., he would order its destruction with "fire, fury, and frankly power the likes of which this world has never seen before." In 2017, he refused to recertify that Iran is in compliance (Iran *is* in compliance!) with the July 2015 breakthrough Joint Comprehensive Plan of Action agreed to by the Permanent Members of the UN Security Council, plus Germany (P5+1). He apparently hopes Congress will ultimately kill it. Is Trump bluffing about wanting an enormously enlarged nuclear arsenal, or about nuking North Korea, or about pulling down the temple around the landmark Iran nuclear deal?

Was he also bluffing in the spring of 2018 about wanting to negotiate nukes out of North Korea without the U.S. giving up anything significant in return? Does Trump have anything in mind for this initiative other than soaking up the publicity of a meeting with Kim Jong-un? He'd better, because Kim and the North Koreans

---

[194] Chris Matthews, interview with Donald Trump, at a forum in Milwaukee, Wisconsin on March 30, 2016. Cited in Daniel Ellsberg, The Doomsday Machine: Confessions of a Nuclear War Planner (New York: Bloomsbury, 2017), p. 330.

[195] Ibid., pp. 331-332.

may call his bluff.[196] And how does Trump think the North Korean leader will react to the appointment of über-hawk John Bolton as national security advisor, a man who has called repeatedly for a U.S. preemptive strike against North Korean nuclear facilities (and also against Iran's, even *after* the landmark 2015 deal, with which the Iranians are in full compliance)? Is Bolton the embodiment of a Trumpian bluff with a walrus mustache? Should Kim believe that he is? Or is Bolton a red flag signaling that the North Koreans should circle their wagons and get ready for war?[197]

Trump and His Many Missile Crises

Trump, like Khrushchev with his missiles, like Kennedy with his naval blockade, may be bluffing. Trump had a reputation as a bluffer when he was a real estate developer. Many readers of this book may, like us, believe Trump is bluffing most, or nearly all, of the time. Many believe, perhaps correctly, that the current occupant of the White House is best described as America's Bluffer-in-Chief.

But if you are Kim Jong-un, or Vladimir Putin, or Hassan Rouhani, or any other leader of a nuclear nation, what are you to think of Trump's nuclear expostulations? Will you bet that Trump is bluffing? How will you convince your hard-liners that Trump is bluffing? And if you don't believe he is bluffing, or you can't convince your relevant constituents that he is bluffing, then what? What if you and/or your associates conclude that you cannot afford to bet that he is bluffing? The Cuban Missile Crisis strongly suggests that you will prepare for nuclear war and that every preparation you make for that war raises the odds that the war will actually happen.

James G. Blight and **Janet M. Lang** have written 15 books on the history of recent U.S. foreign policy, seven of them on the Cuban Missile Crisis including, most recently, *Dark Beyond Darkness: The Cuban Missile Crisis as History, Warning and Catalyst* (2018). They were the principal advisers on Errol Morris' 2004 Academy Award-winning documentary, *The Fog of War*. Their short films on the Cuban Missile Crisis are at: https://www.youtube.com/user/armageddonletters. They are professors in the Department of History and the Balsillie School of International Affairs at the University of Waterloo. They have been married for 41 years.

---

[196] Kaitlyn Schallhorn, "Trump on North Korea: From 'Rocket Man,'" to 'Fire and Fury.'" Fox News, March 12, 2018. This assemblage of Trump's tweets and occasional other remarks about North Korea illustrates vividly what happens when a mindset and syntax similar to that of teenage boys facing off in a playground game are, by the black magic of Trump's occupancy of the White House, merged with the threat of nuclear war. Immersion in this long string of inconsistent, uninformed, often totally incoherent verbiage renders one, as the saying goes, as sober as a deacon. The unreal becomes surreal when you realize that Fox News, Trump's personal glorification machine, presents the string of tweets admiringly, as if they overflow with morsels of nuclear wisdom to be savored.

[197] See Peter Beinert, "The Deeply Underdeveloped Worldview of John Bolton," The Atlantic, April 29, 2018.

Images from the Cuban Missile Crisis

These images record the gravity of the situation President Kennedy dealt with during 10 fateful days in October of 1962. How deliberative and circumspect should we expect President Trump to be if faced with a similar crisis? Notice that the generals are in uniform in the President Kennedy's administration whereas in President Trump's administration the generals now are costumed in civilian garb.

President John F. Kennedy meets with members of the Executive Committee of the National Security Council (EXCOMM) regarding the crisis in Cuba. (L-R) President Kennedy and Secretary of Defense Robert S. McNamara, Cabinet Room, White House, Washington, D.C. *By Cecil Stoughton Public domain, via Wikimedia Commons*

CIA reference photograph of Soviet medium-range ballistic missile (SS-4 in U.S. documents, R-12 in Soviet documents) in Red Square, Moscow. *By Central Intelligence Agency Public domain, via Wikimedia Commons*

President Kennedy meets in the Oval Office with General Curtis LeMay and reconnaissance pilots who flew the Cuban missions. Third from the left is Major Richard Heyser who took the photos on which the Cuban missiles were first identified. *Courtesy of CIA, public domain*

U-2 reconnaissance photograph of Cuba, showing Soviet nuclear missiles, their transports and tents for fueling and maintenance. *By CIA Public domain, via Wikimedia Commons*

President Kennedy signs the Proclamation for Interdiction of the Delivery of Offensive Weapons to Cuba at the Oval Office on October 23, 1962. *Public domain.*

More than 100 US-built missiles having the capability to strike Moscow with nuclear warheads were deployed in Italy and Turkey in 1961. *Public domain*

Chapter 13

One Week in August: How a Self-Made Nuclear Crisis Exposed Donald Trump's Psychopathology

By Seth D. Norrholm, Ph.D.

For the purposes of this chapter, I have decided to focus on Trump's behavior regarding North Korea during the week of August 6-12, 2017, a time I believe to be one of the most telling (and frightening) weeks of his tenure in office to date.

August 6-12, 2017

August 8, 2017 (televised comments via multiple media outlets)
At a time when nuclear tensions were escalating and with it fear and anxiety in citizens throughout the U.S. mainland, Hawaii, Guam, Japan, and the Korean peninsula, a defiant Trump, with arms locked across his chest, made the following harrowing statement toward North Korea: "They will be met with fire, fury, and frankly, power the likes of which this world has never seen before." It should be noted that Donald Trump, the civilian, reportedly has long had a fascination with nuclear weapons because they epitomize power and dominance, two traits that he values above all others (Starrs 2018, Blake 2017, Neidig 2016, Wong 2016)

August 10, 2017 (televised comments via multiple media outlets)
As a nation and the world at large attempted to *wrap their heads around* what was unfolding, Trump then threw more *fire and fury* into the conflict by suggesting that his previous comments from two days before were not "tough enough," and he stated this:
"Let's see what [Kim Jong-un] does with Guam. He does something in Guam, it will be an event the likes of which nobody has seen before—what will happen in North Korea."

The bombastic, hyperbolic Trump, who made these inflammatory statements while at his golf course in Bedminster, New Jersey, was engaged in a media street fight with Kim Jong-un while a bewildered nation looked on in amazement, terror, and confusion. And why not? This was a president whose own narcissistic tendencies had fueled a machine in which "alternative facts" and "gaslighting" were introduced into the public lexicon, and members of the media and American citizenry were forced to decide between what to believe and what not to believe.

Now Trump had started a self-made nuclear crisis in which leadership and credibility were critical while sitting atop an administration in which both were dangerously lacking. Even Trump's "generals"—Defense Secretary Jim Mattis, National Security Advisor H.R. McMaster, and White House Chief of Staff John Kelly—were forced to clean up after the president in the form of "a calming presence" and backpedaling (Powell 2017). Secretary of State Rex Tillerson, Mattis, and McMaster were forced to convince leery allies that a nuclear conflict was not imminent, that Trump was just "hot," and diplomatic measures would still be pursued. It was also widely reported that Mattis and McMaster had to explain the utterly catastrophic nature of a pre-emptive strike on the Korean peninsula to the president.

August 11, 2017, 7:29 AM (via Twitter)
As Trump's bellicose week continued into Friday, he again *upped the ante* and laid few fears to rest by sending out this early-morning tweet:
"Military solutions are now fully in place, locked and loaded, should North Korea act unwisely. Hopefully Kim Jong Un will find another path!"

This tweet came just hours after Defense Secretary Mattis had attempted to soften the president's words of the week by restating that diplomacy was still the primary option for addressing North Korean nuclear threats (Merica, Liptak, and Dewan 2017).

Consider this thought experiment for a moment: What if Trump's latest selection for National Security Advisor—remember he's already had two in a year's time—John Bolton, a known war hawk, had been in the White House during that dangerous week? What if instead of being restrained by his advisors, he had been egged on? The outcome and its deadly consequences are frightening to think about.

Since August 2017

November 8, 2017 (via Trump South Korea speech; Twitter)
The beginning of November 2017 marked a flare-up in tensions between the Trump and Kim administrations. Much of this was related to President Trump's visit and address to South Korea's National Assembly during which he stated (and later tweeted), "This is a very different administration than the United States has had in the past. Do not underestimate us. And do not try us." Not surprisingly, North Korea's state-run Central News Agency issued this statement:

"The U.S. must oust the lunatic old man from power and withdraw the hostile policy towards [North Korea] at once in order to get rid of the abyss of doom. ... The U.S. had better make a decisive choice ... if it does not want a horrible nuclear disaster and tragic doom."

It is important to note at this point that both Donald Trump and Kim Jong-un display behaviors publicly that could be described as dangerously narcissistic and sociopathic (Robertson 2017, Norrholm and Hunley 2017). In that vein, they both demand adoration and fierce loyalty from their followers, both show an apparent lack of empathy unless the caring act provides secondary gain (i.e., makes them look good), and both appear to derive pleasure from psychologically and/or physically harming others. There is one striking difference that is relevant to this book and its implications. Trump's extreme narcissism with its related malignant features has produced *self-made* crises that would likely have been avoided were a different U.S. president elected in November 2016. Kim Jong-un, who is the latest in a despotic legacy, must employ propaganda techniques in order to maintain his reign and to ensure the continued existence of the Kim line. Historically, much of the propaganda aimed at the oppressed North Korean people has included an *us versus them* mentality and sought to convince the populace that America is hell-bent on destroying North Korea, most likely through the use of nuclear weapons.

Until the Trump administration took power, much of this was largely baseless propaganda. However, President Trump, through his saber-rattling rhetoric and incendiary tweets, has reinforced this piece of propaganda and provided added legitimacy to Kim's claims at home. This places more American lives at risk and further underscores the dangerousness of Trump's behaviors and actions.

November 11, 2017, 8:48 PM (via Twitter)
Numerous mental health professionals and media pundits have described Donald Trump as a "man-child" in large part because of the immature manner in which seventy-one-year-old father and grandfather conducts himself. In previous writings, for example, David Reiss and I have described three elements of extreme narcissism that are associated with immaturity of this type: a collapsed perception of time, impressionistic thinking, and need for validation (Norrholm and Reiss 2017). To put it simply, the extreme narcissist acts "in the moment" with little respect for the linear passage of time and does so based on how he feels *at that moment* and how others *respond to him at that moment*. Impressionistic thinking is a type of reasoning that relies on emotions to define reality rather than logic, facts, rational thought, or consistency. Children often show impressionistic thinking, because we learn to sense and feel before we can communicate verbally, before developing a more mature type of thinking based on respect for reality, logic, and consistency.

Taking these factors into account—in addition to other narcissistic features discussed previously—it is not surprising that Trump sounds like a child in this tweet in response to Kim Jong-un calling the president "an old lunatic" as mentioned previously:

"Why would Kim Jong-un insult me by calling me 'old,' when I would NEVER call him "short and fat?' Oh well, I try so hard to be his friend – and maybe someday that will happen!"

January 2, 2018 (via Twitter)

Kim tweeted: "The entire area of the U.S. mainland is within our nuclear strike range … the United States can never start a war against me and our country."

A glaring problem with an extreme narcissist as president is that foreign policy maneuvers and perceived attacks are taken *personally* and come with the potential for *ego injury* that a narcissist strives to protect against. Time and time again, Trump's response to perceived attacks and possible ego injury is the rage *tweetstorm* and nothing close to resembling State Department-sanctioned diplomacy.

Trump's fixation on physical qualities that suggest dominance such as larger physical size, whether it is overall height or the size of a particular body part, spilled over into his "nuclear button," raising the eyebrows of U.S. Department of Defense officials as well as trained Freudian psychoanalytical thinkers nationwide:

"North Korean Leader Kim Jong Un just stated that the 'Nuclear Button is on his desk at all times.' Will someone from his depleted and food starved regime please inform him that I too have a Nuclear Button, but it is much bigger & more powerful than his, and my button works!"[198]

January 14, 2018 (via Wall Street Journal; Twitter)

In early 2018 during an interview with the *Wall Street Journal* when he claimed, while being audiotaped, that "I probably have a very good relationship with Kim Jong-Un of North Korea (Bender et al. 2018)," a statement with no basis in fact or experience as the two leaders have not met in person as of this writing and communication has largely been through indirect means such as social or state-run media. Rather than clarify any misunderstanding about what he said or its

---

[198] It does not take a Freudian psychoanalyst to detect the implicit references to genital size and function in the above tweet. However, it is worth noting in the context of fitness for duty and demeanor that Trump is the first major candidate-turned-president to openly boast on national TV about the apparent size of his genitals.

intent, Trump chose to attack the *Wall Street Journal* for using one of his Presidential catch phrases, "FAKE NEWS!"

March 6, 2018, 10:11 AM (via Twitter)

To Donald J. Trump, any public appearance, statement, or tweet is intended for *his* audience. As I have discussed many times and with other mental health professionals, Trump sees himself as the eternal emperor in his own mind and of his own world. The rest of us are just players or spectators in and around his stage. His statement to the governor of Guam, whose island was potentially in North Korean *nuclear* crosshairs during that white-knuckle week of August 2017, suggested the governor should be grateful to be basking in Trump's publicity.

"I have to tell you, you have become extremely famous all over the world. They are talking about Guam; and they're talking about you. … I can say this: You're going to go up, like, tenfold with the expenditure of no money (Cagurangan 2017)[199]."

Nowhere in this statement is reassurance in the form of practical security and safety measures for Guam or words of comfort, evidencing the total lack of empathy found in the malignant narcissist.

"Possible progress being made in talks with North Korea. For the first time in many years, a serious effort is being made by all parties concerned. The World is watching and waiting! May be false hope, but the U.S. is ready to go hard in either direction!"

In this tweet Trump indicates that he is willing to "go hard in either direction"—keeping in mind that in one direction is a full-fledged nuclear conflict with the possible loss of hundreds of thousands, if not millions, of North Korean, South Korean, Japanese, Chinese, and American lives. To Trump this momentous fork in the road would appear to be six of one vs. half a dozen of another, precisely because he is devoid of basic human sympathy for the potential victims of a war he might start.

---

[199] Later in August 2017, Trump would go on to describe the devastating Hurricane Harvey in terms of its place in history based on its duration, intensity, damage, and expense—sounding more like a "fanboy" than a concerned leader. In fact, Trump would go on to praise FEMA administrator Brock Long for now being "famous" after the storm hit southeast Texas.

March 8, 2018, 9:08 PM (via Twitter)

"Kim Jong Un talked about denuclearization with the South Korean Representatives, not just a freeze. Also, no missile testing during this period of time. Great progress being made but sanctions will remain until an agreement is reached. Meeting being planned!"

President Trump accepted the invitation to a potential meeting with Kim Jong-un with little to no consultation with advisors and in direct contradiction with statements put out by then-Secretary of State Tillerson. In other words, this was a significant example of Trump displaying impressionistic thinking as discussed earlier in this chapter. After months of juvenile and unsophisticated name calling, rage tweeting, and hurling nuclear war rhetoric, Trump chose to employ a reality TV tactic and "pop in" to the White House briefing room to announce the upcoming summit with the North Korean dictator Kim. No official State announcement complete with rationale, thought process, or analytical process was provided. The White House, through spokesperson Sarah Huckabee Sanders, was forced to "backpedal" the next day by placing conditions on the occurrence of a Trump/Kim meeting. In other words, they were forced to play catch-up with the president and his impulsive actions. Because of his impressionistic thinking and the fact that it "felt good" to Trump *in that moment* to blurt out a meeting acceptance, planning and reason had to be incorporated *after* the decision was made public.

Time will tell what ultimately happens, but we have been shown ominous warning signs in just over a year. This was readily apparent during a week in August of 2017 when our nation moved as close to a nuclear conflict as we have been since the Cuban Missile Crisis—and this crisis was largely avoidable and self-made by a dangerously narcissistic, would-be king who acts on impulse and impressionistic thinking in the moment without thought of long-term consequences.

Seth Davin Norrholm, Ph.D. is an Associate Professor of Psychiatry and Behavioral Sciences at Emory University School of Medicine, a full-time faculty member in the Emory Neuroscience Graduate Program, and a member of the Emory Clinical Psychology Graduate Program. Dr. Norrholm has spent 20 years studying trauma-, stressor-, anxiety-, depressive-, and substance use-related disorders and has published over 90 peer-reviewed research articles and book chapters. An expert in human fear, Dr. Norrholm specializes in addressing fears associated with primary psychiatric diagnoses and personality disorders. Dr. Norrholm has been featured on NBC, ABC, PBS, CNN.com, Politico.com, *The Huffington Post*, Yahoo.com, *USA Today*, WebMD, The History Channel, and *Scientific American*.

References

Michael C. Bender, Louise Radnofsky, Peter Nicholas, and Rebecca Ballhaus, "Donald Trump Signals Openness to North Korea Diplomacy in Interview." *The Wall Street Journal*, January 11, 2018.

Aaron Blake, "Trump's loose talk on nuclear weapons suddenly becomes very real." *The Washington Post*. October 11, 2017, https://www.washingtonpost.com/news/the-fix/wp/2017/10/11/trumps-loose-rhetoric-on-nuclear-weapons-has-become-a-very-real-concern/?utm_term=.007c9a04cdb9.

Mar-Vic Cagurangan, "Trump to Guam Governor: North Korea Threats Will Boost Tourism 'Tenfold,'" *The New York Times*, August 12, 2017. https://www.nytimes.com/2017/08/12/world/asia/trump-guam-governor-phone-call.html.

Dan Merica, Kevin Liptak, and Angela Dewan. "Trump warns North Korea: U.S. military 'locked and loaded," *CNN.com*, August 11, 2017.

Harper Neidig, "Scarborough: Trump asked adviser why U.S. can't use nuclear weapons," *The Hill*, August 3, 2016.

Seth Davin Norrholm, S.D. and Samuel Hunley. "The Psychology of Dictators: Power, Fear, and Anxiety," *Anxiety.org*. January 12, 2017, https://www.anxiety.org/psychology-of-dictators-power-fear-anxiety.

Seth Davin Norrholm, and David M. Reiss. "Eternal Emperor in His Own Mind: The Distorted Reality of Donald Trump," *The Huffington Post*, May 27, 2017, https://www.huffingtonpost.com/entry/eternal-emperor-in-his-own-mind-the-distorted-reality_us_5929abfee4b07d848fdc0429.

Bill Powell, "Trump's Generals Can Save The World From War—And Stop The Crazy." *Newsweek*, August 12, 2017.

Ian H. Robertson, "Personality and Potential Nuclear Confrontation" *Psychology Today*, August 12, 2017.

Jenny Starrs, "White House dismisses criticism of Trump's North Korea 'Nuclear Button' tweet." *The Washington Post*, January 3, 2018. https://www.washingtonpost.com/politics/white-house-dismisses-criticism-of-trumps-north-korea-nuclear-button-tweet/2018/01/03/fa51d7d2-f0a2-11e7-b390-a36dc3fa2842_story.html?utm_term=.862b47dd77c7.

Kristina Wong, "Trump says he wouldn't take use of nuclear weapons 'off the table,'" *The Hill*, March 30, 2016.

The United States conducted the Swordfish test of the RUR-5 ASROC nuclear depth bomb off San Diego in 1962. *Public domain, via Wikimedia Commons*

Chapter 14

The Bully-In-Chief:
Trump and Kim Jong-Un Could Destroy the World
to Prove Who Has the Bigger Button

By Philip Zimbardo and Rosemary Sword

Since well before the 2016 presidential election, we've been part of the mental health community intent on educating and warning the public about the dangerousness of Donald J. Trump in his role as president of the United States. Our specialties are time perspective theory [200] and therapy.[201] Through this lens, we are convinced that Donald Trump is an *extreme present hedonist*—a person who lives in the moment, making decisions impulsively with no reflection on past mistakes, and, worse, no thought of future consequences. Extreme present hedonists share a worrisome set of personality traits: low self-esteem, a strong tendency toward self-aggrandizement, and for some, a propensity toward addiction, as well as bully behavior.[202]

We've witnessed how Trump's low self-esteem causes him to spout outrageous claims of grandiosity that fly in the face of fact. We've seen how he has bullied celebrities, politicians, employees in the highest echelons of government, citizens, athletes, and world leaders. We fear that this dangerous mix of tendencies may cause him to push *the button* because it will make him feel more powerful, more in control *in the moment* when he feels trapped and under attack by Special Counsel Robert Mueller. This is our concern. And it is grave.

In this chapter we'll explore how Trump's bully behavior presents a unique window into his psychology and the resultant heightened nuclear risk we all face should the perfect storm of circumstances arise.

Let's start with a little background on President Trump and North Korea's supreme leader, Kim Jong-un,[203] which reveals a startling degree of similarity

---

[200] Zimbardo, P; Boyd, J. (2008) The Time Paradox. New York, NY. Rider.

[201] Zimbardo, Phillip; Sword, Robert; Sword, Rosemary. (2012) The Time Cure (San Francisco, CA. Wiley.

[202] Zimbardo, P, Sword, R. (2017) "Unbridled and Extreme Present Hedonism" in The Dangerous Case of Donald Trump: 27 Psychiatrists and Mental Health Experts Assess a President, Lee, B X (Ed) pp. 25-50 New York, NY. Thomas Dunn Books.

[203] Sophia L. Perssio, "North Korea's Kim Jun Un was a Smoking, Raging Teenager" in Newsweek, New York: Newsweek.com, September 16, 2017, http://www.newsweek.com/north-koreas-kim-jong-un-was-smoking-raging-teenager-660039.

between them.[204] [205] They both are privileged, entitled heirs to power who are clearly narcissistic, cocky, grandiose, with explosive tempers known for their bully behavior. That autocrats and dictator-wannabes display these same behaviors isn't surprising. It takes a bully to be a successful dictator.

To be clear, bullying is not a partisan issue. It is a behavior described as the use of power through strength or influence to intimidate another person. It is practiced not only by humans, but by other primates, and other mammals. In the animal kingdom, where pecking order is an important aspect of survival, or to obtain sexual privileges, bullying can lead to shunning, beatings, expulsion from a troop of chimpanzees or congress of baboons, and ultimately even death of the victim.[206] [207] Unfortunately, the same behavior and its varying outcomes are also too true of humans.

In the schoolyard, when the bully and his/her minions gang up on a student, the victim may, from that point forward, cringe and try to disappear whenever the bully materializes. As the victim's self-esteem plummets, the bully's increases. In some instances, as a self-preservation strategy, the victim may reluctantly join the bully's gang, if the bully agrees. (This may lower the victim's self-esteem or, conversely, cause an uptick due to social acceptance. Concurrently, the bully's self-esteem increases.) In other instances, victims may try to divert the bully's attention by turning on a different possible victim in an attempt to take the heat off themselves. (The initial victim's sense of relief may override feelings of guilt at causing another person's victimization.) In the meantime, the witnessing bystanders who do nothing to correct the situation become, through their inaction, complicit in the bully's activity. This inadvertent complicity allows the bullying behavior to continue. So it is important to realize that for every bully and victim there are many observers who remain silent passive bystanders.[208]

In 2015, bullying reached an unprecedented high-level mark in modern history due to its unabashed use in American politics by Donald Trump as he

---

[204] Catherine Bosley and Fredrik Dahl, "Future North Korean Leader Attended Swiss School: Friends," London: Reuters, December 19, 2011, https://www.reuters.com/article/us-korea-north-swiss/future-north-korean-leader-attended-swiss-school-friends-idUSTRE7BI14920111219.

[205] Philip Zimbardo and Rosemary Sword, "Unbridled and Extreme Present Hedonism," 31.

[206] Jane Goodall, "Social Rejection, Exclusion and Shunning Among the Gombe Chimpanzees" in Science, San Francisco: California Academy of Sciences, 1986, 227, https://www.sciencedirect.com/science/article/pii/0162309586900506.

[207] Franz deWahl, "Primates - A Natural Heritage of Conflict Resolution" in Science, Washington, D.C.: Science, Vol 289, July 2000, 586, http://www.emory.edu/LIVING_LINKS/publications/articles/deWaal_2000b.pdf.

[208] Rosemary Sword and Philip Zimbardo, "The Bystander Effect" in PsychologyToday.com, New York: Psychology Today, February 27, 2015, https://www.psychologytoday.com/us/blog/the-time-cure/201502/the-bystander-effect.

tainted our presidential debates and campaign with his expert bullying tactics.[209] We have all witnessed and experienced bully behavior, but what has been new on the bully scene is the use of cyberbullying, with technology replacing face-to-face confrontations.[210]

In 2018, these same schoolyard bully tactics and behaviors can be applied to our current governance. Trump, the bully in power, has an already established penchant for using social media to damage others. He doesn't need to threaten a subordinate to make them do what he wants. The victim is aware of Trump's bully past behavior—and the results—so the impending negative tweet or statement about the intended victim is enough to keep the victim squelched or *in line*. As is happening in our schoolyards by witnessing bystanders, being *in line* may mean keeping silent instead of speaking out against the injustice.

To the extent that bullying enhances the power of the bully, it might appear to be a rational strategy. But it has severe limitations and severe potential costs for a leader and the society he leads. First, the bully leader's behavioral options are extremely limited. If he is publicly challenged, he must ferociously counterattack or lose all face and power. Secondly, the bully operates on the principles of present-tense hedonism, responding to what feels good in the moment—aggression—without calculating the probable long-term consequences.

What can we expect when two bullies confront one another? The answer is obvious and, indeed, frighteningly predictable: neither will back down without a fight.

In March 2018, Trump fired his national security advisor, H.R. McMaster, one of the "adults in the room" who we were told might tackle Trump on the way to the nuclear football, and replaced him with John Bolton[211], a tempestuous bully himself who has publicly argued for a first strike against North Korea and war with Iran. "Bolton is precisely the kind of bully that Trump finds attractive and admirable. And suddenly, with his appointment, the White House is an even darker place," wrote Joe Conason, in his article in the *National Memo*, "A Chickenhawk Bully Who Reflects Trump Perfectly." We are greatly concerned that rather than be a voice of reason and moderation, Bolton will encourage Trump's worst bullying instincts by egging Trump on to show Kim *who's boss,* and that the world may be destroyed by two dueling, insecure, immature bully dictators.

[209] Philip Zimbardo and Rosemary Sword, "Unbridled and Extreme Present Hedonism," 41-42.

[210] Sherry Gordon, "6 Types of Bullying," in Very Well Family, Tennessee: Verywell.com, February 25, 2018, http://bullying.about.com/od/Basics/a/6-Types-Of-Bullying.htm.

[211] Mark Landler and Maggie Haberman, "Trump Chooses Bolton for 3rd Security Advisor as Shake-up Continues" in The New York Times, New York: The New York Times, March 22, 2018, https://www.nytimes.com/2018/03/22/us/politics/hr-mcmaster-trump-bolton.html.

Given that bully tactics are the default settings for world leaders Kim and Trump, we may be closer to nuclear war than we think. In a speech, Kim called Trump a "mentally deranged U.S. dotard."[212] In retaliation Trump sarcastically— and backhandedly—tweeted that Kim is "short and fat";[213] and he has repeatedly referred to Kim as "Little Rocket Man." Trump clearly considers himself to be the "Big Rocket Man." As Trump tweeted, "North Korean Leader Kim Jong Un just stated that the 'Nuclear Button is on his desk at all times.' Will someone from his depleted and food starved regime please inform him that I too have a Nuclear Button, but it is a much bigger & more powerful one than his, and my Button works!" If we were psychoanalytically inclined, we would have to wonder if all of this is a contest about who has the biggest penis.

A war of words between two bullies typically escalates into physical conflict. Neither can back down.

Trump has been erratic in the way he deals with Kim Jong-un—from disparaging bully tactics to suddenly and quite eagerly wanting to meet with him. If the meeting never takes place, or if it fails to produce agreements, the bully tactics will resume as each man blames the other for the failure. In addition, because Trump is a present-tense hedonist,[214] he also might escalate military conflict if it momentarily relieves the psychological pressure created by other factors, most notably the Mueller investigation, and enhances his sense of esteem, power, and dominance in the short term. His April 2018 ordering of missile attacks against Syria before there was confirmed external observers' evidence of nerve gas used against civilians by the Assad government is a potent example of Trump's rush to action.

Millions may die to prove who has the bigger button—Trump or Kim. When Marco Rubio challenged Trump as having small hands, implying he might therefore have a small penis as well, Trump assured us "there's no problem there, I can assure you."[215] But Trump's insecurities may be a big, big problem, at a scale so horrible we can barely imagine it.

Perhaps Trump's hedonistic addiction to around-the-clock tweeting is a good diversion as his personal playground, so that we can all know what this

---

[212] Alex Ward, "Here's the full text of Kim Jong Un's unprecedented threat against Trump" in Vox.com, Washington, D.C.: Vox, September 22, 2017, https://www.vox.com/2017/9/22/16349460/kim-jong-un-statement-trump-dotard-full-text.

[213] Alex Ward, "Trump's latest tweet storm called Kim Jon Un 'short and fat'" in Vox.com, Washington, D.C.: Vox, November 12, 2015, https://www.vox.com/2017/11/12/16639462/trump-kim-north-korea-russia-twitter.

[214] Philip Zimbardo and Sword, Rosemary, Living & Loving Better, 2017, N. Carolina: McFarland, 40.

[215] Gregory Krieg, "Donald Trump defends the size of his penis" on CNN, Atlanta: CNN, March 4, 2016, https://www.cnn.com/2016/03/03/politics/donald-trump-small-hands-marco-rubio/index.html.

preposterous president of the United States is ruminating about prior to his grandiose acting out.

Philip Zimbardo, Ph.D., professor emeritus at Stanford University, is a scholar, educator and researcher. Zimbardo is perhaps best known for his landmark Stanford prison study. Among his more than 500 publications are the bestsellers *The Lucifer Effect,* and *The Dangerous Case of Donald Trump*, as well as such notable psychology textbooks as *Psychology: Core Concepts, 8th edition* and *Psychology and Life,* now in its 20th edition. He is founder and president of *The Heroic Imagination Project* (heroicimagination.org), a world-wide nonprofit teaching people of all ages how to take wise and effective action in challenging situations.

Rosemary Sword is codeveloper of *Time Perspective Therapy* and co-author of related books such as *The Time Cure,* Wiley 2012; *Time Perspective Theory,* Springer, 2015; *Living and Loving Better,* McFarland, 2017; and *The Dangerous Case of Donald Trump, Macmillan, 2017.* Sword and Zimbardo write a popular column for *Psychology Today* and contribute to *AppealPower.com* (European Union online journal), *Psychology in Practice,* a new Polish psychological journal, and *Happify.com.* She is also developer of *Aetas: Mind Balancing Apps* (discoveraetas.com) and a private practice time perspective therapist.

References

Bosley, Catherine, Dahl, Fredrik, "Future North Korean Leader Attended Swiss School: Friends." *Reuters*, December 19, 2011, https://www.reuters.com/article/us-korea-north-swiss/future-north-korean-leader-attended-swiss-school-friends-idUSTRE7BI14920111219.

deWahl, Franz, "Primates - A Natural Heritage of Conflict Resolution" in Science, Washington, D.C.: Science, Vol 289, July 2000, 586, http://www.emory.edu/LIVING_LINKS/publications/articles/deWaal_2000b.pdf.

Goodall, Jane, "Social Rejection, Exclusion and Shunning Among the Gombe Chimpanzees," San Francisco: California Academy of Sciences, 1986, 227, https://www.sciencedirect.com/science/article/pii/0162309586900506.

Gordon, Sherry, "Six types of bullying every parent should know about." *Very Well Family*, February 25, 2018, https://www.verywellfamily.com/types-of-bullying-parents-should-know-about-4153882.

Krieg, Gregory, "Donald Trump defends the size of his penis," Atlanta: CNN, March 4, 2016, https://www.cnn.com/2016/03/03/politics/donald-trump-small-hands-marco-rubio/index.html.

Landler, Mark, Haberman, Maggie, "Trump Chooses Bolton for 3rd Security Advisor as Shake-up Continues," *New York Times*, March 22, 2018, https://www.nytimes.com/2018/03/22/us/politics/hr-mcmaster-trump-bolton.html.

Perssio, Sophia L., "North Korea's Kim Jun Un was a Smoking, Raging Teenager," *Newsweek*, September 16, 2017, http://www.newsweek.com/north-koreas-kim-jong-un-was-smoking-raging-teenager-660039.

Sword, Rosemary, and Zimbardo, Philip, "The Bystander Effect." *Psychology Today*.com, February 27, 2015, https://www.psychologytoday.com/blog/the-time-cure/201502/the-bystander-effect.

Ward, Alex, "Here's the full text of Kim Jong Un's unprecedented threat against Trump," *Vox*.com. September 22, 2017, https://www.vox.com/2017/9/22/16349460/kim-jong-un-statement-trump-dotard-full-text.

Ward, Alex, "Trump's latest tweet storm called Kim Jon Un 'short and fat,'" *Vox*.com, November 12, 2015, https://www.vox.com/2017/11/12/16639462/trump-kim-north-korea-russia-twitter.

Zimbardo, Philip, Sword, Richard, and Sword, Rosemary, *The Time Cure*, 2012, San Francisco: Wiley, 36, 53-54, 60.

Zimbardo, Philip and Sword, Rosemary, *Living & Loving Better*, 2017, N. Carolina: McFarland, 40.

Zimbardo, Philip, and Sword, Rosemary, "Unbridled and Extreme Present Hedonism," in *The Dangerous Case of Donald Trump: 27 psychiatrists and mental health experts assess a president*, edited by Bandy X. Lee, New York: Thomas Dunn Books/Macmillan, 2017, 25-50.

Chapter 15

American Carnage: The Wars of Donald Trump

By Melvin Goodman

"I've had a lot of wars of my own. I'm really good at war. I love war…," Trump declared at a campaign rally in Iowa in 2015. Perhaps we should believe him, since he seems to be perpetually embattled with virtually everyone (but Putin), including his own Justice Department. But what of real war? Will he find he loves that too?

When former Secretary of State Rex Tillerson famously referred to President Donald Trump as a "f…ing moron," it was in response to the president's case for expanding U.S. nuclear forces and justifying the use of such forces that expanded and directed the Pentagon to draft plans for the use of nuclear weapons even with non-nuclear states and cases where an adversary used non-nuclear weapons. Dick Cheney once raised such ideas, and they were immediately shot down by the national security team.

But President Trump has installed a virtual "war cabinet" that favors the use of force.

Secretary of State Mike Pompeo has long been an uberhawk who favors hard power over diplomacy. Even if he were inclined to pursue diplomacy, he will inherit a dysfunctional Department of State as a result of Tillerson's campaign to reduce the budget for diplomacy and to make no appointments to many of the most important leadership positions of the department. More than forty countries are currently without a U.S. ambassador, including such key countries as Germany and South Korea.

Trump nominated Pompeo's deputy at CIA, Gina Haspel, to be the CIA director. Haspel commanded the worst of the CIA's secret prisons during the Global War on Terror and was a key decision maker in the destruction of the ninety-two torture tapes. Pompeo favors the return of torture as a means of "gathering of vital intelligence."

The mainstream media point to Secretary of Defense James Mattis as the moderating "adult in the room." But Mattis earned his nickname "MadDog," and his loss of command in the Obama administration, because he favored expanding the war in Iraq to Iran. Mattis commanded U.S. Marines in Iraq who were responsible for a large number of civilian fatalities, including one case where he dismissed murder charges against American soldiers who shot unarmed men, women, and children at close range.

Overall, this is the most bellicose presidential cabinet in U.S. history.

The most sensitive national security positions will be occupied by individuals who favor the use of military force, who played a major role in the use of torture and abuse, or who recommended regime change and even the use of nuclear weapons.

The most frightening Trump appointment thus far has been John Bolton as national security advisor, the third most powerful position in Washington after the president himself and the White House chief of staff. When President George W. Bush nominated Bolton to be the U.S. ambassador to the United Nations, a Republican-controlled Senate made certain that he could not win confirmation. Like Trump, Bolton was perceived as a bully who sought retribution against those who contradicted him. His State Department colleagues placed him in the "kiss up; kick down" category. Two former secretaries of state, Colin Powell and Rex Tillerson, refused to accept Bolton as a deputy secretary because of his extremist views and his brutal treatment of underlings. Richard Painter, former Bush official, said, "John Bolton was by far the most dangerous man we had in the entire eight years of the Bush Administration," adding "Hiring him as the president's top national security advisor is an invitation to war, perhaps nuclear war."

Bolton is just the man to enable Trump's worst instincts. One of the primary tasks of the national security advisor is to be an honest broker, bringing different views to the president. This is clearly not Bolton's *modus operandi*. He described his job of national security advisor as making sure that the bureaucracy doesn't impede the decisions of the president.

The mere thought of Trump and Bolton discussing national security and the use of force in the White House is simply frightening. Both men have displayed impulsive and explosive behaviors, and Trump's fixation on undoing the legacy of Barack Obama points to an obsession. Where Nixon's biographers described him as sharp and analytical with a remarkable memory, Trump's biographers point to dangerous elements of irritability and aggressiveness as well as a pattern of deceitful behavior in his personal and professional life. Bolton is even more willing to resort to force than Trump.

Both Trump and Bolton have engaged in irresponsible talk about nuclear weapons. Trump told interviewers that there is no point in having nuclear weapons if we're not willing to use them. Bolton still defends the use of force in Iraq and favors preemptive attacks against both Iran and North Korea. Bolton has penned several editorial articles to make the case for a first strike against both countries. In previous roles, he played a key role in politicizing the intelligence to justify the war in Iraq and, as U.N. ambassador, regularly misused intelligence to make false statements in the General Assembly and the Security Council regarding Syrian and Cuban weapons systems.

The irresponsible remarks of both Trump and Bolton regarding force and the use of nuclear weapons have brought back memories of the madman theory of policy. Early in Richard Nixon's presidency, he told his chief of staff, Bob Haldeman, that his secret strategy for ending the Vietnam War was to threaten the use of nuclear weapons. Nixon opined that President Eisenhower's nuclear threats in 1953 brought a quick end to the Korean War and that he planned to use the same principle of threatening maximum force. Nixon called it the "madman theory," getting the North Vietnamese to "believe … I might do anything to stop the war."

Ironically, Daniel Ellsberg, who famously leaked the Pentagon Papers, may have been responsible for introducing the theory in his lectures in 1959 to Henry Kissinger's Harvard seminar on the conscious political use of irrational military threats. Ellsberg called the theory the "political uses of madness," and he noted that any extreme threat would be more credible if the person making the threat were perceived as not being fully rational. Ellsberg couldn't imagine that an American president would ever consider such a strategy, but he believed that irrational behavior could be a useful negotiating tool. Kissinger, who became Nixon's national security advisor ten years later, said that he "learned more from Dan Ellsberg than any other person about bargaining."

But while Kissinger was a measured, reserved, cerebral, rational strategist, evidence has been accumulating that Donald Trump is none of those things. Many contributors to this volume have the professional expertise to diagnose him, and do so, more fully than I can. But his impulsive need to make vengeful attacks on those who challenge him, his lies and paranoid conspiracy theories, his attacks on minorities, women and immigrants, indeed his combative stance with virtually everyone points to someone who cannot conduct a rational and considered exercise of power.

Trump is not a theoretician, so we are not talking about a considered "madman" approach. Rather, we have to consider the frightening possibility that we have an actual "madman" as president, and a Cabinet that will enable his combative madness. It's not a grand strategy but a warning sign of the real carnage to come.

Trump says he loves war. We should believe him.

Melvin A. Goodman has a Ph.D. from Indiana University. His 42-government career includes service with the CIA, the Department of State, the Department of Defense, and the U.S. Army. His seven books on international security include *Whistleblower at the CIA: Inside the Politics of Intelligence, National Insecurity: The Cost of US Militarism*, and *The Failure of Intelligence: The Decline and Fall of the CIA*. He is an adjunct professor of government at Johns Hopkins University and a senior fellow at the Center for International Policy.

Operation Cue: A few minutes after detonation the atomic blast in Operation Cue looked like this, May 5, 1955. *National Archives*

Chapter 16
Taking Trump's Finger off the Nuclear Button

By Tom Z. Collina

Most Americans do not realize that the president of the United States has unlimited authority to launch U.S. nuclear weapons at the time of his choosing, with no real checks or balances from anyone. President Donald Trump could order a nuclear war as easily as a Domino's pizza.

This situation is both dangerous and unnecessary. Simply put, the risks of having nuclear weapons ready to launch within minutes outweigh any perceived benefits, especially if the sole decision-maker cannot be trusted. It is time for a change.

President Trump, with John Bolton as his national security advisor, now has the same frightening power as all presidents in the atomic age. At the height of the Watergate scandal in 1974, President Richard Nixon boasted about his nuclear prowess: "I can go back into my office and pick up the telephone and in 25 minutes 70 million people will be dead."[216]

Under his own authority, with just one phone call, President Trump could unleash thousands of nuclear weapons, each one many times more powerful than the Hiroshima bomb. Short of mutiny, no one can stop him. Once launched, the missiles cannot be recalled.

This is not fake news. This is not even a matter of debate; there is bipartisan unity on this point. Senate Foreign Relations Committee chair Bob Corker (R-Tenn.), and then-ranking member Ben Cardin (D-Md.), agreed late last year that the president has the ability to launch U.S. nuclear weapons on his own authority. "The president has the sole authority to give that order, whether we are responding to a nuclear attack or not," said Corker. "Once that order is given and verified, there is no way to revoke it."[217]

Sen. Cardin said, "Based on my understanding of the nuclear command-and-control protocol, there are no checks—no checks—on the president's authority. The system as it is set up today provides the president with the sole and ultimate authority to use nuclear weapons."

---

[216] Richard Rhodes, "Absolute Power," The New York Times, March 21, 2014.

[217] Tom Z. Collina, "The Most Dangerous Man in the World," Defense One, Nov. 14, 2017.

But never before have so many questioned the fitness of a commander-in-chief to unilaterally control the largest killing machine ever created, with the unquestioned capacity to end life on earth.

Sen. Corker has been worried about Trump and nuclear weapons for some time. Last fall, he said, "We could be heading towards World War III with the kinds of comments that he's making."[218]

And as Sen. Chris Murphy (D-Conn.) put it last year, Americans are concerned that President Trump "is so unstable, is so volatile" that he might order a nuclear strike that is "wildly out of step" with our national security interests. "Let's just recognize the exceptional nature of this moment in the discussion that we're having today," he said.[219]

The Nuclear Button

Despite what we may see in the movies and on TV, there is actually no "nuclear button." This is a metaphor for a complex system of phones, codes, and messages that enable the president to order, and his or her military staff to carry out, a nuclear attack. It starts with a briefcase known as the "football," carried by a military aide who is near the president at all times, which contains nuclear strike options and authentication codes that the president needs to issue launch orders. The president must also have a special code printed on a card, called the "biscuit," that is in the president's possession around the clock.

Once the president issues orders, the well-oiled military machine takes over. The orders travel down the chain of command until they reach launch officers in missiles silos, pilots on bombers, and captains on submarines who have trained for this moment. Only widespread mutiny could stop this process from reaching its grim end. The whole process would take just minutes.

Some have suggested that military leaders would not necessarily carry out a presidential launch order. Gen. C. Robert Kehler, former head of Strategic Command, has sought to reassure the public that "the military does not blindly follow orders" and that illegal orders would not be implemented. Don't count on it. Officers who might be tempted to question a presidential order of this kind should be reminded of Harold Hering, who, in 1973, was training to be an Air Force nuclear missile launch officer. He dared to ask his instructors: How can I be certain that any launch order I receive comes from a sane president? He was fired.[220]

---

[218] "Read Excerpts From Senator Bob Corker's Interview With The Times," The New York Times, Oct. 9, 2017.

[219] Tom Z. Collina, "The Most Dangerous Man in the World," Defense One, Nov. 14, 2017.

[220] Michael S. Rosenwald, "What if the president ordering a nuclear attack isn't sane? An Air Force major lost his job for asking," The Washington Post, Aug. 10, 2017.

And, as Dr. Peter Feaver from Duke University puts it, in the world of military officers, "there is a presumption that the [nuclear launch] orders are legal."

We don't have many real-life examples of nuclear launch orders to look at (thankfully), but orders to launch conventional weapons are plentiful. In April, President Trump ordered Secretary of Defense James Mattis to launch a conventional attack against Syria. Congress had not authorized the attack, making it arguably illegal under Article I of the Constitution. Rather than resisting the order, Mattis justified it on the grounds that "the president has the authority under Article II of the Constitution to use military force overseas to defend important U.S. national interests."[221] This is an extreme position that could cover just about any use of military force, and thus most legal scholars would call it unconstitutional. That did not stop Gen. Mattis.

The reality is that when it comes to using the bomb, the president has almost complete autonomy with no institutional checks and balances. There are no interagency meetings, congressional hearings, Supreme Court decisions, or United Nations votes. As Bruce Blair, a former Air Force nuclear missile launch officer, has said, "The presidency has evolved into something akin to a nuclear monarchy."[222]

Yes, there are many systems in place to prevent nuclear weapons from being launched by an unauthorized person or by accident. But currently there is no way to prevent a president from starting nuclear war.

Dethroning the Nuclear Monarchy

How can we remedy this situation? It is long past time to bring democracy to decisions about the bomb. It no longer makes sense, it if ever did, to have so much power in the hands of one person. It is just too dangerous.

Kennette Benedict of the *Bulletin of the Atomic Scientists* observes that for decades Americans have ceded the authority to start a nuclear war to a single person. Congress has no voice in the most important decision the United States government can make. As it stands now, Congress has a larger role in deciding on the number of military bands than in initiating nuclear catastrophe.

This situation completely contradicts the checks and balances created by the U.S. Constitution. Even though they could not imagine the dangers of nuclear war, the framers of the Constitution understood the dangers of tyranny and gave the power to declare war to Congress—not to the president. With British rule fresh in their minds, they believed that ceding such power to the executive would result in a state of perpetual conflict and that the only way to check that power was citizen participation in any decision to go to war.

---

[221] Bruce Ackerman, "Trump Can't Make War Whenever He Likes," The New York Times, April 16, 2018.

[222] Bruce Blair, "What Exactly Would It Mean to Have Trump's Finger on the Nuclear Button?," Politico, June 11, 2016.

"Our Founding Fathers would be rolling over in their graves if they knew the president could launch a massive, potentially civilization-ending military strike without authorization from Congress," Rep. Ted Lieu (D-Calif.) said in 2016.[223]

Rep. Lieu and Sen. Edward Markey (D-Mass.) have introduced a bill that would prohibit the president from launching nuclear weapons without a declaration of war from Congress, except in response to a nuclear attack. The bill would legally block the president from using nuclear weapons first in a crisis, without authorization from the people's elected representatives.

Some might argue that Congress would never provide this authority and thus the president could never use nuclear weapons first. Fine. As Vice President Joe Biden announced before he left office, "It's hard to envision a plausible scenario in which the first use of nuclear weapons by the United States would be necessary. Or make sense."[224]

And as Sen. Markey said, "Neither President Trump, nor any other president, should be allowed to use nuclear weapons except in response to a nuclear attack. By restricting the first use of nuclear weapons, this legislation enshrines that simple principle into law."[225]

In an effort similar to the Markey-Lieu bill, Rep. Adam Smith (D-Wash.), ranking member of the House Armed Services Committee, introduced legislation in 2017 that simply states that "it is the policy of the United States to not use nuclear weapons first."

These ideas have begun to gain popularity outside Washington, D.C., as well, with cities and states across the country poised to pass resolutions in support of limiting the president's nuclear authority.

Without congressional deliberation and citizen participation in the gravest decisions of life and death, our democracy is greatly diminished. Benedict suggests that citizens are treated as children who don't deserve a voice in how our country's nuclear weapons are deployed. That is not how the world's greatest democracy should work.

Congress must end the nuclear monarchy, exercise its constitutional responsibility and demand its rightful role in nuclear weapons policymaking. The likely outcome is a greatly reduced chance that any president, including President Trump, would use nuclear weapons first. The certain outcome is a restoration of our democratic institutions.

---

[223] Rebecca Kheel, "Dems tie nuclear first-strike bill to concerns about Trump," The Hill, Sept. 17, 2016.

[224] Joe Biden, "Remarks by the Vice President on Nuclear Security," Jan. 11, 2017.

[225] Rebecca Kheel, "Dems seek to limit Trump's options for using nuclear weapons," The Hill, Jan. 24, 2017.

Avoiding Accidental Nuclear War

In addition to acts of Congress, there are steps the White House should take to reduce the inherent risks of current launch procedures. Only the executive branch can reduce the very real risk that a false alarm could lead to a nuclear launch—that is, accidental nuclear war.

The main reason the president has nuclear autonomy is to allow him or her to launch the weapons quickly—within minutes—before a surprise Russian attack could wipe out U.S. land-based forces. But this is a vestige of the past. Even if all U.S. land-based missiles were destroyed, the United States could still respond to an attack with nuclear weapons based on submarines, safe under the ocean. These sea-based weapons alone would deter any Russian attack.

Former Secretary of Defense Bill Perry says often that U.S. land-based ballistic missiles are redundant and should be retired. As Perry wrote in 2016: "These missiles are some of the most dangerous weapons in the world. They could even trigger an accidental nuclear war."[226]

As Perry explains, false alarms have happened before and can happen again. "While the probability of an accidental launch is low, human and machine errors do occur. I experienced a false alarm nearly forty years ago, when I was under secretary of defense for research and engineering. I was awakened in the middle of the night and told that some Defense Department computers were showing 200 ICBMs on the way from the Soviet Union. For one horrifying moment I thought it was the end of civilization. Then the general on the phone explained that it was a false alarm. He was calling to see if I could help him determine what had gone wrong with the computer."

Once these vulnerable land-based missiles are gone, the president would no longer be faced with the time-urgent decision to launch them before they could be destroyed by incoming missiles. And since sea-based weapons are invulnerable, there would be no need to launch quickly. The president could wait days.

At a minimum, the United States should take its nuclear weapons off high alert. In 2016, more than 90 prominent American scientists, including 20 Nobel laureates, sent a letter to President Barack Obama warning him that keeping weapons ready to launch "increases the risk that one or more nuclear-armed missiles could be launched accidentally, without authorization, or by mistake in response to a false warning of an incoming attack. A launch could, in turn, trigger a retaliatory nuclear attack."[227]

The United States should also announce that it will never use nuclear weapons first in a conflict, but only to deter their use by others. This could serve to reassure

---

[226] William J. Perry, "Why It's Safe to Scrap America's ICBMs," The New York Times, Sept. 30, 2016.

[227] Tom Z. Collina, "How to Slow President Trump From Pushing The Nuclear Button," Defense One, June 30, 2016.

Moscow and, if Russia reciprocates, help both nations back away from the nuclear brink.

Many would say that President Trump should be the last person to entrust with the authority to launch U.S. nuclear weapons. In fact, he is probably the only one who is. This makes Trump the most dangerous man in the world—not just to others, but to the United States itself. It is time for Congress to exercise its democratic authority under the Constitution to limit the president's dangerous nuclear autonomy. And it is time for the White House itself to reduce pressures on presidential decision-making that could lead to accidental nuclear war.

President Trump is not a normal president. He should not be entrusted with the same level of nuclear authority given to previous presidents. Some argue that we should not change long-standing policies based on the experience of one leader, since we might then need to change them back again when a new leader is elected. But 25 years after the end of the Cold War, it is time to change nuclear launch policies for Trump and all future presidents. Trump has awakened us to this clear and present danger, but, unless we act now, that danger will persist after he exits the White House.

Tom Z. Collina is Director of Policy at Ploughshares Fund in Washington, D.C., and has 30 years of experience in nuclear weapons, missile defense and nonproliferation policy and research. Prior to joining Ploughshares Fund in 2014, Tom worked at the Arms Control Association, the Institute for Science and International Security and the Union of Concerned Scientists. He has published hundreds of articles and appears frequently in the national media, including The New York Times, CNN, and NPR. He has testified before the U.S. Congress and regularly briefs congressional staff. Tom has a degree in International Relations from Cornell University.

1950s Civil Defense Pamphlet Photo Images

One wonders how comforting the 1950s government-issue pamphlet might have been. The last page urges the reader to "FOLLOW THESE SIMPLE RULES."

Fallout is nothing more than particles of matter in the air, made radioactive by nuclear or thermonuclear explosions. When an atomic or hydrogen bomb is exploded close to the ground, thousands of tons of atomized earth, building materials, rocks, and gases are sucked upward, sometimes to a height of 80,000 feet or more. They help form the mushroom cloud which is always seen with one of these explosions.

Some of these radioactive particles spill out in the immediate area of the explosion soon after it occurs, but others may be carried by the upper winds for many miles. Sooner or later, however, they settle to earth. This is called fallout.

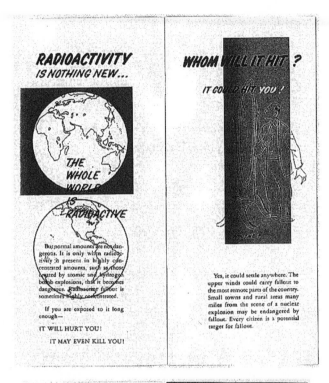

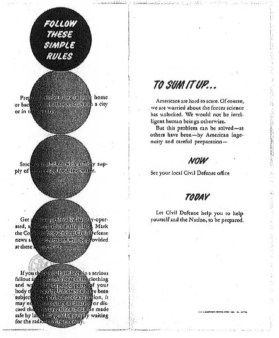

A 1955 pamphlet entitled "Facts about Fallout," issued by the Federal Civil Defense Administration, warns Americans about the dangers of radioactive fallout in the event of a nuclear explosion, and gives suggestions citizens can take to protect themselves. *National Archives*

Chapter 17
Is Donald Trump a Fascist?

By Bård Larsen

The Nobel Prize-winning author Sinclair Lewis published the novel *It Can't Happen Here*, about the fascist populist Buzz Windrip, who wins a landslide presidential election following extensive election trail promises about social and economic reform, as well as bringing about a new dawn for patriotism and traditional values. Swiftly, Windrip dismantles American institutions, builds an alliance with Berlin and establishes a German-style dictatorship.

Another book, written by Philip Roth, is both more subtle and relevant to our time. In *The Plot Against America* from 2004, Charles Lindbergh runs for president on a Republican ticket in 1940. The incumbent president is defeated, none other than the Euro-friendly, anti-fascist Franklin D. Roosevelt, who with his arrogant faith in the ineffability of democracy underestimates the appeal of Lindbergh. In fact, the flying ace and Nazi-friendly anti-Semite Lindbergh was central to the America First movement.

This movement preached U.S. noninterventionism in the war in Europe. In *The Plot Against America*, Lindbergh runs on an isolationist platform featuring an underlying conspiracy theory targeting a global Jewish scheme. President Lindbergh signs a treaty with Germany, but unlike in Sinclair's story, Roth's USA isn't swayed into totalitarianism. Instead, the rule of law is partially subverted, freedom of speech curtailed, and the Jews "relocated." Through counterfactual narratives depicting his own Jewish family, Roth describes how fear and prejudice eat at the heart of American society and pave the way for a gradual dismantling of the liberal order.

According to an article by Simone Zelitch in the weekly periodical *Forward*, Donald Trump can be construed as a synthesis of the literary characters of Windrip and Lindbergh.[228] The point of contention is, of course, whether this comparison is relevant. At worst, Roth's and Sinclair's counterfactual narratives will go on to achieve prophetic status.

But is Trump really a fascist?

---

[228] Simone Zelitch, "How Philip Roth Predicted the Rise of Donald Trump". Forward, July 6, 2016, https://forward.com/culture/343681/how-philip-roth-predicted-the-rise-of-donald-trump/

Is Trump a fascist?

Trump's political agenda is paradoxical in the sense that it is both demagogical and rather devoid of substance. Most worryingly, it isn't Trump's zany antics that are the worst of it, but rather his volatile and narcissistic personality. Trump is apparently unable to meet the fundamental democratic requirements of political finesse and negotiation. Trump isn't wired for democracy ("I alone can fix it"). From observing Trump's behavior, it's not a big leap to imagine that he'd seize upon dictatorship—or kleptocracy—with both hands if it were served up on a silver platter.

Following World War II, the philosopher Theodor W. Adorno and some of his colleagues attempted to map the psychological profile of fascism, or rather, they developed an analysis of what they coined *the authoritarian personality*. Among these, Adorno, et. al., highlight a strong ego (narcissism) overriding one's own insecurity, poor impulse control, an aggressive and cynical view of humanity, rigidity, constant displays of toughness, anti-intellectualism, conspiratorial thinking, a tendency to stereotype and exclude certain groups, as well as intolerance and a general disdain for nuances.

Other features of classical fascism are less relevant to Trump. For example, he is not a traditionalist, right-wing ideologist or an outspoken supporter of the one-party state. Trump differs from the fascists of the 1930s. However, he is entirely in line with the radical right-wing populist authoritarian trends of our time. Today's authoritarianism comes in the form of quasi-democratic or fully pseudo-democratic societies, where the leader's goal is to control state institutions while giving them a sheen of constitutional legitimacy, as we see in today's Russia, Turkey and, increasingly, even Poland and Hungary. Trump has already succeeded in moving America in that direction.

The Economist downgraded American democracy from "full democracy" to "flawed democracy" in its recent report that also notes an alarming trend worldwide—more countries are moving away from democracy than toward it. In its recent report on global democracy, the foundation Freedom House points that the U.S. democratic standards are eroding at an accelerated pace and worldwide there is an increased loss of liberty.[229] Where America was the unparalleled global guardian of democracy, the report asserts that Trump's authoritarian hubris has encouraged and emboldened illiberal and reactionary regimes.

---

[229] Ishaan Tharoor, "Trump Is Speeding the Global Erosion of Democracy, Watchdog Says," The Washington Post, January 18, 2018, https://www.washingtonpost.com/news/worldviews/wp/2018/01/18/trump-is-speeding-the-global-erosion-of-democracy-watchdog-says/?utm_term=.2a7b71aaa36e

Can it Happen Here?

Though it's fair to say that the Founding Fathers wrought the Constitution in such a way as to prevent *fixers* like Trump from expanding their powers, there is still cause for concern. The postwar era in the Western world (and in particular the fall of the Berlin Wall) has been largely dominated by the permanence and sanctity of the liberal state founded on laws, a perception so rational and steeped in history that no one would freely dismiss it. However, many examples of such a dismissal exist, admittedly in countries where democratic traditions haven't taken root properly. Could the same happen in a country with a liberal history? Historians who have worked with authoritarian ideologies and the collapse of civilizations are not convinced by the undaunted optimism that meets them.

Many are wondering whether the U.S. president has a *plan*, a strategy underpinning his many antics, or whether he's acting on impulse. In all likelihood, the two aren't mutually exclusive. There are those who claim that Trump won't be a threat to the major political institutions. Trump has no inner, ideological, authoritarian core, and autocracies are built on the antidemocratic ideology of pure purpose.

Perhaps it would rather be fair to say Trump is an authoritarian by instinct. The reason he spends almost all his energy (on Twitter and other media) on undiplomatically showcasing his thin skin is that he can't stand being contradicted. It's one thing to be disappointed in political failures, but the main bulk of his social media invective is directed at entirely unrelated matters, down to the most banal and personally vindictive, like athletes and actors. This includes many of his attacks on liberal institutions: the press, freedom of speech, Congress, and the courts. Trump considers the liberal order a personal insult. Trump's authoritarianism isn't even particularly opportunistic in a classical sense; it is downright personally instinctive.

Steps on the road Authoritarian Rule.
Step 1: what is truth?

The thing most of us notice is Trump's trifling with lies and truth.[230] Lying is not uncommon, but on the whole, we are aware of when we're lying. In Trump's world, randomized mendacity is more than a tool to be used cynically. Trump is building a narrative around himself where both lies and truth are informed by emotional impulsiveness.

It's challenging to respond to a head of state who lies constantly. The historian Timothy Snyder is of the opinion that Trump's lies are shuffling tyranny. These are dark matters. Postfactualism paves the way for systemic change, Snyder said in an

---

[230] David Leonhardt and Stuart A. Thompson, "Trump's Lies," The New York Times, December 14, 2017, https://www.nytimes.com/interactive/2017/06/23/opinion/trumps-lies.html

interview with Trevor Noah on *The Daily Show*. Without access to facts, there can be no trust. No trust, no order. No order, no democracy: "So if you want to rip the heart out of a democracy directly, if you want to go right at it and kill it, what you do is you go after facts. And that is what modern authoritarians do."

Achieving the first step of autocracy, erasing truth, requires three actions: First, you lie yourself, all the time. Second, you say it's your opponents and the journalists who lie. Third, everyone looks around and says, "What is truth? There is no truth. And then, resistance is impossible, and the game is over."[231]

Step 2: Dehumanize the "others"

During the annual CPAC conference for American conservatives (now reactionaries) in February 2018, where even the radical nationalists Nigel Farage and Marion LePen held the podium, Trump gave an uncommonly long speech. For most of the audience, the high point was his recital of the entire lyrics to the Sixties song "The Snake" with theatrical passion (which wasn't a first).

"The Snake" was written in 1960 by the soul singer and civil rights activist Oscar Brown Jr. The lyrics describe a snake freezing to death, who cunningly convinces a gullible woman to let him into her house. Safely inside, after the woman has given him warm milk and honey, he delivers the fatal bite. As she is lamenting her imminent death, the snake chides her: "Oh, shut up, silly woman! You knew damn well I was a snake before you took me in." Brown Jr. was an artist who enjoyed using powerful allegory as a means in stories about everyday challenges, which in this song roughly translates into "There's no such thing as a free lunch."

The song and the history of the artist don't matter to Trump. This is where demagoguery comes into play. Trump always declaims The Snake in a very specific context, namely that of refugees and migrants ("think of it in terms of immigration"). Syrians and Mexicans are the cunning snake, and the American people are the gullible and charitable hosts who offer shelter, milk, and honey, only to be rewarded with a lethal bite. With his metaphors, the U.S. president explains that there are people inside the nation's borders representing a lethal threat to American lives.

Dehumanization means stripping individuals of human properties. There's ample reason to use the term sparingly. It is a very serious matter to accuse someone of this, and yet at times the cry of "Wolf!" goes up. In Trump's case, however, this accusation is spot-on.

A clear and rather depressing example of why can be found in Julius Streicher.

---

[231] Maxwell Stratchan, "In 60 seconds a 'Daily Show' Guest Brilliantly Exposed the Danger of Post-Truth," Huffington Post, May 17, 2017, www.huffingtonpost.com/entry/daily-show-fascism-post-truth_us_591c54abe4b0a7458fa48cbe

Streicher was one of the most hard-core anti-Semites of the Third Reich. A propagandist of some repute, he was editor of the rabidly anti-Semitic periodical Der Stürmer (The Attacker). His views were so radical even the top brass of the Nazi party was put out by them (the billboards for Der Stürmer were taken down during the 1936 Olympics).

Der Stürmer was characterized by crass caricatures, often comparing Jews to inhuman or unpleasant creatures. For example, the caricature "Brood of Serpents" was published in September 1934, reading: "The Jew's symbol is a worm, not without reason. He seeks to creep up on what he wants." Same publication, March 1935: "Don't Let Go!" (Nicht auslassen!): "Do not grow weary, do not loosen the grip. This poisonous serpent may not slip away. Better that one strangles it to death, than our misery begin anew."

Is it reasonable to compare Donald Trump to Julius Streicher? On the face of it, such a comparison appears melodramatic and absurd.

No, Trump is definitely no Nazi, but in this instance, he has employed the same analogy and the same jargon as Julius Streicher.

The recital of "The Snake" is essentially portraying a group as vermin or predators, depending on one's view of venomous reptiles. This is not intended to make a humorous jab at a political opponent, but rather to agitate from the podium. Trump knows his audience, which encompasses the white power segment and other right-wing extremists in the U.S. Firearms are ubiquitous and largely present in the hands of those who think Trump's snake analogy is an apt one for the existential threats that beset them. In another time, in another society, Trump's snake analogy would have appeared as a plausible prologue to crimes against humanity.

Step 3: International Bully

Trump embraces autocrats and rarely, if ever, speaks critically of them.[232] During his state visit to the Philippines, Trump was treated to a sentimental love song by President Rodrigo Duterte, another Streicher-like demagogue.[233] Trump was moved by this. Idealizing autocrats makes rational sense in Trump's worldview: In the unfree and nepotist states there is a peacock with no statesmanlike qualities but yet unlimited power and the prospect of retaining it for the rest of his life.

But the corollary is that his massive ego requires that he be the most powerful and dominant cock in the walk—the strongest of the strongmen.

---

[232] Zack Beauchamp, "Trump is embracing a new generation of strongmen," Vox, February 27, 2018, https://www.vox.com/world/2018/2/27/17058182/xi-jinping-term-limits-trump

[233] "Philippines' Duterte sings love song for Trump: 'You are the light'," The Guardian, November 13, 2017, https://www.theguardian.com/world/2017/nov/13/you-are-the-light-philippines-duterte-sings-love-song-for-trump

The notable exception is Vladimir Putin, but even there he must pound his chest and brag about winning an arms race with Russia, and proclaiming in open defiance of the observable facts "no one is tougher on Russia than me."

He also wants everyone to know that no one has been tougher than he on North Korea. And there he may be right. His bellicose threats and taunting tweets have put the world on edge. It is obvious that North Korea represents a very real and unmanageable threat. Still, a worst-case scenario involves a major war landing in our laps, triggered by a president with a personal and irrational antipathy toward a cookie-cutter totalitarian on the opposite side of the world who offered him offense.

Trump appears more volatile than ever after alleged talks with "The Rocket Man" in Pyongyang, and after axing the pragmatic Secretary of State Rex Tillerson in favor of John Bolton. The latter has gone on record to support a first-strike policy against North Korea.

The concept of dominant bilateralism was recently coined by the Norwegian researcher Anders Romarheim at the Norwegian Institute for Defence Studies. Trump seeks to dominate other nations through the fusion of trade and security, thereby reaping the benefits of his power base through bilateral dominance:

"Trump's intimidating behavior towards other states is reminiscent of Russian gunboat diplomacy of the post-Soviet sphere. Could the liberal world order we have come to take for granted be replaced by the uncompromising power politics of two dominantly bilateral twins? One in the Kremlin and the other in the Oval Office."[234]

Romarheim continues: "Trump is executing policies, both foreign and domestic, as though there were no counterweights to them. When the counterweights come into play, one wonders what will happen as Trump faces international humiliation."

In the authoritarian calculus of might makes right, war can offer an exhilarating opportunity to both demonstrate and expand one's power. "I've had a lot of wars of my own. I'm really good at war. I love war…, but only when we win," Trump told the audience at a campaign rally. We don't know if the Trump presidency will lead to a war sparked by his ego.

No one knows what the end of Trump's presidency will spell. For example, there is a well-founded concern over how the incompetent and volatile Trump administration will be able to handle or take advantage of a profound international crisis, say, North Korea or a massive terrorist strike. On whose behalf will he act? That of the autocratic opportunist (himself), or the well-being of the nation?

---

[234] Anders Romarheim, USA og Norge i Trumps verden, Internasjonal Politikk, March 2017, https://tidsskriftet-ip.no/index.php/intpol/article/view/696/1611

Should Trump be charged with colluding with the Russians, his fall would be of biblical proportions. Therefore, he could do almost anything in his power to obstruct the investigation. It is hard to imagine that the U.S. institutions will not at some point represent a direct challenge to Trump's presidency and authoritarian style of leadership. Meanwhile, Trump is bringing chaos to the public. This could be the intention of the GOP radicals: that even the opposition takes the gloves off and society crumbles, paving the way for radical solutions as the only plausible course. Staving off chaos has the potential for a great deal of power. It is the strongman's raison d'être.

The worst-case scenario when a fire is lit under Trump's feet will then be war, the ultimate lightning rod to domestic issues. There is little, if anything, in Trump's character to make us truly doubt that even the most destructive consequences are a price he's willing to pay. Not to mention that Trump correlates with all the obvious signs of the Dunning–Kruger effect.

The presidency makes Trump the potential chopping block for the nation, where he has set out to revive the American Dream and American greatness singlehandedly, omnisciently, and in record time. The prospect of failure is immense, and the discrepancy between his own self-image and logical realism is likely unparalleled in postwar history. In short, no other position in the world would be more challenging for a man of a vulnerable ego and short fuse.

Whether it be war or peace, America will have to reinforce the democratic instituions and repair the divided society and broken public discourse Trump has sought to destroy.

Bård Larsen is a political commentator, author, and historian. He is working as a fellow at the Norwegian think tank Civita. His main subjects are author-itarianism, human rights, and democratic erosion. He graduated from the University of Oslo on a thesis about the Armenian Genocide.

Chapter 18

The Relentless Victim: How Donald Trump Reinforces North Korea's Narrative

By Paul French

Arirang and North Korean National Psychology

Most years, usually from August through to early September, Pyongyang's giant 114,000-capacity May Day Stadium hosts the spectacular Arirang Grand Mass Gymnastics and Artistic Performance. Thousands of North Koreans, from as young as five years old to senior citizens, participate in Arirang, which is perhaps best known for the 30,000 Pyongyang schoolchildren who form huge revolutionary mosaic pictures by holding up colored cards. Rehearsals start many months before opening night. Gymnasts, acrobats, dancers, opera singers, and marching ranks of armed men and women tell a version of the story of Arirang.

Arirang itself is a Korean folk song, perhaps as much as six centuries old, about a "Land of Morning Calm" that overcomes distress and disaster to emerge as a strong and dignified nation. It was a song used to symbolize resistance to Japanese colonial rule on the Korean peninsula between 1910 and 1945. In Pyongyang nowadays the Arirang folk story is retold to show the rise of the Democratic People's Republic of Korea (DPKR) under Kim Il-sung, through the leadership of son Kim Jong-il, and now his grandson Kim Jong-un. The evening-long spectacle weaves together the ancient myth of Arirang with the later national origin myth of Kim Il-sung's defeat of the Japanese and creation of the DPRK. Featured heavily is the North's resistance to "American imperialism," sixty years ago. To the audience it feels as if that war finished only recently; it is part of the daily collective memory of every North Korean, even those born more than half a century after the armistice was declared.

Through massive gymnastic and acrobatic displays, curiously dated-looking mass waltzing, and revolutionary patriotic songs, it is made clear that the North Korean nation emerged from anti-imperialist struggle and warfare; that the nation still remains threatened by anti-socialist, anti-revolutionary imperialist enemies (primarily the United States and its proxies Japan and South Korea) that threaten to destroy the Northern state and prevent the *natural* and *universally desired* unification of the Korean people. Arirang is the origin story of the DPRK, writ large and loud, in full Technicolor. It is part-Broadway show, part-military tattoo, part-kitsch revolutionary opera. It is completely state propaganda. It is enacted every night by tens of thousands of performers to audiences of perhaps a few hundred (Workers' Party of Korea officials, honored fraternal guests from the North's few

161

remaining international allies, and a handful of curious tourists). It shows the North as a victim of aggression, a country encircled by enemies that threaten nuclear war, a nation proudly and defiantly ready to fight back with everything from pitchforks to ICBMs. It is regime survival at its most raw. President Trump would be well advised to get the DVD. This gigantic show of national psychology, theatrical victimhood, and supposed encirclement by hostile forces is at the core of North Korea's self-image and shared common national identity.

Perpetual War

For the United State, the Korean War is an event of history. A largely forgotten episode that ended sixty-five years ago, spawned a few B-movies and the TV show *M*A*S*H*. Despite the 36,914 American war dead (according to Pentagon numbers) and the Korean War Veterans Memorial on the National Mall, the conflict is massively overshadowed by the later Vietnam War and the enduring legacy of World War II. Amid all the recent debate, rhetoric, tweets, and confusion over the Trump administration's policy on North Korea the 1950-1953 war and the uneasy armistice agreement—the war has never officially ended—has never been referred to. Yet in the DPRK the notion of the Korean conflict as a perpetual war, one that continues through different means and requires a constant state of readiness and preparedness is omnipresent. It goes to the heart of the North's threat perception and goes a long way to explaining its diplomatic bombast, rhetorical attacks, and sense of victimhood.

The North sees the armistice since 1953 as literally that, a cessation during which the United States and its allies—the southern Republic of Korea(ROK), Korea's former colonial master Japan and an aggressively anti-Pyongyang United Nations—are merely biding their time before forming a coalition to attack again. Pyongyang sees the regular ROK/U.S. joint military exercises on land and sea (that involve over 300,000 South Korean and 15,000 U.S. troops) as clear evidence of this intent; similarly, the perceived notion that Washington will permit Japan to remilitarize; the increased sanctions championed by United States at the U.N., and the deployment of the American THAAD anti-missile system in the ROK.

This attitude of perpetual war readiness permeates every aspect of DPRK life, from the military uniforms, long rows of medals, and never-ending titles of the senior leadership up to and including *Great Marshal* Kim Jong-un. This is further reinforced with the centrality of universal conscription to everybody's life and the constant reiteration of Article 86 of the DPRK Constitution, "national defence is the supreme duty and honour of citizens." War readiness and civil defense preparedness are integral to the education syllabus from infancy to university while South Korean spies and infiltrators and Japanese-paid counterrevolutionaries are central to much of the country's cultural output, including movies, television, novels, poetry, art, and mass events such as the Arirang gala described above.

In all these political, social and cultural forms the DPRK is victimized, targeted, at point of imminent (quite possibly nuclear) attack from outside forces either led by or guided by the United States. The current U.S. administration's failure to understand or engage with the North's *theatrical victimhood* has been a major miscalculation. The failure to understand this key element of the North's collective social national psychology is a fundamental error and has, when combined with President Trump's rather offhand and ill-informed remarks and tweets, severely exacerbated the tensions on the Korean peninsula and the wider East Asian region. Additionally, this failure to understand the North's collective psychology of encirclement and perceived threat has made it harder for America's key ally, Seoul, to enter into a joint strategy with Washington for dealing with Pyongyang. Hence North-South talks before, during, and after the 2018 Winter Olympics in Pyeong-chang have continued without the United States.

Pyongyang's state of perpetual war and its theatrical victimhood closely mirror that notion of endless conflict described by the English writer George Orwell in his dystopian novel *Nineteen Eighty-Four* (1949). In that novel the three "superstates" of the world, Eurasia, Oceania, and Eastasia, are in a presumed perpetual state of war with each other. This constant warfare is largely based on rockets whose randomness of timing and strike location keep the people of Eurasia in constant civil defense mode and on a war footing. This allows for food rationing, limited power supplies, curfews, and other restrictions usually reserved for wartime to become effectively perpetual too. Orwell is recalling the Nazi V2 rockets fired at London in the latter stages of World War II, though North Korean rhetoric and iconography can obviously call upon nuclear rockets and ICBMs.

To completely dismiss this threat perception in North Korea is difficult given the almost total devastation of Pyongyang and much of the North during the Korean War and the debates that occurred during 1950 within the Truman administration around whether to use nuclear weapons on the peninsula. While this almost total devastation and the threat of nuclear bombardment may not be particularly well known in America, it is extremely well known and constantly reiterated in the DPRK's media and education system. The *theatrical victimhood* of the North's own historical narrative may seem remote and alien to the outside world, yet it is comprehensible and does sustain a certain logic, when the nation's history is understood.

In Orwell's novel it is not always clear who is actually firing the rockets and it is suggested that perhaps the superstate's governments launch them themselves to maintain the fear and tension. North Korea's notion suggested nearly every day via the television and print media, as well as workplace *study sessions* and *political meetings* and, regular civil defense drills, is that an American-inspired attack, perhaps nuclear, is highly likely, if not imminent. Perpetual war, or perhaps more accurately in today's DPRK the perpetual threat of war, is in fact a strategy used by the state to continuously promote its own political agenda.

As well as the symbolism and iconography—the ubiquity of military uniforms, war films, constant public campaigns to improve vigilance against attack and subversion, civil air raid precautions, the high level of militarization of society, and war threat iconography, on-street signage, propaganda posters, slogan banners, etc.—the North positions itself as a victim seeking peace, but one left with no alternative but to prepare for war. This is the only way to preserve the revolution and the nation. Clearly it is a regime survival strategy by the Pyongyang leadership that is used in part to justify shortages of food, medicines, and blankets as well as just about every consumer good, plus the rationing of essential food, power cuts (described as conservancy), inadequate public transportation, and just about every shortage and indignity in North Korea life.

Naturally in a nation claiming to be *encircled* by enemies, the curtailing of personal travel, imports (of food, goods, and culture), ideas, and news is shown as necessary and unavoidable. This allows the Pyongyang regime to avoid any contact or engagement with the outside world. When it does choose to engage in one way or another, the victimhood is maintained. For instance, when the North found itself in the midst of a horrendous and tragic, though entirely avoidable, famine in the mid-to-late 1990s (engendered by unproductive collective farming, outdated notions of agriculture, insufficient fertilizer, and mass deforestation leading to severe flooding of arable land), it was forced to accept food aid. In 1997, when the United States Agency for International Development (USAID) sent food aid packages to the DPRK, each pack was labelled "Gift of the People of the USA." Over 30 million USAID food packs entered the DPRK. In 2003 Andrew Natsios, the then-administrator of USAID, told the Subcommittee on East Asian and Pacific Affairs of the Senate Committee on Foreign Relations that each pack was seen by the reluctant Pyongyang regime as a potential source of "informational contamination" but the government was desperate in the face of starvation. He added that DPRK officials had been known to tell people that the USAID packs were American reparations for the Korean War.

Victim Psychology

Naturally this strategy of self-isolation becomes more accentuated if the actual rhetoric coming from the DPRK's perceived enemies is harsh, aggressive and militaristic, as it has been overwhelmingly since the accession of the Trump administration. Talk of "bloody noses," "short, sharp shocks," "knockout blows," and so on do nothing but reinforce the victim mentality, the idea that the United States is attempting to bully North Korea. It plays directly into the hands of Kim Jong-un and serves to strengthen the DPRK's communal psychology of isolation and being embattled.

Victim psychology generally refers not to a person who is an actual victim of a terrible act—natural disaster, rape, war, etc.—but rather to someone who avoids personal responsibility by blaming others. This might not be an entirely accurate diagnosis of the DPRK or of Kim Jong-un, but it does offer some insight into the country's communal psychology. North Korea did indeed suffer in the civil war, although that was a conflict Kim Il-sung (with the backing of the Soviet Union) triggered. However, the deliberate and state-sponsored prolonging of this victimhood for over six decades—as well as its promotion through general education, military, work, and social life, all forms of entertainment, media, and propaganda, and its reinforcement constantly in political messages from the leadership to the people—perpetuates a highly melodramatic notion of victimhood. The message is clear: the world is against us; the forces of imperialism and reactionary capitalism work tirelessly to destroy us; the United States of America remains intent on dominating us. With highly limited access to any information outside the country and the constant reinforcement of this message by the state from birth to old age, North Koreans have few informational tools with which to counter the regime's overwhelming historical narrative.

Threat Perception

President Trump, by engaging in rhetoric as equally bombastic as that emanting from Kim Jong-un and Pyongyang, presumably meant to appear tough and to bolster his own domestic political base. Perhaps even (and maybe most worryingly) the president believed he could somehow *win* a trading of insults in some sort of high-stakes, high-level schoolyard style encounter? Whatever this stance may ultimately do for his own political standing and image at home (even if at later stages he attempts to walk back his previous rhetoric in order to achieve some sort of deal with the DPRK), it has been a gift to Pyongyang's narrative crafters who have been able easily to weave his comments into their own ongoing narrative of encirclement, threat of war, and victimhood to bolster and seemingly legitimize the Kim Jong-un regime. Through his actions—tweets, tough guy rhetoric, inflammatory name calling—President Trump has, for the moment, made North Korea and the Kim regime stronger rather than weaker.

Paul French is the author of *North Korea State of Paranoia: A Modern History* (Zed Books), first published in 2005 and in four subsequent updated editions. He is also the author of *Our Supreme Leader: The Making of Kim Jong-un* (2016). Educated in London and Glasgow, French lived in China for two decades and first visited the DPRK in 2002. He is a regular commentator on North Korean issues for the BBC and France 24. In 2017 his narrative-drama, *Death at the Airport: The Plot Against Kim Jong-nam* was broadcast on BBC Radio 4.

Chapter 19

Trump and North Korea: The Offer for Talks Was Impulsive, But Could it Work?

By Stephan Haggard

Those who watch the Korean peninsula for a living have a decidedly mixed view of President Donald Trump's off-again, on-again approach to North Korea. The downsides are well known and go far beyond the Koreas. U.S. policy toward the Asia-Pacific region has been sustained by a broad, bipartisan consensus on some basics: support for the alliances; a belief in the positive and integrative effects of an open Pacific economy; and commitment to institutions that integrate China and other countries in the region to a rule-based order. That President Trump has been cavalier with respect to this consensus is an understatement.

And of course, there is the question of the sheer incoherence of the administration's foreign policy and foreign policy process: the rotating cast of principles; a hollowed-out State Department; and even an empty ambassadorial position in Seoul. Coercive diplomacy always involves the complex task of imposing costs on an adversary while simultaneously proposing an off ramp. Mixed messages are part of the terrain. However, efforts to ascribe a coherent strategy to Trump's approach to North Korea are hard to sustain. The administration has shown a manifest lack of deliberation as the president's various statements on the issue appear virtually random.

Trump's decision to meet with Kim Jong-un was impulsive and made on the spot.[235] It followed the transmission of the offer by two South Korean envoys, before any of the foreign policy and defense principals had a chance to assess the risks and formulate a measured response. Secretary of State Rex Tillerson was in Africa at the time. Neither Japanese Prime Minister Shinzo Abe nor Chinese President Xi Jinping was informed in advance. Indeed, the fear of many analysts is less that Trump would initiate a conflict—the concern of many others in this volume—than that the words of the president are increasingly ignored as white noise. Yesterday fire and fury or a bloody nose; today a summit. If the storm is going to shift course, why not just wait it out?

---

[235] Mark Landler, "North Korea Asks for Direct Nuclear Talks, and Trump Agrees," New York Times March 8, 2018 at https://www.nytimes.com/2018/03/08/us/politics/north-korea-kim-jong-un-trump.html

All of that said, it is also important to admit that U.S.-North Korea policy has been in a rut, and Kim Jong-un has been the beneficiary. The George W. Bush administration was outmaneuvered for several years before seeking a negotiated settlement through the Six Party Talks. That well-meaning effort faltered in 2008, and the Obama administration never succeeded in picking it back up. The reasons for this failure lie largely at the doorstep of North Korea, but they hinge at least in part on the inability of the Obama administration to either bring adequate pressure to bear on the North or to issue credible offers to negotiate.

Enter Trump. Despite the white noise of the president's Twitter account, Secretary Tillerson articulated a broadly coherent strategy toward the problem, which drew heavily on ideas that had long been floating around Treasury and among sanctions hawks. These were combined with advice on negotiations that emanated from within the State Department and was consistent with Chinese objectives.

The first prong in the strategy was a ramping up of sanctions pressure. One set of measures, first visible in 2016, was facilitated by China's growing disaffection with North Korea. Over the course of 2016-2017, Xi Jinping conceded to U.N. Security Council resolutions, which for the first time placed serious restraints on North Korea's commercial trade. By late 2017 sanctions measures had been instituted at the multilateral level that cut off key North Korean exports, particularly of coal and iron ore.

Yet, Beijing was increasingly operating under constraints associated with secondary sanctions on the part of the United States as well. Secondary sanctions are those aimed not at the target, but at third countries that trade with the sanctioned country. Again, this authority had been granted to President Obama but largely went unused; the Trump administration embraced it with relish, particularly in a sweeping executive order issued in the fall of 2017.[236]

Given that North Korea has come to rely so heavily on China, China's change of heart has been pivotal to subsequent developments. Beijing was by no means embracing a U.S. pressure-only approach, however. To the contrary, both at the U.N. Security Council and at the Mar-a-Lago summit, China had its own price for cooperation: that the United States was open—meaning seriously open—to negotiations with the North. Despite the president's tough talk, Secretary Tillerson reiterated not only a willingness to talk to North Korea, but to address North Korean – and Chinese—concerns. In particular, he committed to the so-called "Four Nos": that the United States does not seek regime change, collapse, or accelerated

[236] Stephan Haggard, "Sanctions: Things Are About to Get Interesting," Witness to Transformation blog, September 21, 2017 at https://piie.com/blogs/north-korea-witness-transformation/sanctions-things-are-about-get-interesting-really.

unification, and that it has no ambition to station troops above the 38th parallel were North Korea to suddenly collapse.

How does this posture square with "fire and fury" and more-or-less open discussion of pre-emptive or preventive options that appeared to gain ground in late 2017? The short answer is that it doesn't. Some of the more outrageous comments could—on closer inspection—be read as nothing more than a restatement of the U.S. extended deterrent: that we would respond forcefully to a North Korean attack and would respond with nuclear weapons to a North Korean nuclear attack. If pending negotiations fail, the risk of a return to military options certainly increases. But the military options on the peninsula are not particularly good, as Defense Secretary James Mattis and other military leaders have repeatedly pointed out. And the idea that the United States would undertake a first *nuclear* strike against North Korea seems a particularly remote probability, and even more so given the open discussion of the possibility that such an order could well be ignored by the military.[237]

So, what are the risks of hosting a summit? Some critics have focused on the fact that recognition—pictures of a tin-pot dictator smiling and schmoozing with the president of the United States—would itself be an epic public relations coup for Kim Jong-un. North Korea has long craved American respect not only for material reasons but out of a desire to be treated as an equal.

The way that Kim Jong-un's secret trip to Beijing was covered by state media in North Korea—conveniently avoiding any discussion of substantive issues such as denuclearization—suggest that such a public relations coup is indeed a risk. But in the larger scheme of things, these optics are ultimately not that important. The core question is whether the summit is capable of delivering progress on the mutual interests of the parties, which center on denuclearization for the United States and some form of security assurances and sanctions relief for North Korea.

The short answer is "no." Given the lack of preparation, the most that the summit can do is to outline some broad principles and objectives and set in motion a subsequent negotiating process, one that is likely to last for some time. Those principles and objectives will be deeply parsed for inappropriate concessions. In the end, though, the broad parameters are well known and have in fact been inscribed in prior documents, most notably the 2005 Joint Statement of the Six Party Talks.[238] North Korea will commit to some process of denuclearization, appropriately monitored by third parties in the form of International Atomic Energy

---

[237] See for example Richard Betts and Matthew Waxman, "Safeguarding Nuclear Launch Procedures: A Proposal," Lawfare, November 19, 2017 at https://www.lawfareblog.com/safeguarding-nuclear-launch-procedures-proposal

[238] Joint Statement of the Fourth Round of the Six-Party Talks, Beijing September 19, 2005 at https://www.state.gov/p/eap/regional/c15455.htm

Agency inspectors. The United States will agree to some gradual relaxation of sanctions, normalization of relations, and the replacement of the armistice with a peace regime on the peninsula.

The fact that North Korea claims it is willing to talk about nuclear weapons does not provide much comfort. For many years, Pyongyang's conception of "denuclearization" included measures that would fundamentally weaken the alliance. The "devil in the details" is how the complex quid pro quos of an agreement will be sequenced: whether in a prolonged phased process or through a more ambitious bargain in which a package of concessions would be exchanged at the same time, as was largely the case in the wrongly maligned Iran deal. The possibilities that North Korea would simply stall are apparent, and American negotiators are thinking about what up-front actions might be required for negotiations to be meaningful.

It should be stated at the outset that no one who follows the Korean peninsula thinks that the prospects for such an ultimate agreement are particularly high. North Korea has broken out, making it that much harder to negotiate away its nuclear program, stocks of fissile material and the weapons themselves. In addition to the nuclear program, we have the equally if not more troubling problem of negotiating some limits on North Korea's missile program. The record of North Korea keeping past commitments is tarnished to say the least.

And by far the greatest risk of the enterprise is that China will decide that sanctions relief is appropriate given whatever progress is on offer. Such a move would fundamentally weaken the pressure that appears to have brought North Korea to the table in the first place.

Yet some of the risks also reside on the U.S. side. The turnover in Trump's foreign policy team has brought in two figures who are decidedly more hawkish than their predecessors: Mike Pompeo at State and John Bolton at the National Security Council. Bolton's appointment is particularly worrisome, given his political posturing on the North Korea issue and his open disdain for negotiated settlements such as the Iran nuclear deal. One real risk of the summit is that either in advance of it or in its wake, Bolton pushes for preconditions or terms that essentially kill negotiations before they begin.

Yet with all of these risks, it is worth remembering that Kim Jong-un's pursuit of nuclear weapons and an intercontinental missile capability has been relentless. Few doubt that if the country does not already have such a capability, it is close. If critics don't like the narrow path through a summit to negotiations, what precisely is the alternative?

In sum, those watching North Korea have few illusions about the Trump administration's ability to pull off this particular coup. There is a 15-year record stacked against success. If the post-summit negotiating process gets derailed for reasons emanating either from North Korea or the United States, then risks of a military confrontation rise. So do the concerns raised by others in this volume about the capacity of President Trump to manage a serious foreign policy crisis.

But for now, what we have is the first step in a process, however flawed, which is much more than we have had since the Six Party Talks collapsed in 2008. If Trump fails, we are no worse off than we were before. If he pulls it off, we will have to give the devil his due.

Stephan Haggard is the Krause Distinguished Professor at the School of Global Policy and Strategy at the University of California San Diego. He has written widely on the political economy and international relations of East Asia. His work on North Korea with Marcus Noland includes three books: *Famine in North Korea* (2007), *Witness to Transformation: Refugee Insights into North Korea* (2011) *and Hard Target: Sanctions, Engagement and the Case of North Korea* (2017). He runs the Witness to Transformation blog at http://www.piie.com/blogs/nk/ with Marcus Noland and currently has a regular column with Joongang Ilbo.

Chapter 20

The Art of the North Korea Deal:
If Trump Can Understand Kim's Fears,
We Can Have Peace on the Korean Peninsula

By Harry J. Kazianis

While tensions in Northeast Asia have clearly subsided since the fall of 2017, any mix of factors, especially the personalities and competing geopolitical ambitions of U.S. President Donald Trump and North Korean leader Kim Jong-un could still set the stage for potential military conflict that could claim the lives of millions of people.[239]

The aim of this chapter is to analyze the nature of both leaders' strategic and ideological thinking as well as national security goals and aspirations with a focus on how these factors drive tensions in Northeast Asia. Utilizing such analysis as a lens, this work will explore possible factors that could lead to a potential agreement that decreases tensions on the Korean peninsula once and for all through the ending of North Korea's most dangerous military programs.

Into the Mind (and Goals) of Kim Jong-un

In many situations, when national security experts analyze an international affairs issue or a specific leader, most hairpin back to their training in graduate school, looking to complex political science theories while forgetting the basics of human nature. Of course, many times, obvious answers are there for the taking, but the *experts'* training tells them to look much deeper, for a more sophisticated explanation. Why we do this is simple: We aren't comfortable with rational but simplistic reasoning.

The above logic clearly applies in our attempt to understand Kim Jong-un, the leader of a nation that has tested countless ballistic missiles over the last few years that have driven Northeast Asia to the brink of war.[240] Additionally, his nuclear weapons tests, as well as allegedly killing his half-brother with chemical weapons, have drawn conclusions that the young dictator is crazy, suicidal, and, most

---

[239] Please see: http://theweek.com/articles/692872/how-preemptive-strike-north-korea-could-end-killing-millions

[240] Please see: http://theweek.com/articles/692872/how-preemptive-strike-north-korea-could-end-killing-millions or thinking on this issue: https://www.theatlantic.com/international/archive/2018/01/hr-mcmaster-trump-north-korea/549341/

terrifying of all, undeterrable even when confronted with nuclear annihilation if he were to unleash his atomic arsenal.[241]

I would argue such analysis is wrong. Kim Jong un is rational in that his goal above all else is survival, but not in the traditional understanding of the term. Kim's idea of survival is more akin to a Mafia street captain who seeks to hold onto power—almost out of a fictional drama. Here is where the so-called experts or political scientists get it wrong, as Kim is not looking to the greats of geopolitics or history for guidance but seems to emulate another historical but fictional figure, none other than Michael Corleone from of *The Godfather*.[242]

While it might seem strange, such a comparison does give us a working template to understand Kim's behavior and make predictions about his future actions. But many will ask: How does one compare someone who starves his own people, runs concentration camps akin to Nazi Germany, brainwashes millions, and regularly tests nuclear weapons and missiles to a fictional Mafia don?

Indeed, some context is needed. The fictional Corleone, in many respects, has the same problem as Kim, just on a much smaller scale. The North Korean dictator is fighting to survive in a world where he has many outside rivals trying to ensure his demise. In Corleone's case, it was rival families trying to destroy him, but in Kim's situation, he fears America, South Korea, Japan, and most likely China plotting his downfall—and his death. To ensure his survival, Corleone and Kim will do anything—morality be damned. Both will lie, cheat, steal, breaking any law, or kill anyone to achieve the protection of their position or survival. Clearly, for both Corleone and Kim, survival is all that matters.

This explains why North Korea wants nuclear weapons platforms and missiles to carry them to all parts of the planet, while, at the same time he must impoverish his own people who, many times, do not have enough food to eat.

Such a situation creates come very clear dangers. If Kim feels boxed in or feels invasion or a military attack that will lessen his chances of survival is imminent, he may feel he has no choice but to strike. And Kim would likely choose to attack with the majority of his nuclear, chemical, and likely biological weapons, starting a horrific conflict not seen since the last Korean War—or perhaps World War II.

---

[241] For my past thinking on this issue, please see: http://nationalinterest.org/feature/why-north-korea-building-icbms-ask-michael-corleone-20208

[242] Trump's best enunciation of such overtones: https://www.nytimes.com/2016/04/28/us/politics/transcript-trump-foreign-policy.html?mtrref=www.google.com&gwh=7727 CEAE90926C504B4BB6EBE5B1505A&gwt=pay

The Art of the Amateur: Donald Trump Takes on North Korea

President Trump, while certainly learning on the job since taking office in January 2017, is certainly a national security and foreign policy novice. Unfortunately, thanks to an awful mixture of bad timing and growing North Korean capabilities, the Trump administration is now tasked with having to decide on an approach to Pyongyang that could lead to war or a presidency filled with years of up and down tensions, taking away much of the available international affairs bandwidth needed to tackle other issues in the Asia-Pacific region and beyond.

Here is where we must get a sense of Trump's thinking on national security issues. With little to no experience or training on the fine art of foreign policy making along with a constantly changing mix of advisors, Trump may not have a clearly defined worldview. He does, however, seem to embody some characteristics of the realist school of international affairs, broadly defined today as embodying a mix of pragmatism, a downgraded focus on human rights, a tendency to avoid regime change campaigns, and a rejection of moralistic overtones in design making.[243]

At the same time, the president seems to utilize his experience in business combined with his past career as reality TV star to make dramatic national security pronouncements in what seems to be to an attempt to gain leverage over his competition. For example, during the campaign and as president, Trump has taken a number of positions that had drawn the ire of key allies, including challenging the value of the NATO alliance, making veiled threats to withdraw troops from treaty allies in territories in Asia, taking maximalist positions on trade agreements that have been codified decades ago such as NAFTA, and so on.

I would argue this mix of Trumpian Realism combined with a flair for the dramatic thanks to his time on television and business instincts to stake out a tough opening position as leverage, may in many traditional situations serve him well. However, such tactics could be troublesome when it comes to dealing with North Korea. For example, if Trump in a crisis were to take an aggressive position on a key issue during an emergency, like threatening to attack Kim if he were to ever test another ballistic missile in the future, or recycle his "fire and fury" language from 2017, Kim's survival instinct could kick in. In such a situation, Kim may consider launching a first strike on U.S. and allied assets in Northeast Asia first, knowing that if the U.S. were to attack first, Kim would lose most of his military might. This would, of course, engender a U.S. counterresponse, which would utilize nuclear weapons if North Korea were to employ such weapons first—resulting in the death of millions of innocent people as well as the release of radioactive materials that could spread throughout Asia and the Pacific Rim.

---

[243] For background: https://qz.com/1004330/north-korea-is-sitting-on-trillions-of-dollars-on-untapped-wealth-and-its-neighbors-want-a-piece-of-it/

The Deal that Could Be Struck Between Kim and Trump

Trump Must Bend, Kim Must Trust
Despite the large differences in strategic thinking between both Kim and Trump, there is some possibility of bridging the gaps between their positions if one thinks creatively and one side is able to come to grips with the other's quest for security.

At this point, it would be incumbent on President Trump to tap into his pragmatic, realist instincts and begin to see the security situation on the Korean peninsula from the mindset of his opponent, something many able businessmen are able to do when trying to land an agreement. If Trump can empathize and begin to understand Kim's security goals, while at the same time lessen to some extent his reality TV-based flair for the dramatic, there is the possibility of a deal that would ensure there is no possibility of armed conflict on the Korean peninsula.

At the same time, Kim would need to begin to show some signs of trusting his mortal enemies in Washington as well as in Tokyo and Seoul. Considering the recent diplomatic thaw since January, this is now all in the realm of possibility.

The Foundation
The bedrock of any deal would be to somehow guarantee the regime survival and security of North Korea while at the same time certify that Kim's weapons of mass destruction and ability to threaten South Korea, Japan, and the United States is eliminated. While many such proposals have been offered in the past, there is at least, if one seeks to ensure the mutual security of all interested parties as stated above, a viable path forward. There would be six components to such a plan:

The Ending of Kim's Nuclear Weapons Program: This would include a full accounting of Kim's total nuclear weapons arsenal, bomb-making materials, atomic infrastructure and all nuclear weapons technological transfers done in the past. Kim would also need to agree to an intrusive inspections regime that would allow for twenty-four-hour, seven-day-per-week, 365-day-a-year inspections of any part of North Korean territory. No part of the so-called hermit kingdom would be out of bounds.

The Ending of Kim's Missile Program: North Korea would also need to give up any stockpiles of ballistic and cruise missiles, research and development of new weapons and pass along any information regarding past weapons or research sales—especially to Iran.

The Ending of Kim's Chemical and Biological Weapons Programs: While the world's collective attention is fixed on Pyongyang's nuclear weapons and missile programs, Kim's other weapons of mass destruction—specifically, chemical and most likely biological weapons—must also be eliminated. Kim would need to, in a similar fashion to the above, provide a full accounting of his weapons and surrender them as well as his ability to make such weapons. He would also need to provide any documents that show any weapons or technology transfers to outside actors, whether it be nonstate actors, terrorist groups, or nation states like Iran, Syria or others.

Removal of Artillery Pointed at Seoul: With a metro population of over 25 million people, the citizens of Seoul must also be protected in any final agreement with North Korea. Kim would need to destroy, or at least move out of range, the thousands of artillery platforms pointed at the Seoul metropolitan area. This is essential for South Korea's security for, if left in place, it would leave what amounts to thousands of large "guns" pointed at the collective heads of millions of people and could be used to strike at a moment's notice.

All U.S., Japanese or Foreign Prisoners Must Be Released: Over the years, the Kim regime has abducted foreign nationals as well as imprisoned other foreigners who were in North Korea for various legal reasons. Pyongyang would need to provide a full accounting of such prisoners and release them in an expedited manner.

What Does North Korea Get? A Great Deal—Over Time: Obviously, the above would amount to a massive loss of military capabilities by North Korea—leaving it very open to attack and war of regime change. However, if Pyongyang were to agree to such terms, Kim could very well get the security he desires.

While Pyongyang would likely have a long list of demands for giving away most of its most deadly weapons, the United States and its allies could provide strong incentives, including: 1. The ending of all sanctions; 2. A formal peace treaty ending the Korean War; 3. Full diplomatic recognition by the United States and an exchange of ambassadors; 4. The dismantling of the Demilitarized Zone and withdrawal of U.S. forces to a more southern position in South Korea; 5. A nonaggression pact, something long demanded by North Korea, signed by Washington, Seoul and Tokyo; 6. Economic assistance to the tune of billions of dollars to rebuild North Korea's rotten infrastructure whole reintegrating Pyongyang into the global economy; 7. Investment in North Korea's natural resources, which many experts see as worth trillions of dollars, money that could go a long way into rebuilding the country, and finally[244]; 8. Energy and food assistance for a predetermined period of time to ensure North Korea's stability.

Such a deal, grand in scope as well as in scale, would be phased in over time, allowing all sides to begin to form mutual trust, build key relationships, and move past decades of historic animosity. North Korea would need to meet certain benchmarks over set periods of time, and provided it that it met them, the U.S. and its allies would reward the regime with one or a mixture of the above incentives.

---

[244] There is extensive documentation of North Korea's prison camp system. The best work on this subject comes from The Committee for Human Rights in North Korea, a Washington, D.C. based non-profit, whose work can be found here: https://www.hrnk.org/publications/hrnk-publications.php

In fact, if Kim did meet all of the above disarmament goals as outlined, one could see U.S. forces cut by substantial numbers over a period of years—if not removed entirely if Kim were to keep his side of the bargain.

Why Such a Deal Could Be Impossible

While such an agreement, at least on paper, seems to meet the security requirement of all geopolitical actors involved on the Korean peninsula, putting such ideas on paper does mean they are political viable nor possible. In fact, many outside factors could come into play that could very well hamper such a deal from ever being fully followed, supposing such an agreement could be forged in the first place.

First, we must consider North Korea's history of violating almost every international agreement it has signed with the U.S. and its allies. Likely tied to its obsession with survival, if the Kim family feels it can gain an advantage by cheating or undermining an agreement—just like the Corleones—there is a high probability they will do it. Therefore, the Trump administration must ensure all incentives in a comprehensive agreement would be matched deed for deed—Kim makes a concession, and the U.S. and its allies make one. There can be no giveaways to North Korea or economic incentives to enter an agreement, as the regime would seek to simply pocket them for no reciprocal action on its part. Anything America and its allies could give to North Korea to strengthen its security must be built on matching actions only.

However, Kim will have his own concerns, pointing to history—a history of America also breaking its word on past nuclear deals. North Korea has pointed out on multiple occasions how Washington brokered an agreement with Libya in 2003 for its abandonment of its own nuclear weapons program, only to be see its own regime changed years later in an effort led by Washington in its allies. North Korea also is happy to detail America's wars of regime change against Afghanistan and Iraq as evidence it can never give up its nuclear weapons.

President Trump will also have a tough time convincing many in his own party that there is any hope of a peaceful settlement with North Korea. Many will point to over 100,000 people in what amount to political prison camps, some would say gulags, confirming that indeed North Korea is the world's most prolific abuser of human rights.[245] Many will ask the question: How can we trust a nation that treats its own people more like slaves than citizens? And considering President Trump has named former Ambassador John Bolton as national security advisor, someone who has advocated for regime change against North Korea, there is reason to be skeptical that any agreement is possible.

---

[245] Author interviews.

Is Trump Capable of Empathy? Separating 'Reality TV' Trump from 'Human' Trump

Considering President Trump's unique usage of Twitter, proneness to changing his position depending on the situation as well his penchant for being unpredictable, there are many who would argue that our president is not capable of empathy. Indeed, many voices on the left as well as various "Never Trump" commentators argue that the president cares more about how he looks in the media, his poll numbers, and his 2016 election win than taking the time to understand a potential adversary or opponent. And in a negotiation with North Korea, not having that key ability could set the stage for disaster.

There are, however, many on the right, and several who work closely with the president who have pushed back against this argument. According to at least two White House staffers I know personally, they argue quite empathically that President Trump, while not a conventional commander and chief in the slightest sense of the word, can show and has shown empathy. As one White House source put it to me, on background:

"Look, Trump is not professorial like Obama, nor does he have the conservative background like George W. Bush—but he has a heart. Think about how he reacted when he saw innocent Syrians being gassed—he responded not once, but twice. My boss might not know every world leader or the GDP of South Africa, but he has a heart, he is empathetic, and he clearly tries to see it from his opponents' or other persons' perspective. How could he not have gotten this far if he did not? He cares, he cares about the men and women of this nation who have been forgotten by the elites here in Washington and both political parties. If that is not empathy, I don't know what is."

Another White House staffer, also speaking anonymously, was a little blunter:

"I get a little frustrated at questions like this—which I feel I answer too often—because people don't get Trump. You should know that there is the public Trump—Mr. Social Media who is on the attack 24/7 and always wants to keep his enemies off balance, and the more private, should I say human, Trump. This is a man who does have a heart, but he does not exactly put it on the table for the whole world to see. Being a businessman, he can't just show his emotions, feelings, or personal investments in the attitudes in feelings in others right on the table. As president, I am sure he keeps his own, more personal feelings to himself. I can tell you he does have an empathy chip, as I have seen it on numerous occasions—it just does him no good to put it on display."

Reasons for Hope, or War

While clearly there would be many outside factors and powerful actors who would rally against any agreement, there is reason for at least some optimism. There is a growing recognition, at least among U.S. officials, those close to governments of American allies in Asia and those close to the Chinese government that a repeat of tensions in 2017 could be the spark that starts a second Korean

War. Considering the cost in human life, economic, diplomatic, and, indeed, radioactive fallout, all sides have a strong incentive to step back from the brink and act boldly to forge some sort of agreement. While we cannot estimate how difficult it will be to craft such a deal, all sides have strong incentives to try. However, it will take the Trump administration, and indeed the president himself, to shift his own strategic thinking and actions, and look into the mind of Kim Jong-un. For it might just be simple empathy that provided a path to peace in Asia.

Harry J. Kazianis is Director of Defense Studies at the Center for the National Interest and Executive Editor of its publish arm, *The National Interest*. He also serves as Senior Fellow at the China Policy Institute and Fellow for National Security at the Potomac Foundation. In the past, Kazianis served as a foreign policy adviser to the 2016 presidential campaign of Senator Ted Cruz and Editor-In-Chief of *The Diplomat*. He has authored over 400 op-eds, reports and monographs on national security issues and is a frequent guest on CNN, Fox News, CNBC and many other news outlets.

Chapter 21

Madman or Rational Actor?
Kim Jong-un's Nuclear Calculus

By Ken E. Gause

In order to understand North Korea's strategic calculus, two factors must be assessed: Kim Jong-un's rationality as the supreme decision maker and the political framework within which he operates. These are factors that will fundamentally impact how North Korea thinks about a range of issues, including its burgeoning nuclear program.

Therefore, care must be taken to explain the logic behind the extrapolations made with regard to North Korea's calculus as time progresses in order to create a firm foundation for findings on how the regime might act in the future, especially if and when it secures a viable nuclear deterrent.

Is Kim Jong-un a rational actor?

This question has been raised by outside observers throughout the Kim Jong-un era. In September 2017, the young leader's rationality was questioned as he entered into a very personal exchange with the American president after the latter, in front of the United Nations, referred to him as "Rocket Man," saying he had placed his country on "a suicide mission," and threatened to "totally destroy" North Korea unless Pyongyang backs down from its nuclear challenge. Kim responded in a personally delivered message in the name of chairman of the State Affairs Commission in which he called the president a "dotard" and threatened the "highest level of hardline countermeasure in history."[246] Words such as "madman" and "irrational actor" appeared in the world press as it sought to game out what would come next. Analysts are left wrangling with how best to characterize Kim Jong-un in terms of his boundaries and what drives him to action.

There are a number of profiles that have been created in an attempt to explain Kim Jong-un's actions. The most obvious departure from the way his father operated is Kim Jong-un's open persona. He conveys an impression of an outgoing,

---

[246] Personal statements by the supreme leader occur annually on New Year's Day. Personal statements during a crisis are extremely rare, if not unprecedented. Therefore, the dynamics behind it are worthy of analysis for what it says about his decision-making calculus and whether it is driven in part by emotion over intellect.

people-friendly, and ambitious leader, markedly different from Kim Jong-il's isolationist, solitary, and secretive image. Kim Jong-un appears to be comfortable giving speeches and interacting with large groups of ordinary citizens, whereas his father only gave one publicly recorded speech that lasted twelve seconds. This aspect of Kim Jong-un's leadership style harkens back to his grandfather, Kim Il-sung. Defector reporting also paints a picture of a young and impetuous Supreme Leader who is sometimes quick to make decisions without seeking advice. Other profiles describe him as thin-skinned and easily angered, especially if his authority or legitimacy is challenged. The stories of his purges of senior leadership officials fit this personality profile. That said, he apparently understands the tremendous power of the position he holds but also understands that there are constraints established by his father and grandfather that the system imposes. How eager he is to challenge some of these constraints remains unclear. His decision to reveal the failure of the Unha-3 missile test in April 2012 may have been his own decision or could have resulted from the fact that he listened to advisors who advocated for transparency, given the unprecedented openness leading up to the launch. But is he a rational actor?

There is a wide literature on the issue of rationality and decision making. Rationality is an exceptionally difficult term to define, and there is a lack of consensus about how it can be applied when looking at adversary actions and interactions with the international community. A 1991 RAND study of adversary behavior analysis outlines several points individual scholars have raised in their attempts to codify rationality.

- Rationality requires decision-analytic thinking preceded by a reasonable search for adequate options.
- Rationality requires considering the utilities of various outcomes, the probability of those outcomes for each option, and a calculation such as how to maximize expected utility.
- The concept of limited rationality posits that decisions will have a super-ficially logical basis—i.e., a "reasonable" relationship between objectives and decisions. It does not imply that the decisions are wise and sound. Rather, it implies only that the decision making has satisfied certain minimum criteria for what passes in the real world as rationality.[247]

In the case of Kim Jong-un, case studies demonstrate that he is a rational actor if we accept the premise that his decisions are driven by a desire to perpetuate two centers of gravity (or key objectives): the survival of the regime and the

---

[247] Paul K. Davis and John Arquilla, Thinking About Opponent Behavior in Crisis and Conflict: A Generic Model for Analysis and Group Discussion (Santa Monica: RAND Note N-3322-JS, 1991).

continuation of Kim family rule.[248] His actions might not lead to the most efficient outcomes, but they point to his adherence to a "limited rationality" that is traceable in terms of their motivation.[249]

Case 1: The execution of Jang Song-taek. On December 12, 2013, Jang Song-taek, Kim Jong-un's uncle and *de facto* number two man in the regime, was tried by a special military tribunal of the Ministry of State Security and executed, according to state media. His execution was the most significant since purges carried out in the 1950s by Kim Il-sung, Kim Jong-un's grandfather and North Korea's founder. Since 1960, purged top officials have not usually been killed, and the denunciations of purged figures have not typically been so extreme and public. Although high-ranking leaders, including members of the Kim family, have been deposed before, their demise has not been this public or dramatic.

Jang's purge was followed by claims in the international community that Kim Jong-un was a bloody tyrant who was willing to attack his own family on a whim. Subsequent information coming out of the regime suggests a complicated story of betrayal and growing threat to Kim Jong-un's authority within the regime. An investigation into Jang's affairs conducted in 2012 and early 2013 revealed his growing control over a number of hard currency operations, many of them at the expense of other power brokers within the regime.[250] This had led to a growing tension within the second echelon of power and a steadily intensifying power struggle among Jang's forces, the military, party, and internal security apparatuses. In addition, Jang had shown increasingly less deference to Kim Jong-un and his legitimacy as the sole leader of the regime. Finally, Jang's relations with the Chinese leadership were increasingly questioned by the Kim family,[251] especially after he reportedly failed to secure Kim family funds from Chinese banks. Therefore, Jang was becoming a disruptor within the regime. Kim Jong-un's decision to purge his

---

[248] If we were to posit that Kim's decisions were driven by other factors, such as ensuring the prosperity and well-being of the North Korean people, then one could question whether he is a rational actor.

[249] These three case studies were chosen because they either describe events that led the international community to label Kim Jong-un as "crazy" or "irrational" or they demonstrated limited rationality in terms of decision making. Of the handful of high-profile events that have occurred since Kim Jong-un came to power, not one fits the characteristics of an irrational act—i.e., fundamentally went against Kim Jong-un's core interests.

[250] For a detailed description of this investigation see Ken E. Gause, North Korean House of Cards: Leadership Dynamics Under Kim Jong-un (Washington, DC: The U.S. Committee for Human Rights in North Korea, 2015).

[251] In February 2018, the Japanese media cited Chinese sources that alleged that Jang Song-taek had conspired with the Chinese leadership to remove Kim Jong-un and replace him with his older half-brother, Kim Jong-nam. See Unattributed report, "China Official Says North Korean Succession Row May Be Behind Kim Jong Nam Murder," NHK World Online, February 13, 2018.

uncle and dismantle his growing fiefdom was a rational act. To allow Jang to continue to pursue his agenda would have inhibited Kim's ability to fully consolidate his power.[252]

Case 2: The Sony hack. In November 2014, a hacker group which identified itself by the name "Guardians of Peace" demanded that Sony Pictures pull its film *The Interview*, a comedy about a plot to assassinate North Korean leader Kim Jong-un, and threatened terrorist attacks at cinemas screening the film. On November 24, the Guardians of Peace leaked a release of confidential data from the Sony Pictures film studio. The data included personal information about Sony employees and their families, e-mails between employees, information about executive salaries at the company, copies of then-unreleased Sony films, and other information. After major U.S. cinema chains opted not to screen the film in response to these threats, Sony elected to cancel the film's formal premiere and mainstream release, opting to skip directly to a digital release followed by a limited theatrical release the next day. U.S. intelligence officials, after evaluating the software, techniques, and network sources used in the hack, alleged that the attack was sponsored by North Korea. North Korea denied all responsibility.

In the open source, the perpetrator of the Sony hack is still open to debate and whether or not North Korea carried out the hack, it no doubt supported the attack, the motivation of which demonstrates an effort to control escalation while sending a message of retribution to the international community. The timing of *The Interview*'s release raised issues for North Korea. It was during the period of its diplomatic charm campaign designed to secure international aid for the regime, a critical component to Kim Jong-un's ability to consolidate his power. If the regime were to conduct an overt aggressive provocation, it would have undoubtedly ended any hopes of securing this aid. Instead, Kim Jong-un (if he in fact ordered the attack) opted for a covert means of exhorting revenge. By resorting to a cyberattack, the regime obscured its fingerprints from the operation, pinpointed the target, allowed Pyongyang to claim innocence, all the while keeping the regime's diplomacy on track. Since the attack, the international media have become reticent about lampooning Kim Jong-un and his regime. Given Kim's calculus, which includes protecting his image and legitimacy within the regime, the Sony hack makes rational sense.

Case 3: The assassination of Kim Jong-nam. On February 13, 2017, Kim Jong-nam, Kim Jong-un's older half-brother, died after being attacked by two women in Malaysia with VX nerve agent during his return trip to Macau at klia2, the low-cost carrier terminal at Kuala Lumpur International Airport. The Malaysian

---

[252] During the period of the regent structure, Kim Jong-un often complained that his actions were constrained by the "old guard." Author's discussion with source with firsthand knowledge of this issue, September 2017.

government pointed to North Korea as being behind the assassination. The subsequent investigation provided evidence of North Korean involvement, although Pyongyang vehemently proclaimed its innocence. A standoff between the two countries followed, in which North Korea prevented Malaysian nationals from leaving the country until Malaysia released Kim Jong-nam's body into its custody along with three North Korean nationals believed to be tied to the attack. A deal was struck in which both sides agreed to release their "hostages" and Kim's body was returned to North Korea. The only people arrested for the assassination were the two women (one Indonesian and the other Vietnamese) who carried out the attack.

Of all the high-profile actions by North Korea during the Kim Jong-un era, the assassination of Kim Jong-nam is the most opaque in terms of its motivation. The theories range from sending a message to the North Korean expatriate population in the wake of several senior-level defections to a standing order issued by Kim Jong-un soon after coming to power. The reasoning has led many to question Kim Jong-un's sanity and label him a "crazed lunatic." However, some sources point to a more rational explanation for Kim Jong-un's decision to get rid of his older half-brother. If it is true that Kim's power consolidation has entered its final phase, this would be the time in which he needs to ensure that the House of Kim is in order. Any pretenders to the throne need to be eliminated. An older sibling, especially one who had fallen out with the regime and does not owe his loyalty to Kim Jong-un, would be considered a potential threat. In the months leading up to the assassination, North Korean defector organizations had reportedly reached out to the older Kim to head a so-called *government in exile*. Kim Jong-nam's ties with China could also have been worrisome given increasing tension between the two neighbors. Finally, Kim Kyong-hui, Kim Jong-un's aunt, was Kim Jong-nam's protector within the regime. She has not been seen in public since September 2013 and is rumored to either be dead or in a hospital. In any case, her political influence is rumored to have waned, giving her nephew the latitude to make preparations for his final push for consolidation. If true, this ruthless act is an example of limited rationality. The execution of the assassination was not done in the most effective manner, but in the end, it served to promote Kim Jong-un's ultimate interests.

Nuclear Program a Rational Choice?
There are some analysts who argue that assuming that North Korea (and more particularly its leaders) is a rational actor, it should have abandoned its nuclear program when it was offered the incentives to do so. However, rather than making the rational choice of giving up its nuclear program in exchange for economic and security benefits in the mid-2000s, North Korea committed the fallacy of retaining its nuclear arsenal, which would render the regime more vulnerable in the long

run. This line of argument ignores the strategic lens through which Kim Jong-un and his predecessors view the situation.

Any assessment of the rationality of Kim's decision-making on the nuclear program requires an understanding of why North Korea wants these weapons. North Korean official media often cite Pyongyang's nuclear weapons as the reason for the regime's continued survival and blame the fall of the regimes in Iraq and Libya for their decisions to give up their nuclear programs. In addition, Pyongyang has stated publicly that the U.S. strikes against the Syrian regime in 2017—most recently in April 2018—reaffirm its need to continue advancing its nuclear and missile programs as a way to deter similar strikes against North Korea.

At a more operational level, possession of nuclear weapons makes up for (at least in part) a deteriorating conventional force that is largely stagnant in its underground fortifications. The notion of a "bolt from the blue" that once characterized North Korean military doctrine has largely given way to the ability to land artillery on Seoul and thus keep South Korea's capital hostage. But this conventional deterrent does not deter regime change from across the Pacific. Therefore, Kim likely subscribes to the notion that for North Korea to complete its deterrent posture, it needs to deter long-range strikes from the United States while ensuring that conventional forces on the peninsula cannot move north of the demilitarized zone (DMZ). A viable nuclear program with a proven capability to strike the U.S. homeland fills this need.

Beyond motivations tied to the survival of the regime, there are secondary drivers of North Korea's nuclear and ballistic missile programs. Not only do nuclear weapons elevate North Korea's geopolitical status, they potentially increase its strategic leverage. The regime views nuclear weapons as a guarantee that it will remain a significant player and be able to interact with China and the United States as an "equal" while achieving a position of strategic advantage via escalation dominance over Japan and South Korea.

Nuclear Employment and Potential for Miscalculation

Over the next few years, assuming that the regime does not collapse or give in to denuclearization, Kim Jong-un's nuclear doctrine will come into focus. Whether he will seek to use his nuclear deterrent beyond its defensive role to backstop a campaign of coercion is a point of contention and debate within the Pyongyang-watching community. Whether the North Korean nuclear capability will be tied to a concept of first (or preemptive) strike or remain a second-strike weapon is not entirely clear and probably depends on the circumstances. From the few doctrinal pronouncements that have been made public on nuclear employment, it appears as if Kim has given himself great latitude. How much stock Kim places on his newfound capability to change the calculus of his adversaries, in the minds of many, will reflect his understanding of the balance of power in the region and his realistic ability to change the status quo. Only if he is delusional, the argument goes, will he attempt to engage in an unprovoked game of high-stakes chicken.

It should be noted that testing the boundaries with a newfound weapon system, such as a nuclear deterrent, is not without precedent. One illustrative example is Pakistan, which effectively declared itself a nuclear state in 1998 by conducting its own nuclear tests weeks after a successful nuclear test by India. The following year, emboldened by its new status, Pakistan sought to seize disputed territory in Kashmir. It sent forces across the border to take up positions in Kargil, a district in the Indian state of Jammu and Kashmir near the Line of Control separating Pakistani and Indian military forces. Once discovered, Pakistan claimed that the forces were local militants and denied responsibility. While there is some evidence that India was careful to control the escalation of the conflict in response to Pakistan's thinly veiled nuclear threats, it did not deter India from responding with airpower to push Pakistani forces out of its territory. While Pakistani military leaders appeared to believe that their lack of a credible conventional deterrent, combined with India's growing military capabilities, made limited nuclear options a necessity, Pakistan's failure to extract any gains from the operation demonstrated that its nuclear arsenal did not affect the dynamics of the conflict in the ways its leaders had hoped. Not only was Pakistan repelled, but India has since taken steps to provide itself with more options for deterring or responding to low-level conventional provocations by Pakistan to prevent escalation to nuclear war.

The simple fact that Kim Jong-un might explore what he can get with his country's new capability does not make him irrational. In fact, it is something that is very likely to happen. The question is under what circumstances and how will Kim probe and test his advantage. The circumstances under which North Korea might resort to coercion and nuclear blackmail will be to get out of a box.[253] The increased sanctions are already beginning to be felt inside North Korea. By the time that North Korea fully develops its nuclear deterrent, the maximum pressure campaign (assuming that engagement has failed) will be in full swing. Kim Jong-un will be increasingly concerned about the impact that the pressure will have on his ability to control the regime and enforce his legitimacy. This will likely foster a strong motivation for Kim to see what he can get if he pushes back, using the nuclear deterrent to confound the response of his adversaries. But will he be indiscriminate in how he uses this nuclear threat? That is where rationality comes into play.

---

[253] It should be noted that contrary to conventional wisdom, North Korea has given no indication that it plans to use its nuclear program for coercion. An examination of regime pronouncements during 33 military incidents since 2008 turned up little or no evidence that the regime attempted to use nuclear threats to affect the outcome of the standoff or incident.

Most likely Kim Jong-un will act in accordance with his two primary objectives: regime survival and perpetuation of Kim family rule. This means that he will only move up the escalatory ladder to a point at which he believes the United States will be deterred from retaliation. Up until that point, North Korea might explore a pressure campaign designed to extract concessions (economic and security), primarily from South Korea. North Korea's strategy could include conventional military attacks against South Korean assets.

If Kim Jong-un tries such attacks and fails or comes to believe that the United States and South Korea are prepared and willing to respond with overwhelming force much further down the escalatory ladder to his provocations (via an allied strategic messaging campaign), then like Pakistan, he is likely to learn the extent to which the nuclear deterrent gives him an ability to use his conventional forces as part of a brinksmanship strategy. His attempts to force the international community to accept North Korea as a nuclear power or even extort concessions will collide with the overriding elements of Kim's strategic calculus. If his actions up to this point are any indication, Kim Jong-un will act rationally in pursuit of regime survival and perpetuation of Kim family rule.

The other angle many analysts take in making judgments on Kim's rationality is how he would employ his nuclear weapons once he has an established deterrent. Under what circumstances would he choose to launch a nuclear weapon? Can he be trusted with his finger on the nuclear button to be a rational actor? North Korea's military thinkers have identified two purposes for nuclear weapons use in wartime: 1) to repel invasion or attack from a hostile nuclear weapons state (e.g., the United States) on its own territory; and 2) to make retaliatory strikes against an enemy that has already struck first using regime-threatening forces (presumably nuclear) against North Korea. In March 2013, Kim Jong-un speaking at a Central Committee Plenary meeting provided insight into North Korean thinking about its nuclear program. It appears he reserves the right to preemption under certain circumstances. One of the circumstances he alluded to was the notion of "imminent threat." He allegedly said, "The U.S. was testing my self-control and getting on my nerves (in March 2013 during the Foal Eagle exercise), but there was no limit to the psychological pressure I could withstand" because "the U.S. threat was not imminent." During the crisis of 2013, North Korean media alluded to the fact that the regime had developed a set of standing operating procedures for the authorization of the employment of nuclear weapons in wartime. According to Rodong Sinmun, "the nuclear weapons of the DPRK can be used only by a final order of the Supreme Commander of the Korean People's Army."

In recent years as U.S. and South Korean rhetoric has heated up to deal with the growing North Korean missile and nuclear testing program, North Korean doctrine has allegedly internalized the need for a first (or preemptive) strike capability to forestall any decapitation strategy. How this would play out and what red lines Kim would have that if passed would trigger a nuclear attack remain unknown or ambiguous at best. But regardless of whether North Korea has a first strike policy or not, there is no evidence that Kim Jong-un would act irrationally when it comes to the nuclear button. At the bottom line, regime survival remains first and foremost his guiding objective.

If Kim Jong-un is a rational actor, what about the possibility that he could misperceive or misinterpret actions by the United States and South Korea? If President Trump were to engage in the so-called *Bloody Nose* strategy of carefully selected targeting of North Korean sites tied to the nuclear and missile program in an effort to stall their progress, would Kim respond in a way that could be considered wildly disproportional and arguably irrational?

It depends on how the United States conducted its attacks. If the attacks were preceded by a strategic communications campaign that made it clear that the motive for the attack was not regime change, and Kim saw evidence that this was true, North Korea would likely respond in a rational manner. This would probably not entail an immediate, overt response, which would just lead to a U.S.-ROK response. Instead, Kim would likely choose another domain and another time to exact retribution, most likely in a covert manner. Sinking a ship or conducting a cyberattack would allow North Korea to keep its response somewhat proportional, give Pyongyang deniability (at least initially), and confound the United States and ROK from easily moving up the escalatory ladder. Such tactics were used in 2010 with the sinking of the *Cheonan*, in 2014 with the Sony hack, and in 2015 with the landmine attack along the DMZ. Although violent, these attacks reflected a rational approach to escalation in a challenging asymmetric relationship.

If tensions erupt in a crisis, Kim's motivation will be deterrence, at least at the outset of a crisis, and ultimately survival. If Kim judges that risk is already high—such as following limited strikes designed to impact North Korea's nuclear program—he may be more risk tolerant in his decision making. The asymmetry in motivation between North Korea and its adversary (the United States or a U.S.-led coalition)—North Korea's survival, and that of Kim and the regime, would be existentially threatened in a way that its adversary would not (except perhaps in the case of South Korea)—might result in North Korea effectively achieving escalation dominance, or at least Kim believing that he has achieved it. In other words, Kim may recognize and exploit the fact that the United States has a higher deterrence threshold despite its larger nuclear arsenal. As a result, Kim may feel more comfortable conducting overt conventional military actions, sensing U.S. reluctance to escalate out of fear of exposing South Korea to a barrage of artillery or, ultimately, exposing itself to nuclear escalation.

If U.S. and alliance strikes on North Korea come without warning and for no apparent reason, the potential for misperception is great. Kim Jong-un, if he felt that the regime's survival was under threat, could become irrational (as perceived from the outside). But because survival of the regime is one of his prime objectives, a nuclear strike could make limited rational sense as a retaliation for a mortal attack on the regime. This could lead to the so-called *circling the drain* scenario. With little hope of surviving, Kim could unleash nuclear attacks and cyberattacks designed to cause great harm to the international order. Even if he abdicated his leadership post, commanders at lower echelons could employ an overwhelming conventional attack on Seoul as part of the regime's *dead man switch*.

Over the next year or two, North Korea will try to change the status quo. This could come through a freeze of its nuclear program in return for economic and security incentives. It could come through a campaign of escalation and provocation. Much will depend on the policies and actions of Washington and Seoul. Regardless of the direction, Kim Jong-un will remain a rational actor, punching and counterpunching with decisions designed to ensure the regime's survival and his role as leader. That's the good news. The bad news is that a nuclear strike could make limited rational sense to him if he perceives Trump as a mortal threat to his regime.

Ken Gause is the director of the Adversary Analytics Program at the CNA Corporation, a defense research organization based in Arlington, Virginia. He has studied and written on North Korean leadership affairs since the late 1980s and is the author of three books: *North Korean House of Cards: Leadership Dynamics in the Kim Jong-un Era*; *Leadership Dynamics Under Kim Chong-il: Power, Politics, and Prospects for Change*; and *Coercion. Control. Surveillance, and Punishment. An Examination of the North Korean Police State*.

Chapter 22

Nuclear Deterrence and Leadership Behavior: How Presidential Actions Raise or Lower the Risk of War

By James E. Doyle, Ph.D.

Can the personality and behavioral instincts of individual leaders raise or lower the risk of nuclear war? This is a critically important question due to the enormous responsibility and decision-making power bestowed on individual heads of state in nuclear-armed nations. In fact, the theory of nuclear deterrence is based squarely on theories and assumptions regarding human behavior. Since nuclear deterrence has been enshrined in the national security strategies of the world's leading nations, these assumptions have gone largely unexamined. With Donald Trump, Vladimir Putin, and Kim Jong-un all with their fingers on the nuclear trigger simultaneously, it is high time to reassess how individual leaders and their personalities can influence the risk of nuclear war.

How Deterrence Works in Theory

Nuclear deterrence is more a psychological than military contest, although functional nuclear forces are certainly required for its successful operation. To deter attack by a potential nuclear-armed aggressor, a defender must threaten unbearable nuclear retaliation. The threat of retaliation is essential because there is no effective defense against the nuclear weapons of the United States or Russia or China, for example. The attacker is restrained mainly by the knowledge that the defender possesses both the capability and the will to launch a devastating nuclear counterattack. This means that parties in a nuclear deterrent relationship must maintain nuclear forces and convincingly declare their willingness to use nuclear weapons if their core interests are threatened or attacked.

At the very foundation of this balance of terror is a critical assumption about human behavior. The assumption is that national leaders and statesman with responsibility for the security of their citizens will behave rationally to maximize positive outcomes and minimize negative outcomes for their nations and allies. If this assumption is false and leadership behavior is random, ill conceived, or malign, then, given the consequences of nuclear war, reliance on nuclear weapons for security would be suicidal.

But the theory of nuclear deterrence is even more convoluted. It trumpets two truly dubious beliefs. First, it holds that knowledge of the extreme destructive power of nuclear weapons actually focuses the human mind and sculpts the bureaucratic process of national decision making in a positive manner. In other words, because the stakes of a nuclear crisis are absolute, threatening the very existence of the states involved and lives of their leaders and citizens, nuclear weapons actually *improve* human decision making in a crisis. Nuclear theologians thus claim that nuclear deterrence makes national leaders more cautious, risk averse and desirous of diplomatic solutions to military crises. They claim that this nuclear threat-induced caution is responsible for the lack of direct conflict between great powers since World War II.[254] Historical evidence supporting this view is weak, however, and a so-called "nuclear peace" comes with the constant risk of catastrophic destruction.

Notably this assumption of rationality and caution is made regardless of the national, cultural, or religious background of nuclear-armed leaders. And as will be discussed below, a record of criminal, irrational, or erratic behavior in certain individual leaders is often disregarded in favor of the conclusion that they can still be deterred from reckless nuclear decisions. But this also disregards the possibility of a narcissistic leader who might act recklessly because he perceives an existential threat to his personal hold on power.

The second notion is that national leaders may be able to temporarily strengthen deterrence or coerce their rival in periods of tension or crisis by acting in a manner that leads their rival to doubt their rationality and believe they are capable of unpredictable, aggressive actions even when stakes of a crisis are not extreme. This consideration, called by deterrence theorist Thomas Schelling "the threat that leaves something to chance," tempts some leaders to engage in nuclear brinksmanship. Of course, this possibility logically contradicts the belief that nuclear risks make leaders more cautious and risk-averse. The danger is that risk-prone individuals, usually attempting to strengthen a weak or doubtful deterrent threat, will miscalculate and trigger an inadvertent nuclear war.

If you find these arcane features of nuclear deterrence alarming or hard to believe, you are not alone. Scholars and strategists have warned about the paradoxes, illogic, and tautologies of nuclear deterrence theory since the beginning of the atomic age.[255] History is replete with examples when honor, anger, or national self-respect prevailed over pragmatic calculations of material loss and gain as the reason for resorting to force. Indeed, deterrence theory's assumption of rationality is somewhat ahistorical when the causes of conflict are concerned.

---

[254] Jonathon Tepperman, "How Nuclear Weapons Can Keep You Safe," Newsweek, August 28, 2009, http://www.newsweek.com/how-nuclear-weapons-can-keep-you-safe-78907

[255] "Deterrence: A Political and Psychological Critique," in Robert Axelrod, Robert Jervis, Roy Radner, and Paul Stern (Eds.): Perspectives in Deterrence (New York: Oxford University Press, 1989).

Unfortunately, history teaches that decision makers often convince themselves, in spite of contradictory evidence, that they can successfully challenge strongly held positions of an adversary without provoking war. The chances of these miscalculations increase when leaders confront acute political and strategic vulnerabilities and are naturally confrontational or feel powerless to back down. They falsely assume that their adversaries will recognize this and back down instead.

Rather than asserting that nuclear deterrence is likely to hold no matter who has their finger on the button, it is perhaps more useful to ask what leadership traits, organizational structures, or doctrinal positions might mitigate or exacerbate the very human tendency toward emotionalism and misperception during political crises with a risk of nuclear weapons use. Assessing what is known about past nuclear crises is helpful to this thought experiment. However, it does not provide a deep source of perspective for future crises because most close calls with nuclear arms occurred between the United States and the Soviet Union. The United States now faces multiple potential nuclear adversaries, most notably Russia, China, and North Korea.

Lessons from Past Nuclear Crises

Over the past 70 years nations have prepared to use or threatened to use nuclear weapons several times during crises. In a small number of cases nuclear war was narrowly avoided. It is vital to remain aware of this historical record and to search these episodes for insights that can help prevent nuclear crises or nuclear use in the future. One such insight is that correctly interpreting communications with adversaries and understanding their intent during a crisis is difficult. Although often minimized in nuclear deterrence theory, the party trying to deter and the challenger are likely to have inherent differences in cognitive bias, approaches to problems, capacities for empathy, and perspectives on the balance of risk and reward at stake in the dispute. The probability of misunderstanding is high because human beings tend to misunderstand statements and information in situations of extreme tension.

The chances of miscalculation are always high when potential nuclear adversaries lack consistent dialogue on divisive issues and try to act unilaterally to improve their position.

This was clear in 1962 during the Cuban Missile Crisis when Soviet Premier Nikita Khrushchev ordered the emplacement of nuclear-armed missiles in Cuba. The Soviets were trying to restore the perception of strategic nuclear parity with the United States and to extend deterrence to Cuba in the way Washington had extended deterrence to West Germany by vastly raising the stakes of a U.S. invasion of Cuba. But the Soviets sent nuclear missiles to Cuba secretly, in an attempt to confront the U.S. with a *fait accompli* that could only be reversed by threat of war.

Nuclear deterrence theory fails to adequately explain why the Soviets would undertake such reckless action. This was not a cautious, risk-averse policy designed with an eye toward the need to avoid raising nuclear tensions. It was a deliberate attempt at deception that was not anticipated by the United States and a gamble that the recently elected U.S. President Kennedy would back down.

What saved the world during this crisis was Kennedy's ability to react in a firm but calm and deliberative manner to the dangerous Soviet challenge. Based on incomplete knowledge, several of Kennedy's senior military commanders advised him to launch an aircraft attack on the incomplete missile sites in Cuba. President Kennedy rejected this option. He feared that some Soviet missiles might survive the attack, and since the military threshold had been crossed, they would be launched at U.S. forces, precipitating a full-scale nuclear war. In the early 1990s it was learned that Soviet commanders of already operational tactical nuclear-missile bases had been given the authority to launch their missiles if attacked. If US air strikes had been ordered, it is very likely that a nuclear exchange would have followed, potentially escalating to direct attacks on US and Soviet cities. Kennedy's prudent decision to refrain from the direct use of military force and to instead block further Soviet naval shipment to Cuba avoided nuclear war and provided more time to resolve the crisis.

Kennedy demonstrated this remarkable restraint again at the very height of the crisis, the day that brought the world to its closest point with nuclear war. On Saturday, October 27, 1962, the twelfth day of the crisis, a Soviet anti-aircraft missile battery shot down an American U-2 spy plane over Cuba. The American pilot was killed. Declared American policy in such an event was to retaliate by launching an attack on the anti-aircraft missile battery. Chairman of the U.S. Joint Chiefs of Staff Gen. Maxwell D. Taylor recommended that the U.S. Air Force attack the anti-aircraft missile site the next day. Secretary of Defense Robert McNamara argued that an invasion of Cuba had become inevitable.[256] But President Kennedy chose not to attack the missile site and waited for a response to his direct communication with Soviet Premier Khrushchev. The crisis ended when Khrushchev agreed to remove the nuclear missiles from Cuba in exchange for U.S. pledges not to invade the island and to privately remove U.S. nuclear-armed Jupiter missiles from Turkey.

In the case of the Cuban Missile Crisis, President Kennedy ignored the advice of his military leaders to escalate by bombing the missile sites in Cuba. In future Cold War crises senior military personnel in America and the Soviet Union would need to question or ignore the information being provided by early warning radars, which on multiple occasions indicated falsely that a nuclear attack was under-

---

[256] "Summary Record of the Eighth Meeting of the Executive Committee of the National Security Council," October 26, 1962, John F. Kennedy Presidential Library and Museum, http://microsites. jfklibrary.org/cmc/oct27/doc2.html

way.[257] For example, on September 26, 1983, a Soviet early-warning satellite indicated an attack by five U.S. nuclear missiles. Tensions were high between the two countries. The Soviet Union had recently mistakenly downed a South Korean passenger plane, killing all aboard. The Soviet officer on duty, Lt. Col. Stanislav Petrov, decided on the basis of intuition to disobey protocol and refrain from relaying the warning up the chain of command. Had he done so, the Soviet General Staff may have requested the authority to launch a retaliatory strike on the basis of a warning that proved false. Petrov would later state that he doubted the radar warning because "when people start a war, they don't start it with only five missiles."[258]

What Petrov displayed was extraordinary judgment and a sense of personal professionalism that is unlikely to emerge in individuals in the chain of nuclear command unless it is encouraged and practiced. Indeed, one of the key lessons of the Cold War was the benefit of a high level of professionalism exhibited by those dealing with nuclear weapons on both sides and the need to communicate during potentially dangerous situations. U.S. and Soviet political and military commanders recognized the competence on the other side and respected it. In fact, the two nations negotiated and signed two agreements to reduce nuclear risks.

The first was the 1971 Agreement on Measures to Reduce the Risk of Outbreak of Nuclear War. It covers three main areas:

A pledge by each party to take measures each considers necessary to maintain and improve its organizational and technical safeguards against accidental or unauthorized use of nuclear weapons; and

Arrangements for immediate notification should a risk of nuclear war arise from such incidents, from detection of unidentified objects on early warning systems, or from any accidental, unauthorized, or other unexplained incident involving a possible detonation of a nuclear weapon; and

Advance notification of any planned missile launches beyond the territory of the launching party and in the direction of the other party; and

The agreement provides that for urgent communication "in situations requiring prompt clarification," the "Hot Line" (communications link) will be used.[259]

---

[257] "Close Calls With Nuclear Weapons (2015), Union of Concerned Scientists, https://www.ucsusa.org/nuclear-weapons/hair-trigger-alert/close-calls#.WrZbRGaZNE4

[258] Pavel Aksenov, "Stanislav Petrov: The Man Who May Have Saved the World," BBC Russian, September 26, 2013, http://www.bbc.com/news/world-europe-24280831

[259] "Agreement on Measures to Reduce the Risk of Outbreak of Nuclear War Between The United States of America and The Union of Soviet Socialist Republics (Accidents Measures Agreement)," U.S. Department of State, https://www.state.gov/t/isn/4692.htm

A second agreement, the "Agreement Between the Government of the United States of America and the Government of The Union of Soviet Socialist Republics on the Prevention of Incidents On and Over the High Seas," more commonly known as INCSEA, was signed in Moscow in 1972. This agreement served to enhance mutual knowledge and understanding of military activities; to reduce the possibility of conflict by accident, miscalculation, or the failure of communication; and to increase stability in times of both calm and crisis.[260]

After the collapse of the Soviet Union both of these agreements were reconfirmed, and the U.S. and the Russian Federation accepted their obligations. The agreements seek to codify procedures and organizational behaviors that can reduce the risk of conflict by accident or miscalculation. They were prudently entered into after the realization that incidents, human error, and accidents will be a constant feature of relations between potentially adversarial nuclear states and that active steps must be maintained to reduce risk.

Positive and Negative Leadership Behaviors

The record of nuclear crises and near misses clearly demonstrates that human and organizational factors play the critical role in preventing nuclear war. The chances that deterrence will fail are elevated when leaders are risk prone and relations between nuclear-armed states have deteriorated. If we are to have any confidence in the system of nuclear deterrence upon which our survival depends, we must do all we can to ensure that all decision makers with authority for the release and operation of nuclear weapons have the following attributes:

- Rationality
- Emotional stability
- Basic knowledge of nuclear weapons and the consequences of their use
- Experience with crises and a willingness to constantly seek the reduction of tensions
- Ability to process information rapidly and dispassionately
- Open-mindedness to:
  ○ Divergent points of view, including that of the adversary
  ○ Possibility of misperceptions on the part of an adversary
  ○ Possibility that information coming from experts or technology is wrong
  ○ Innovative actions/solutions that create opportunities to de-escalate tensions
- Awareness of the need to maintain operational professionalism during crises

---

[260] "Agreement Between the Government of The United States of America and the Government of The Union of Soviet Socialist Republics on the Prevention of Incidents On and Over the High Seas," U.S. Department of State, https://www.state.gov/t/isn/4791.htm

Traits that are probably undesirable in leaders with authority to order a nuclear strike include:

- Tendency to be easily angered, frustrated, or confused
- Overconfidence or impulsiveness, with a tendency for bravado or brinks-manship
- Possession of an unreasonably confrontational, paranoid, or vindictive nature
- Unwillingness to be challenged, questioned, or to see the situation through the eyes of the adversary
- Unfamiliarity with the consequences of nuclear weapons use
- Unfamiliarity with the record of nuclear near misses due to human and mechanical error and normal accidents
- Inability to command with diplomatic and operational professionalism

The desirable attributes could be critical to preventing nuclear use, but they are just as important if deterrence fails because they would be essential to ending nuclear use at the smallest possible level of damage. The use of 10 nuclear weapons would be a catastrophe; use of 300-500 would end civilization, as we know it.

A Perfect Storm of Nuclear Risk?

It was clear even before the 2016 election of Donald Trump as U.S. president that the leadership of some potential U.S. adversaries lacked several of the positive behavioral traits that help reduce nuclear risks. This is particularly the case with Russian President Putin and North Koran leader Kim Jong-un. Both of these individuals speak belligerently regarding nuclear weapons and have conducted nuclear tests and exercises in a provocative manner.

Following Russia's aggression against Ukraine in 2014, President Vladimir Putin frequently warned the world that Russia remained a nuclear superpower. He suggested that he was prepared to go on a nuclear alert when the Russian military seized Crimea in 2014, implying that Russia reserves the option of nuclear usage to retain the illegally annexed territory. Russia has gone so far as to declare the right to deploy nuclear weapons in Crimea, and reports indicate that Russia has been moving nuclear-capable forces to Crimea and renovating nuclear storage infrastructure in Sevastopol.[261]

---

[261] Russia Threatens Nuclear Strikes Over Crimea," The Diplomat, 11 July 2014, http://the-diplomat.com/2014/07/russia-threatens-nuclear-strikes-over-crimea.
and "Russia says it has a right to put nuclear weapons in Crimea," Los Angeles Times, December 2014, www.latimes.com/world/europe/la-fg-russia-nuclear-crimea-20141215-story.html; "Crimea Could Serve as Location to Deploy Nuclear Weapons, Russia Says," Newsweek, 13 March 2015, www.newsweek.com/crimea-could-serve- location-deploy-nuclear-weapons-russia-says-313545.

Russia has increased its frequency of exercising nuclear-capable aircraft near the airspace of the United States and its allies, and conducted military drills that simulate tactical nuclear employment to terminate a local conflict.[262] It has chosen to violate the 1987 Intermediate Nuclear Forces (INF) Treaty to enhance its theater-range capabilities by deploying a banned ground-launched nuclear cruise missile. Finally, Russia's ambassador in Denmark threatened to target that country with nuclear weapons. It is likely that President Putin's nuclear chest pounding is intended to threaten the NATO alliance, reduce political cohesion within the alliance, and drive a wedge between Washington and its NATO allies.

This is a dangerous political strategy and seems to be directed by Vladimir Putin himself, displaying a risk-prone and bellicose nature that raises alarming questions about how he will behave in any future nuclear crisis. Putin has described an important lesson he learned as a young man in Leningrad: "When a fight is inevitable, you have to hit first."[263] In defending Russia's right to launch a retaliatory nuclear strike against a nuclear attack in March 2018, Putin proclaimed: "Certainly it would be a global disaster for humanity; a disaster for the entire world. But as a citizen of Russia and the head of the Russian state I must ask myself: Why would we need a world if Russia ceased to exist?"[264]

North Korean Leader Kim Jong-un also displays dangerous behaviors that suggest he could trigger a nuclear crisis or miscalculate during attempts at nuclear brinksmanship. Kim Jong-un has personality and behavioral traits precisely opposite from those desirable for leaders with nuclear authority to possess. He is a murderous dictator who has ordered the execution of disloyal family members and government officials deemed to have defied him. He is clearly the top commander of the DPRK's military, and it is doubtful that any individuals or groups would oppose an order from him to employ nuclear weapons.

In August 2017 North Korea threatened: "The day the U.S. dares tease our nation with a nuclear rod and sanctions, the mainland U.S. will be catapulted into an unimaginable sea of fire." Hours later the DPRK warned that it was considering a strike that would create "an enveloping fire" around Guam, the western Pacific island where the United States operates a critical Air Force base manned by

---

[262] Jacek Durkalec, "Nuclear-Backed 'Little Green Men': Nuclear Messaging in the Ukraine Crisis," The Polish Institute of International Affairs, July 2015, http://www.pism.pl/files/?id_plik=20165

[263] Eric Schlosser, "World War III, by Mistake," The New Yorker, December 23, 2016, https://www.newyorker.com/news/news-desk/world-war-three-by-mistake

[264] Will Stewart, "Putin said He Would Annihilate the World with His Nuclear Weapons if Nukes Were Fired at Russia Because 'Why Do We Need a World if Russians Cease to Exist,'" The Daily Mail, March 7, 2018, http://www.dailymail.co.uk/news/article-5472893/Putin-says-hed-annihilate-world-nukes-fired-Russia.html

thousands of U.S. personnel.[265] Kim Jong-un has also said a nuclear launch button is "always on my table" and warned the U.S. it will never be able to start a war.

In a televised New Year's speech, he said the entire US was within range of North Korean nuclear weapons, adding: "This is reality, not a threat."[266]

When he addressed the U.N. General Assembly in September 2017, U.S. President Trump said that if the U.S. was forced to defend itself or its allies, it would have "no choice but to totally destroy North Korea." Referring to Kim Jong-un as "rocket man," Trump said the North Korean leader was "on a suicide mission for himself and for his regime." Kim Jong-un responded to Trump's speech by calling the U.S. president "mentally deranged" and warning that he would "pay dearly" for threatening to destroy North Korea. He also said Trump's comments "have convinced me, rather than frightening or stopping me, that the path I chose is correct and that it is the one I have to follow to the last."[267]

This game of nuclear brinksmanship is dangerous because the leaders of both sides and the national psyche become directly invested in avoiding the embarrassment of backing down if an unintended crisis should emerge. The danger is intensified by the fact that beyond the tense words, both countries are operating their military forces in an aggressive manner near one another. Accidents with ships, aircraft, or missile warning systems can happen at any time, and military commands sent through the chain of communication can be misinterpreted, leading to confrontation or actual use of military force that then escalates out of control.

Following the 2018 Winter Olympics in South Korea, there has been an unexpected thaw in tensions on the Korean peninsula and summit meetings are now planned between Kim Jong-un and South Korean President Moon Jae-in on April 27, 2018 and remarkably between President Trump and Kim Jong-un at a date set tentatively for May 2018. The potential phased dismantlement of North Korea's nuclear program under international verification will be a subject of the talks, but many observers are skeptical that diplomacy can succeed between two leaders who have expressed such animosity toward one another over the past year.[268]

---

[265] Peter Baker and Choe Sang-Hun, "Trump Threatens 'Fire and Fury' Against North Korea if It Endangers U.S.," The New York Times, August 8, 2017, https://www.nytimes.com/2017/08/08/world/asia/north-korea-un-sanctions-nuclear-missile-united-nations.html

[266] Bruce Harrison, Stella Kim, Mac William Bishop and Lauren Suk, "Kim Jong-Un Highlights His 'Nuclear Button,' Offers Olympic Talks, NBC News, December 31, 2017, "https://www.nbcnews.com/news/north-korea/kim-says-north-korea-s-nuclear-weapons-will-prevent-war-n833781

[267] Steven Buser, "Would the Air Force Let Airman Trump Near a Nuclear Weapon?" The New York Times, January 17, 2018, https://www.nytimes.com/2018/01/17/opinion/trump-nuclear-weapons-mental-health.html

[268] Bruce Blair, "Strengthening Checks on Presidential Nuclear Launch Authority," Arms Control Today, January/February 2018, https://www.armscontrol.org/sites/default/files/files/ACT/ACT_JanFeb18_Blair_Prepublication.pdf

President Trump's willingness to issue nuclear threats and his apparent limited knowledge of nuclear weapons realities is equally disturbing in relation to the actions of Vladimir Putin and Kim Jong-un. In 2016 candidate Trump reportedly asked one of his foreign policy advisers, "If we have nuclear weapons why can't we use them?" In January 2018 Trump tweeted "North Korean Leader Kim Jong Un just stated that the 'Nuclear Button is on his desk at all times.' Will someone from his depleted and food starved regime please inform him that I too have a Nuclear Button, but it is a much bigger & more powerful one than his, and my Button works![269]

According to former U.S. Minuteman missile launch officer and Princeton University professor Bruce Blair, preventing such failure depends "in no small measure on qualities of presidential leadership—responsibility, composure, competence, empathy and diplomatic skill—that Mr. Trump evidently does not possess." Mr. Trump appears to disregard the importance of only making nuclear threats when the very existence of the U.S. or its allies is at stake. "He shows no humility toward the civilization-ending destructiveness of nuclear weapons, and offhandedly entertains their use."[270]

Some members of the U.S. Congress are so concerned about President Trump's mental state and vindictive behavior that they held hearings in November 2017 on the ability of the U.S. president alone to authorize a nuclear strike. Senator Chris Murphy, a Connecticut Democrat who said he and others were concerned "that the president of the United States is so unstable, is so volatile, has a decision-making process that is so quixotic, that he might order a nuclear weapons strike that is wildly out of step with U.S. national security interests."[271]

The fact that Vladimir Putin, Kim Jong-un, and Donald J. Trump all control potentially adversarial nuclear forces simultaneously by itself creates a perfect storm of nuclear risk. But this triumvirate of bellicose individuals commands their nuclear nations at a time when several other negative factors combine to inflate the risks of nuclear war to its highest point since the Cuban Missile Crisis. First, relations between the United States and Russia and the United States and North Korea are at their most confrontational in decades. Second, the military forces of these states are operating aggressively close to one another daily, increasing the risk of combat by accident or miscalculation. Third, in the U.S.-Russia case, past

---

[269] "Reducing the Risk of Nuclear War," The Union of Concerned Scientists, January 2016, https://www.ucsusa.org/sites/default/files/attach/2016/02/Reducing-Risk-Nuclear-War-full-report.pdf

[270] Bruce G. Blair, "Trump and the Nuclear Keys," The New York Times, October 12, 2016, https://www.nytimes.com/2016/10/12/opinion/trump-and-the-nuclear-keys.html

[271] "Full Committee Hearing Authority to Order the Use of Nuclear Weapons," U.S. Senate Foreign Relations Committee, November 14, 2017, https://www.foreign.senate.gov/hearings/authority-to-order-the-use-of-nuclear-weapons-111417

agreements to reduce the chance of inadvertent nuclear war that define patterns of communication and rules of the road for exercising and operating military forces are being neglected. In the case of the U.S. and North Korea no such agreements exist. Finally, all three nations are in the process of military buildups, rapidly deploying new weapons that that have unprecedented strategic capabilities for offensive operations. These factors all act to undermine stability, raise tensions, and exacerbate the potential consequences of inevitable human and mechanical errors.

The Path to a Safer Future

Is there a way out of this nuclear nightmare before nuclear weapons are again used in combat? The first step is the urgency of recognizing the unacceptability of the current condition, specifically including the nuclear postures of the United States and Russia and the fact that individual leaders possess the authority to launch weapons that can kill millions.

In the United States and all nations that possess nuclear weapons the mental and emotional fitness of civilian and military personnel who have the responsibility for manufacturing, maintaining, transporting, and operating nuclear weapons is evaluated and monitored through various personnel reliability programs (PRP). For example, the U.S. Department of Defense Directive 5210.42 states[272]: "Only those personnel who have demonstrated the highest degree of individual reliability for allegiance, trustworthiness, conduct, behavior, and responsibility shall be allowed to perform duties associated with nuclear weapons, and they shall be continuously evaluated for adherence to PRP standards."[273] Ironically the U.S. president is not required to be enrolled in the PRP and pass its various evaluations and reviews. This is absurd. If the president is to be given authority over the use of nuclear weapons, then the ability to meet the standards of the PRP program should be a requirement for running for the presidency.

Donald Trump's personality and record of behavior have reignited a domestic debate about fitness for nuclear weapons launch authority. Several bills are under consideration in Congress that would require the involvement of more individuals or even the consent of Congress to launch U.S. nuclear weapons. One proposal is that the use of nuclear weapons would require an order from the president and agreement by the next two people in the presidential chain of succession. Under

---

[272] "Nuclear Weapons Personnel Reliability Program," Homeland Security Digital Library, June 27, 2016, https://www.hsdl.org/?abstract&did=793857

[273] Steven Buser, "Would the Air Force Let Airman Trump Near a Nuclear Weapon?" The New York Times, January 17, 2018, https://www.nytimes.com/2018/01/17/opinion/trump-nuclear-weapons-mental-health.html

normal circumstances, these two people would be the vice president and speaker of the House.[274]

Without a doubt the most reliable way to protect against a rash or irresponsible launch decision or launch on the basis of false warning is to adopt a policy no first use of nuclear weapons. This would allow the U.S. to remove its silo-based missiles from high alert[275] and eliminate the option of launching its nuclear weapons on warning of an attack. The United States could declare that it would launch nuclear weapons only if the detonation of nuclear weapons against the United States or a U.S. ally was confirmed or if the existence of a national ally was threatened by non-nuclear means. This would eliminate the risk that the United States could launch nuclear weapons based on erroneous or misinterpreted warning of nuclear attack. It would also reduce the need for the president and his or her advisors to make a nuclear launch decision under time pressure measured in minutes rather than days or weeks. Such a change in U.S. declaratory policy will not weaken deterrence because even after suffering a first strike that destroyed all U.S. silo-based missiles, the United States would retain the capability of responding with a massive nuclear attack. Invulnerable to a first strike, U.S. submarines at sea carry a majority of U.S. nuclear warheads and can be ordered to retaliate.

The United States should also declare that the sole purpose of U.S. nuclear weapons is to deter and, if necessary, respond to the use of nuclear weapons against the United States or its allies. Congress could take an important step to support a no-first-use policy by passing the H.R.4415[276] - *To establish the policy of the United States regarding the no-first-use of nuclear weapons* stating it is US policy to not use nuclear weapons first, or the Markey-Lieu bill H.R.669[277] - *Restricting First Use of Nuclear Weapons Act of 2017*, which would require that Congress declare war and authorize the first use of nuclear weapons before the president can order such an attack.[278]

---

[274] Bruce Blair, "Strengthening Checks on Presidential Nuclear Launch Authority," Arms Control Today, January/February 2018, https://www.armscontrol.org/sites/default/files/files/ACT/ACT_JanFeb18_Blair_Prepublication.pdf

[275] "Reducing the Risk of Nuclear War," The Union of Concerned Scientists, January 2016, https://www.ucsusa.org/sites/default/files/attach/2016/02/Reducing-Risk-Nuclear-War-full-report.pdf

[276] H.R. 4415, To Establish the Policy of the United States Regarding the No-First-Use of Nuclear Weapons, Congress.gov, November 15, 2017, https://www.congress.gov/bill/115th-congress/house-bill/4415

[277] H.R. 669, Restricting First Use of Nuclear Weapons Act of 2017, Congress.gov, https://www.congress.gov/bill/115th-congress/house-bill/669

[278] "Limiting the President's Ability to Start a Nuclear War," Union of Concerned Scientists, March 2017, https://www.ucsusa.org/sites/default/files/attach/2017/03/Markey-Lieu-First-Strike-Fact-Sheet.pdf

For extreme situations when the U.S. might need to use nuclear weapons first to prevent the collapse of an allied nation, it has been proposed that a consensus of six individuals should be required—the president, vice president, speaker of the House, Senate leader (pro tem), national security advisor, and secretary of defense. The first four in that order represent the legal chain of presidential succession and involve senior congressional as well as executive branch officials to provide balance and broad political legitimacy.[279] This policy would go a long way to reducing the threat that a rogue U.S. president acting on bad judgment could alone launch a nuclear war.

While the United States has no direct influence on the arrangements for nuclear use authority in other nations, the steps outlined above would sharply reduce the perceived need for Russia, China, or North Korea to maintain nuclear forces with the capability to launch under warning of an attack. The removal of U.S. land-based strategic missiles from high alert and their eventual retirement would ease fears in other capitals that this leg of the U.S. nuclear triad would be used to eliminate their nuclear deterrents in a first strike. Such a step would reduce the extreme time pressures for launch decisions and possibly allow potential adversaries to introduce modifications in their own nuclear launch authorities that reduce the risk of nuclear war by miscalculation or rash action by single individual leaders.

Last but not least, the American electorate can choose a president who behaves in a way that lowers nuclear risk. The president we have now heightens it.

James E. Doyle, Ph.D. was a specialist in the Nuclear Nonproliferation Division at Los Alamos National Laboratory from 1997 to 2014. In 2015 Dr. Doyle was awarded the first Paul Olum fellowship from the Ploughshares Fund and was a non-resident fellow at the Belfer Center for Science and International Security at Harvard. His recent works focus on nuclear forces modernization, evolving nuclear threats and strategic planning for the elimination of nuclear weapons.

---

[279] "Bruce Blair, "Strengthening Checks on Presidential Nuclear Launch Authority," Arms Control Today, January/February 2018 https://www.armscontrol.org/sites/default/files/files/ACT/ACT_JanFeb18_Blair_Prepublication.pdf

Chapter 23

Extinction Anxiety and Donald Trump: Where the Spirit of the Depths Meets the Spirit of the Times

By Thomas Singer, M.D.

Call it an epidemic. Anxiety among Americans has skyrocketed since the election of

Donald Trump as president in 2016. An American Psychological Association study found sixty-six percent of adults said the future of the nation was causing them significant stress, the highest levels recorded since the survey began ten years ago.[280] But the word stress doesn't quite capture the magnitude of what is happening inside the psyches of many Americans. It's more akin to terror.

In his *Washington Post* column, "Trump is killing me. Really," Dana Milbank revealed that since the election he had gone from the picture of health to suddenly having dangerously high blood pressure. What astounded him was the flood of letters he got from readers "experiencing all manner of symptoms, real or imagined, of what I called Trump Hypertensive Unexplained Disorder: Disturbed sleep. Anger. Dread. Weight loss. Overeating. Headaches. Fainting. Irregular heartbeat. Chronic neck pain. Depression. Irritable bowel syndrome. Tightness in the chest. Shortness of breath. Teeth grinding. Stomach ulcer. Indigestion. Shingles. Eye twitching. Nausea. Irritability. High blood sugar. Tinnitus. Reduced immunity. Racing pulse. Shaking limbs. Hair loss. Acid reflux. Deteriorating vision. Stroke. Heart attack. It was a veritable organ recital—a large number of people reporting stress-induced illnesses in the Trump era".[281]

Whatever is triggering this collective panic, it seems to be tapping into a level of the psyche that is both deeply primal and widely shared. Freud began his study of the mind with a focus on how we experience and defend against our personal individual anxiety. But what about anxiety for the survival of not just the self, but the species itself and all plant and animal life on the planet?

Apocalyptic fantasies are as old as time, but the term *extinction anxiety,* which originates in such fears, is new. It describes the psychic state of individuals and

---

[280] American Psychological Association, "APA Survey Reveals 2016 Presidential Election Source of Significant Stress for More Than Half of Americans," APA.org, 10/13/16

[281] Dana Milbank, "President Trump is killing me. Really," Washington Post, 9/15/17

groups that are either consciously gripped or unconsciously influenced by the dread of extinction. As we have learned from Freud, anxiety is a warning signal that danger is present and that overwhelming emotions may be felt, giving rise to unmanageable helplessness. The danger may be perceived as arising from internal or external sources and may be the response to a variety of powerful unconscious fantasies.

It is my hypothesis that extinction anxiety is flooding the planet, although it frequently expresses itself in a displaced form of group or cultural anxiety rather than in the direct experience of the fear of extinction. It is timely to give a clinical name to extinction anxiety as a type of warning signal that danger is present whether it is originating in irrational fear and/or irrefutable objective evidence. In his 2017 book, *The Dangerous Case of Donald Trump*, Noam Chomsky writes quite simply:

"There are two huge dangers that the human species face. We are in a situation where we need to decide whether the species survives in any decent form. One is the rising danger of nuclear war, which is quite serious, and the other is environmental catastrophe."[282]

I am not writing this paper to prophesy the end-times. Rather, my purpose in writing this paper is to say that the intense, contemporary anxiety about the approaching end-times is real and needs to be taken with the utmost seriousness.

Donald Trump has been a master of arousing and manipulating extinction anxiety for political and self-aggrandizing purposes. He would not have been able to do this unless there was a huge, global reservoir of extinction anxiety circulating among the world's citizens and waiting to be exploited. Extinction anxiety finds direct expression in environmental groups and those concerned about nuclear war.[283] However, it finds indirect expression in other groups and individuals that fear their own annihilation without a conscious link to their fear of the extinction of the world.

Donald Trump has elevated the fears of many diverse groups around the world by contributing to the belief that their unique identities and very existence are threatened. Whites, blacks, women, men, Latinos, Palestinians, Jews, Muslims, gays, sixty million refugees around the globe are just a few of the groups that Trump seems to have enjoyed toying with by raising concerns about their own survival.

I believe that Trump has been able to tap into a deeper, underlying extinction anxiety that can be viewed as the collective psyche's equivalent of death anxiety in the individual. Extinction anxiety acts as a radioactive background in our global

---

[282] Brandy X. Lee, The Dangerous Case of Donald Trump (New York: Thomas Dunne Books, St. Martin's Press, 2017), 357.

[283] Jen Christensen, "16,000 Scientists Sign Dire Warning to Humanity over Health of Planet," CNN, November 15, 2017, http://www.cnn.com/2017/11/14/health/scientists-warn-humanity/index.html.

society, fueling many of our concerns with an energy we can imagine to be coming from the psyche's equivalent of a nuclear reactor. For instance in the U.S., climate change deniers may be seen as denying the very real possibility of the planet's destruction as a way of defending themselves against the fear of extinction. Aligning himself with this attitude, Trump offers to staunch extinction anxiety by denying it is real. His appointment of Michael Catanzaro, a well-known climate change denier who subsequently resigned on April 18, 2018, as his energy advisor illustrates the president's effort to deny a real problem that threatens our existence.

Denial—whether at the individual or group level—is a most primitive defense in the psyche's arsenal of protecting itself against intolerable suffering and loss, including the fear of death or extinction. Paradoxically then, Trump alternates between raising extinction anxiety around the world by playing one nuclear power off against another (Iran, the United States and the Europeans or China and the North and South Koreans) and denying extinction anxiety and its causes. Meanwhile, he encourages the exploitation of the environment by attempting to undo everything the Environmental Protection Agency has achieved nationally and the Paris Agreement has achieved internationally.

We know that there are fault lines at every level of our global society. The fault lines that demarcate divisions between groups of people and nations run deep along gender, tribal, national, religious, racial, and ethnic lines. I contend that extinction anxiety emerges from the deepest levels of the psyche through these fault lines. They are like channels running between the very source of life and collective psyche on the planet all the way up to the individual. As extinction anxiety courses up and down along these channels, signals of alarm and danger may break through like lava flows that emerge from deep beneath the surface of the earth in volcanic eruptions.

We can also imagine that along these fault lines, extinction anxiety is where the *spirit of the times* and the *spirit of the depths* meet and merge.

The Spirit of the Depths and Extinction Anxiety

The Spirit of the Depths refers to ancient and recurring themes of deepest concern to human beings: themes of death and rebirth, of meaning and meaninglessness , of suffering and joy, of loss and repair, of what is fleeting and what is eternal. From the *spirit of the depths*, humankind has been experiencing apocalyptic fantasies since the dawn of human recorded history. Zarathustra, The Book of Daniel, The Book of Revelations—all are steeped in the apocalyptic vision of the end of time.[284] Perhaps the most moving modern expression of this vision

---

[284] For this section, I am indebted to Richard Stein, M.D., whose "Living on the Edge of the Apocalypse: What Isis, The Christian Right, and Climate Change Deniers Have in Common" appears in The San Francisco Jung Institute Presidential Papers of 2016: https://aras.org/newsletters/aras-

from the spirit of the depths is Yeats' "The Second Coming," written in 1919 at the end of World War 1:[285]

The Second Coming
BY WILLIAM BUTLER YEATS
Turning and turning in the widening gyre
The falcon cannot hear the falconer;
Things fall apart; the centre cannot hold;
Mere anarchy is loosed upon the world,
The blood-dimmed tide is loosed, and everywhere
The ceremony of innocence is drowned;
The best lack all conviction, while the worst
Are full of passionate intensity.

Surely some revelation is at hand;
Surely the Second Coming is at hand.
The Second Coming! Hardly are those words out
When a vast image out of *Spiritus Mundi*
Troubles my sight: somewhere in sands of the desert
A shape with lion body and the head of a man,
A gaze blank and pitiless as the sun,
Is moving its slow thighs, while all about it
Reel shadows of the indignant desert birds.
The darkness drops again; but now I know
That twenty centuries of stony sleep
Were vexed to nightmare by a rocking cradle,
And what rough beast, its hour come round at last,
Slouches towards Bethlehem to be born?

Apocalyptic fantasy from the *spirit of the depths* is alive and well today in the longing of Christian fundamentalists for the end of times in the rapture at Armageddon. If has flourished within Isis and its Islamic apocalyptic vision of the end of times in the yearning to create the Caliphate. These fantasies can be thought of as emerging from the depths of the human psyche that is rooted in the origins of life itself—not just human life but all plant and animal life on the planet. We can also imagine, along with the Hindus, that whatever forces give birth to life on the

---

connections-special-edition-2016-presidency-papers.

[285] William Butler Yeats, "The Second Coming," Poetry Foundation, https://www.poetry-foundation.org/poems/43290/the-second-coming. From The Collected Poems of W. B. Yeats (New York: Macmillan, 1989), 187.

planet can do just the opposite and take back into itself all of life and psyche as in Vishnu's reabsorption into himself of the whole of the created cosmos.

There is little evidence in the public record that Donald Trump has a connection to the *spirit of the depths*. He seems to lack a familiarity with history, religion, or a depth of soulfulness that evinces struggles with themes of suffering, renewal, or transformation that is an essential part of being human. From what we know from those who have had close connections to Trump, he lives in the present, from moment to moment, and his relationships to other people and the life of the planet are primarily transactional. One would not expect the *spirit of the depths* and the *spirit of the times* to meet in any sort of conscious, meaningful interaction in the psyche of Donald Trump. His character is not put together with the wisdom of an *old soul*.

The Spirit of the Times and Extinction Anxiety
The Doomsday Clock

The *Spirit of the Times* refers to the preoccupations, beliefs, and yearnings of a particular age.

Our *spirit of the times* has been anchored in the belief in the rational mind and is dominated by science, technology, and consumerism. It is no accident that the Bulletin of Atomic Scientists has created and maintained a Doomsday Clock since the dawn of the nuclear age in 1947 when the clock was set at seven minutes before midnight. Midnight marks the extinction of the human race. Since its inception, the clock has fluctuated in predicting how much time we have left. In 1953, it was moved up to two minutes before midnight when both the United States and the Soviet Union exploded hydrogen bombs. It drifted back to three minutes before midnight until the election of Donald Trump and it has currently been moved forward to two minutes before midnight.[286]

In the *spirit of the times*, our extinction anxiety is fueled by undeniable objective evidence that life on the planet is seriously endangered. We know, for instance, that we have already entered the "sixth mass extinction event" in which it is predicted that one half of the world's land and marine species could disappear by 2100 unless there is some other annihilating or transforming event that precedes the unfolding of the sixth mass extinction event.[287]

As human beings, we are instinctually and archetypally connected with all life. The threat of the loss of all these nonhuman species contributes to extinction anxiety.[288]

---

[286] Bulletin of the Atomic Scientists, Doomsday Clock, https://thebulletin.org/timeline.

[287] Elizabeth Kolbert, The Sixth Extinction (New York: Henry Holt and Company, 2014).

[288] I am indebted to Jeffrey Kiehl for personal communications about the section on "mass extinction events."

More immediately, on a day-to-day basis, we are flooded with news of devastating fires, massive storms, terrorist attacks, and random mass killings. All of this heightens the horrifying fear that something is terribly amiss in the world. As Yeats wrote:

And what rough beast, its hour come round at last,
Slouches towards Bethlehem to be born?[289]

Not only are we being flooded with way too much information and the staggering explosion of the global population, but also perhaps with too much interconnectivity. Imagine for a moment that all the people you see walking down the street or sitting in a coffeehouse communicating on their cellphones or computers are actually sending out billions of the same daily latent message: "It hasn't happened yet." What if our frantic interconnectivity is a global SOS—an expression of extinction anxiety—and what if we are desperately clinging to one another in an effort to reassure ourselves we are not on a sinking or exploding ship?

I imagine extinction anxiety to be flowing like lava up and down the layers of the ancient and contemporary global psyche that includes evolutionary time, circulating in an accelerating negative feedback loop, up from the *spirit of the depths* to the *spirit of the times*, and back down again, in which guns, storms, droughts, and nuclear threats merge with old and new apocalyptic visions.

Donald Trump and Extinction Anxiety

From one perspective, Trump's political career has been based on his uncanny ability to arouse extinction anxiety while at the same time denying it. He arouses the fears of one group endangering and eliminating another such as white Americans being overrun by people of color and immigrants or people of color and immigrants being bullied and eliminated by white people. At the same time, he denies that human beings are altering the climate or driving other species to extinction so that he and others can exploit the planet for personal gain. He raises the fear of nuclear annihilation with his impulsive aggressivity (Rocket Man) while undoing the nuclear agreement with Iran and promising to nuke North Korea into oblivion or, in an apparent flip of the coin, to end the threat of nuclear war on the Korean peninsula as a matter of showing that he is a master of the big deal. It is hard not to conclude that Donald Trump enjoys toying with extinction anxiety in pursuit of his own narcissistic purposes. We might wonder if Trump's flirtation with global extinction anxiety and denial of it simultaneously do not have their origins in the precariousness of his own inner existence, which we can imagine constantly being threatened by annihilation unless he first annihilates any perceived enemy and emerges as the victor.

---

[289] Yeats, "The Second Coming."

Conclusion

If extinction anxiety is sounding an alarm on behalf of the whole of creation where the *spirit of the depths* and the *spirit of the times* meet at every level of human experience, then our response needs to come from the whole of the psyche in harnessing all of our scientific, political, economic, psychological, and spiritual efforts to forge a unity of deep action on behalf of the creation and against those forces that would destroy it. This effort may well require the extinction of our current worldview, which is focused almost exclusively on materialist reductionisms of all kinds.

No one has sounded the alarm of extinction anxiety more terrifyingly and beautifully at the same time than Cormac McCarthy in his strangely intimate postapocalyptic novel, *The Road*, which has created for me a parallel universe along whose devastated and dangerous road I often find myself walking in reverie. I find myself in a world without electricity, cars, hot water, enough food, and the constant threat of murderous human beings who have lost all their humanity. In the mood of that reverie, I debate whether or not to buy a gun to protect my family—but we Americans already have more guns than people, some 350 million of them, and they don't seem to be protecting us from anything. Surely the wish to own a gun is an instinctive response to defend oneself in the face of heightened extinction anxiety. This is what extinction anxiety does to us!

Anxiety often obscures the source of the terror that induces it. In the last lines of *The Road* McCarthy gives us a poetic vision that lifts the veil of extinction anxiety to let us see what is giving rise to it:

"Once there were brook trout in the streams in the mountains. You could see them standing in the amber current where the white edges of their fins wimpled softly in the flow. They smelled of moss in your hand. Polished and muscular and torsional. On their backs were vermiculate patterns that were maps of the world in its becoming. Maps and mazes. Of a thing which could not be put back. Not be made right again. In the deep glens where they lived all things were older than man and they hummed of mystery."[290]

Thomas Singer, M.D., is a psychiatrist and Jungian analyst in private practice in San Francisco. He is the editor of a series of books which explore cultural complexes in different parts of the world, including Australia (*Placing Psyche),* Latin America (*Listening to Latin America*), Europe (*Europe's Many Souls*), and North America (*The Cultural Complex*). He is working on a book about cultural complexes in Asia. He has edited *Psyche and the City, The Vision Thing*, co-edited the Ancient Greece, Modern Psyche series and co-authored *A Fan's Guide to Baseball Fever*. He

---

[290] Cormac McCarthy, The Road (New York: Alfred A. Knopf, 2006), 306–307.

serves as President of National ARAS, which explores symbolic imagery from around the world. His most recent chapters include "Trump and the American Selfie" in *A Clear and Present Danger* and "Trump and the American Collective Psyche" in *The Dangerous Case of Donald Trump*.

Afterword
Visions of Apocalypse and Salvation

By Leonard Cruz, M.D., M.E.

President Trump is a lightning rod. He galvanizes his base by appealing to instinctual fears of the *other* and he energizes his opponents by what they perceive as demagoguery, race-baiting, misogyny, and a cult of personality. Donald Trump is a charismatic figure capable of evoking apocalyptic visions among conservatives and progressives alike. His presidency may also unleash visions of salvation and catalyze a desperately needed retreat from the brink of annihilation. The contributors to *Rocket Man* are right to sound an alarm and to urge that the command and control of our nuclear arsenal be re-examined. If these chapters succeed in fostering a serious, meaningful, and effective dialogue about removing the president's authority to initiate a first strike, it will have succeeded in its primary objective. But there is a pearl of great price that lays waiting to be discovered. Many confluent forces point toward this potential jewel. Globalization, anthropogenic climate change, emerging infectious diseases, and environmental degradation offer increasingly irrefutable evidence that we live downstream from one another. Marshall McLuhan wrote to Wilfred Watson in 1965, "There are no passengers on spaceship earth, we are all crew."[291]

Apocalyptic visions may be shaping the *Weltanschauung* of top administration officials.

Richard Painter and Leanne Watt point to the unprecedented influence wielded by Rev. Ralph Drollinger, who conducts weekly Bible studies for at least eight members of President Trump's administration. Drollinger, the president's newly minted pen pal, believes that President Trump is anointed by God, and the reverend's apocalyptic overtones become more alarming when they are wedded to the president's unfettered authority to use nuclear weapons. The risk of nuclear warfare and its catastrophic impact arouses intense fear and apocalyptic visions, but it may be giving rise to a new vision, one better suited to our times that values and respects our deep interconnectedness and interdependence.

Utopian visons, like apocalyptic visions, have a long history. They course through the three Abrahamic faiths in the form of *Tikkun Olam* (the Jewish ideal of repairing the world), *City of God* (Augustine of Hippo), *The Virtuous City* (Al-Madina al-Fadila); *The Republic* (Plato); *Utopia* (More); *New Atlantis* (Bacon); *Erewhon* (Butler);

---

[291] Letters of Marshall McLuhan, by Matie Molinaro, Oxford University Press, 1988, p. 325.

Herland (Gilman); and *The Dispossessed* (Le Guin). A deep undercurrent of hope for a better world opens fissures in the individual and collective psyche, and like lava it rises to the surface. This utopian impulse shares a close kinship with apocalyptic visions.

This moment in American history has no precedent. Bard Larsen's chapter identifies the strangely prophetic visions of two great American novelists in foreshadowing some of the circumstances now unfolding. Sinclair Lewis (*It Can't Happen Here*) and Phillip Roth (*The Plot Against* America) recognized a deep reservoir of divisiveness that under the right circumstances can be tapped to propel a despotic leader to power. The safeguards enshrined by our Founding Fathers—the principle of checks and balances of the three branches of government being first among them—become meaningless when party loyalty overtakes the national interest. Such is the case with the continued silence and muted objections Republican leaders display toward the president's misdeeds and the growing evidence of ethical breaches surrounding the Oval Office.

Perhaps more than the political experts and pundits imagined possible, President Trump understood that he could prevail by inciting factionalism among the electorate and incessantly proclaiming false narratives. From his insistence that President Obama's birthplace was uncertain to his recent allegations that the FBI inserted operatives into his campaign, he has proven that a lie retold eventually begins to ring with a quality of believability. I have written elsewhere about the *superiority complex*, a term coined by the Viennese psychoanalyst Alfred Adler, to characterize a compensatory strategy for feelings of inferiority. A superiority complex is characterized by insensitivity to others, an inability to promote collaboration or cooperation, and opposition to a sense of community. "According to Adler, the well-adjusted human being is capable of living in harmony and cooperation with others and acts on behalf of the greater good of society."[292] President Trump's campaign slogan, "Make America Great Again," was rooted in a dark, xenophobic period of our nation's history. His message of America's return to preeminence, the restoration of a less diverse America, and the promise that Trump alone would be a champion for the working class resonated with his base. These distorted, often un-American ideas helped propel Donald Trump to victory. His ability to tout his wealth and Ivy League credentials while aligning himself with the common man made him a mercurial figure capable of playing to any audience of supporters while deriding his detractors.

Dr. Tom Singer informs us that Donald Trump has demonstrated a remarkable capacity to tap the deep psychological currents of *extinction anxiety* that flow like

---

[292] Leonard Cruz. "Trumplethinskin: Narcissism and the Will to Power." A Clear and Present Danger: Narcissism in the Era of President Trump, edited by Leonard Cruz and Steven Buser, Chiron Publications, 2017, pp. 76–77.

lava beneath the surface of our individual and our collective psyches. There does appear to be a deep wellspring of extinction anxiety coursing through each of us individually and collectively; however, there is also a wellspring of hopefulness, a vision of the future distilled in the image of the lion laying down with the lamb.[293] The light of our consciousness illuminates one or the other. The president seems to incline toward provoking extinction anxiety.

Sigmund Freud recognized that unconscious motivation opened a new dimension for ethical inquiry observing that "what is lowest" as well as "what is highest in the Ego can be unconscious."[294] This is true of both our apocalyptic and utopian visions—to a great extent they remain unconscious.

President Trump's impulsive, bellicose behavior has exposed deep flaws in the command and control system of our nation's nuclear arsenal. David Reiss's and Steven Buser's chapters make it clear that the president would not qualify to carry a gun as a policeman or to work in the vicinity of the nuclear arsenal, respectively. He would not be deemed fit for duty. If our elected representatives restrict a president's authority to initiate a first strike, President Trump's alarming behavior may end up paradoxically bringing forth a needed change.

At the eleventh hour the publisher decided to include images of nuclear war and interspersed them in the pages of the text. Spirited debate emerged about publishing images of the bombs dropped on Hiroshima and Nagasaki. Did this sensationalize the gravity of this book's theme? More fearmongering is not what our nation needs. Had the publisher the withheld the images, they might have been complicit with those who naively believe in the limited use of nuclear weapons. I maintain that the notion of see no evil, hear no evil, speak no evil does not extinguish evil; it emboldens it. A frank, mature, and somber examination of the real consequences of nuclear warfare must accept that the result for our species and entire biosphere would be catastrophic. We are living in a period that has been termed the Anthropocene, a geological age during which human activity has been the dominant influence on climate and the environment. There is mounting evidence that the pace at which species are being lost, *extirpation*, is accelerating so much that we are living through a mass extinction. The causes include global warming, ocean acidification, and emerging infectious diseases. Globalization, environmental degradation, and other human activities aggravate these ecological forces. However, the impact of nuclear warfare dwarfs them all. Immediate and massive loss of life would be followed by countless more deaths from the lingering effects of ionizing radiation. Nuclear warfare would produce such an immense quantity of particulate matter—dust and debris—that the energy of the sun would

---

[293] Isaiah 11:6

[294] Sigmund Freud, The Ego and the Id, W. W. Norton, New York, 1962.

be blocked substantially. An almost immediate nuclear winter would ensue.[295] Nearly all life on Earth depends on the capture of the sun's energy for conversion into fuel. Most living systems either photosynthesize or rely on photosynthesizers for survival somewhere in their food chains. Because tactical nuclear weapons might be utilized in an effort to contain the more extreme harmful effects of all-out nuclear conflict, the term *Nuclear Autumn* has been used to characterize the less severe consequences that dozens of smaller detonations might produce. According to David Bressan, even smaller amounts of dust rising into the atmosphere from nuclear explosions would block significant portions of the sun's Earth-bound radiation.

"Reduced crop production could lead to widespread famine in an already struggling world. Changes in temperatures also cause a shift in weather patterns. The precipitation during the monsoon, providing rain for millions of people in Asia, could decrease as much as 20% to 80%. As such large circulation patterns as the monsoon have global effects, also Africa, Australia and the Americas could become drier. Estimated 1 to 2 billion people[296] could face starvation, as much victims as a global nuclear war would claim. Unrest quickly would spread, followed by further conflicts over the limited resources."[297]

I practice addiction medicine, and we frequently meet individuals struggling with addiction where they are in frank, mature, sober fashion by addressing strategies for reducing the harm that comes with excessive, addictive substance use. *Harm reduction* may involve providing a Narcan kit to reverse overdose or test strips to help individuals detect the presence of powerful opioids like fentanyl before injecting a potentially fatal dose. One can hope the individual dealing with addiction will abstain for life, but taking steps to reduce harm makes sense and saves lives. Harm reduction involves straightforward, honest engagement of topics like using clean needles, reducing fatalities from accidental overdose with fentanyl and car-fentanyl, and preventing infectious diseases like hepatitis C and HIV. Saving lives supersedes other long-term goals that may have a broader focus during recovery.

When I apply the principles of harm reduction to the Trump administration, reducing the threat of nuclear war takes precedence over all other efforts to

[295] David Bressan. "Even A Small Nuclear War Would Still Have Effects On Global Scale", Forbes, August 12, 2017, retrieved May 6, 2018 at https://www.forbes.com/sites/davidbressan/2017/08/12/even-a-small-nuclear-war-would-still-have-effects-on-global-scale/#215d1e75507d

[296] http://www.ippnw.org/pdf/nuclear-famine-two-billion-at-risk-2013.pdf

[297] David Bressan. "Even A Small Nuclear War Would Still Have Effects On Global Scale", Forbes, August 12, 2017, retrieved May 6, 2018 at https://www.forbes.com/sites/davidbressan/2017/08/12/even-a-small-nuclear-war-would-still-have-effects-on-global-scale/#215d1e75507d

oppose or support President Trump's policies. Saving our own lives and saving the life of all the fauna and flora of the Earth must be a mandate. No president, most especially **this** president, should be granted the authority to initiate a first strike with nuclear weapons. In a democracy, government derives its power and rights from the governed. Our right to life is one of the three *unalienable* rights announced in the Declaration of Independence. No duly elected president, from Eisenhower to Trump, has been granted the right to deprive the citizens, and everyone else for that matter, of life. If these men possessed the power to initiate worldwide destruction, it is not because the citizens forfeited this right to them. This demands immediate, realistic attention. Failure to address this grave risk potentially renders all other issues moot. Painter and Watt, Gartner, and others point to the very real danger that should President Trump feel humiliated, cornered, or under siege he might resort to the first use of nuclear weapons as a means of re-establishing his powerful position. Addressing the issue of the president's unrestrained authority to launch a first strike is a critically important first step of harm reduction. Here are some sensible harm reductions strategies.

1. Let us secure passage of formal legislation restricting presidential authority to launch a first strike. Two bills were introduced toward that end: *HR 669 Restricting First Use of Nuclear Weapons Act of 2017*[298] and *S. 200 Restricting First Use of Nuclear Weapons Act of 2017.*[299]

2. The midterm election in November 2018 is likely to become a referendum on many things, including President Trump's unacceptable conduct in office. If voters repudiate President Trump's policies and his conduct in office, there is a greater chance that the legislative branch will be cured of its torpor and return to its vitally important democratic function of checks and balances. President Trump's frequent attacks on the judiciary and the free press, pylons of our democratic ideals, cannot withstand an overwhelming turnout of voters who demand a change. If you wish to reduce the harm, get to know the candidates running for office in your region and vote.

3. Because human beings possess awesome, dreadful power over all life on Earth, we must not shrink from our responsibility to mitigate our impact on each other and the entire biosphere. It is hard to conceive of a more urgent occasion since the Cuban Missile Crisis to revisit our command structure over the nuclear arsenal.

---

[298] Ted Lieu, "H.R.669 - Restricting First Use of Nuclear Weapons Act of 2017", US House of Representatives, Retrieved May 6, 2018, https://www.congress.gov/bill/115th-congress/house-bill/669.

[299] Edward Markey, "S.200 - Restricting First Use of Nuclear Weapons Act of 2017", US Senate, Retrieved May 6, 2018, https://www.congress.gov/bill/115th-congress/senate-bill/200.

4. Individually and collectively we can choose to invest in a salvific vision and reject the apocalyptic vision in which nobody wins.

Edward O. Wilson writes in the foreword to Rebecca Costa's 2012 book, *The Watchman Rattle: A Radical New Theory of Collapse:* "Let us accept the title of realists-in-search-of-a-solution. (…) We need to grasp the increasingly complexity of our social and political arrangements, and reach solutions." Like Dr. John Gartner, I grow increasingly concerned that President Trump either cannot or will not wrestle with complex issues. He resorts to simplistic, dichotomous views of us and them, and too often becomes entrenched in emotion-laden, fleeting gut instinct. The president's gut instincts appear to only be well-trained for his own survival, and this must not be allowed to continue unchecked.

Perhaps *Rocket Man: Nuclear Madness and the Mind of Donald Trump* will evoke a fear of the real dangers we live every day and it will inspire a call to action. If a progressive slate of candidates is elected, perhaps they will have the courage to oppose President Trump's repeated attacks on our cherished democratic institutions. These newly elected officials may be more willing to provide checks and balances over the executive branch. In due course, I hope and pray that President Trump will comport himself in ways worthy of the office he holds. If he cannot, I hope he will be replaced by someone who does not disgrace the office.

The Peace of Westphalia was a series of treaties that helped to bring an end to the Thirty Years' War and the Eighty Years' War that ravaged Europe. These agreements established a framework for how nations would rely on diplomacy rather than warfare to resolve disputes. It established several tenets, including that nations and principalities would recognize one another's sovereign borders, and it granted to sovereigns the right to endorse whichever religion they chose from among Catholicism, Lutheranism, and Calvinism. While uninterrupted peace did not result, the ceaseless wars of the preceding century ended, and the principle of keeping aggression in check by maintaining a balance of power was born. The Peace of Westphalia continues to shape diplomacy to this day. According to Henry Kissinger in the *World Order,* "The Peace of Westphalia was a turning point in the history of nations because the elements it set in place were as uncomplicated as they were sweeping."[300]

In the wake of President Trump's tumultuous first year and a half in office we have an opportunity to adopt a new peace that could become as sweeping and transformative as the Peace of Westphalia was centuries ago. Globalization, social media, economic interdependence, and the rising tide of freedom and civil liberties are coalescing and forging a new world order. This new order was conceived by Enlightenment philosophers. It was nurtured in the womb of the American experiment. Now that we face possible extinction at the hands of a fragile, self-

---

[300] Henry Kissinger. World Order. (New York. Penguin Books. 2015). Page 25.

centered, narcissistic man-child, the time has come to finally give birth to this new vision. The opposition that coalesced around President Trump's election and his isolationist, America First agenda may be the needed catalyst to bring forth a new appreciation of our vital interdependence. Our species possesses the capacity for deep self-reflection, and we also possess the means to end our existence. If we meet the challenge of our times with humility, sobriety, and compassion, a new vision for diplomacy and the conduct of international affairs may emerge. If we fail to accept the responsibility for our actions or if we continue to answer the call of the *lesser angels of our nature,* we may be faced with irreversible and deadly results.

President Trump's greatest service to our nation and perhaps to humanity may end up being that his presidency exposed the frailties of our tripartite system of government and our nuclear command and control structure. If President Trump energizes countervailing forces of reason, compassion, and temperance, he may unwittingly evoke utopian visions that can rival the apocalyptic visions he calls forth. A new vision comparable to the Peace of Westphalia will be predicated on the idea that we are one humanity and our common interests transcend national borders, especially when it comes to preventing nuclear annihilation.

Leonard Cruz, M.D. is Editor-in-Chief of Chiron Publications and co-founder of the Asheville Jung Center. He is a contributor to two previous edited volumes, *The Unconscious Roots of Creativity, A Clear and Present Danger: Narcissism in the Era of President Trump*, and co-authored *DSM-5 Insanely Simplified.* After over 35 years in private practice psychiatry, he currently works in the field of addiction medicine.

Contributing Authors

Ruth Ben-Ghiat is Professor of History and Italian Studies at New York University. The recipient of Guggenheim, Fulbright, and other fellowships, she's an expert on fascism, authoritarianism, and propaganda. She writes frequently for the media on those topics and on Donald Trump. Her next book is *Strongmen: How They Rise, Why They Succeed, How They Fall* (Norton). She sits on the Board of Directors of the World Policy Institute.

Steven Buser, M.D. trained in medicine at Duke University and served 12 years as a physician in the U.S. Air Force. He is a graduate of a two-year Clinical Training Program at the C.G. Jung Institute of Chicago and is the co-founder of the Asheville Jung Center. He has worked for over 20 years in private practice psychiatry. He currently works in the field of addiction medicine and serves as Publisher of Chiron Publications.

James G. Blight and **Janet M. Lang** have written 15 books on the history of recent U.S. foreign policy, seven of them on the Cuban Missile Crisis including, most recently, *Dark Beyond Darkness: The Cuban Missile Crisis as History, Warning and Catalyst* (2018). They were the principal advisers on Errol Morris' 2004 Academy Award-winning documentary, *The Fog of War*. Their short films on the Cuban Missile Crisis are at: https://www.youtube.com/user/armageddonletters. They are professors in the Department of History and the Balsillie School of International Affairs at the University of Waterloo. They have been married for 41 years.

Joe Cirincione is president of Ploughshares Fund, a global security foundation. He has worked on nuclear weapons policy in Washington for over 35 years, including for nine years as professional staff on the U.S. House of Representatives Committees on Armed Services and Government Operations. He is a former member of the International Security Advisory Board for Secretaries of State John Kerry and Hillary Clinton. He teaches at Georgetown University and is a member of the Council on Foreign Relations.

Tom Z. Collina is Director of Policy at Ploughshares Fund in Washington, D.C., and has 30 years of experience in nuclear weapons, missile defense and nonproliferation policy and research. Prior to joining Ploughshares Fund in 2014, Tom worked at the Arms Control Association, the Institute for Science and International Security and the Union of Concerned Scientists. He has published hundreds of articles and appears frequently in the national media, including The New York Times, CNN, and NPR. He has testified before the U.S. Congress and regularly briefs congressional staff. Tom has a degree in International Relations from Cornell University.

Leonard Cruz, M.D. is Editor-in-Chief of Chiron Publications and co-founder of the Asheville Jung Center. He is a contributor to two previous edited volumes, *The Unconscious Roots of Creativity* and *A Clear and Present Danger: Narcissism in the Era of President Trump*, and co-authored *DSM-5 Insanely Simplified*. After over 35 years in private practice psychiatry, he currently works in the field of addiction medicine.

Lance Dodes, M.D. is a Training and Supervising Analyst Emeritus at the Boston Psychoanalytic Society and Institute and retired assistant clinical professor of psychiatry at Harvard Medical School. He is the author of many journal articles and book chapters about addiction, and three books on the subject. He has been honored by the Division on Addictions at Harvard Medical School for "Distinguished Contribution" to the study and treatment of addictive behavior and elected a Distinguished Fellow of the American Academy of Addiction Psychiatry. He contributed the chapter "Sociopathy" to the recent bestselling book, *The Dangerous Case of Donald Trump*.

James E. Doyle, Ph.D. was a specialist in the Nuclear Nonproliferation Division at Los Alamos National Laboratory from 1997 to 2014. In 2015 Dr. Doyle was awarded the first Paul Olum fellowship from the Ploughshares Fund and was a non-resident fellow at the Belfer Center for Science and International Security at Harvard. His recent works focus on nuclear forces modernization, evolving nuclear threats and strategic planning for the elimination of nuclear weapons.

Maj. Gen. (retired) William L. Enyart served as an enlisted airman during the Vietnam War and subsequently in the Army National Guard for nearly thirty years. He retired from the military in 2012 as the commander of the 10,000 soldiers and 3,000 airmen of the Illinois National Guard, whereupon he was elected by the voters of southern Illinois's 12th Congressional District to serve in the 113th Congress, where he served on the House Armed Services Committee. He left Congress in 2015. He is an alumnus of the Harvard University Kennedy School of Government U.S. Russia Relations Senior Executive Course, the George Marshall Center Counterterrorism Senior Executive Program, the U.S. Army War College, Southern Illinois University School of Law and Southern Illinois University-Edwardsville. Now in private life, he is an attorney in private practice.

Paul French is the author of *North Korea State of Paranoia: A Modern History* (Zed Books), first published in 2005 and in four subsequent updated editions. He is also the author of *Our Supreme Leader: The Making of Kim Jong-un* (2016). Educated in London and Glasgow, French lived in China for two decades and first visited the DPRK in 2002. He is a regular commentator on North Korean issues for the BBC and France 24. In 2017 his narrative-drama, *Death at the Airport: The Plot Against Kim Jong-nam* was broadcast on BBC Radio 4.

John Gartner, Ph.D. is a psychologist in practice in Baltimore. He taught in the Department of Psychiatry at Johns Hopkins University Medical School for 28 years. He is the author of *In Search of Bill Clinton: A Psychological Biography* and *The Hypomanic Edge: The link Between (a Little) Craziness and (a Lot of) Success in America*. He has also published in *Psychology Today, The Washington Post, Baltimore Sun, USA Today, NY Daily News, Politico, The New Republic, Huffington Post, Salon, Worth*, and *Talk*. He graduated from Princeton University (magna cum laude), received his Ph.D. from University of Massachusetts, and completed his postdoctoral fellowship at New York Hospital-Cornell University Medical Center He is the founder of Duty To Warn.

Ken Gause is the director of the Adversary Analytics Program at the CNA Corporation, a defense research organization based in Arlington, Virginia. He has studied and written on North Korean leadership affairs since the late 1980s and is the author of three books: *North Korean House of Cards: Leadership Dynamics in the Kim Jong-un Era; Leadership Dynamics Under Kim Chong-il: Power, Politics, and Prospects for Change*; and *Coercion. Control. Surveillance, and Punishment. An Examination of the North Korean Police State*.

Melvin A. Goodman has a Ph.D. from Indiana University. His 42-government career includes service with the CIA, the Department of State, the Department of Defense, and the U.S. Army. His seven books on international security include *Whistleblower at the CIA: Inside the Politics of Intelligence, National Insecurity: The Cost of US Militarism*, and *The Failure of Intelligence: The Decline and Fall of the CIA*. He is an adjunct professor of government at Johns Hopkins University and a senior fellow at the Center for International Policy.

Stephan Haggard is the Krause Distinguished Professor at the School of Global Policy and Strategy at the University of California San Diego. He has written widely on the political economy and international relations of East Asia. His work on North Korea with Marcus Noland includes three books: *Famine in North Korea* (2007), *Witness to Transformation: Refugee Insights into North Korea* (2011) *and Hard Target: Sanctions, Engagement and the Case of North Korea* (2017). He runs the Witness to Transformation blog at http://www.piie.com/blogs/nk/ with Marcus Noland and currently has a regular column with Joongang Ilbo.

Gordon Humphrey represented New Hampshire in the United States Senate from 1979 to 1990, serving on the Senate Armed Services and the Foreign Relations Committees, among others. In 1991, he returned home, fulfilling a two-term pledge made when he first ran for office. He regards himself as a Reagan Republican and left the party by registering as an independent the day after Donald Trump was elected president. Prior to public service, Gordon Humphrey was a pilot with a major U.S. airline. Earlier, after four years of military service, he attended George Washington University and specialized flight schools.

Harry J. Kazianis is Director of Defense Studies at the Center for the National Interest and Executive Editor of its publish arm, *The National Interest*. He also serves as Senior Fellow at the China Policy Institute and Fellow for National Security at the Potomac Foundation. In the past, Kazianis served as a foreign policy adviser to the 2016 presidential campaign of Senator Ted Cruz and Editor-In-Chief of *The Diplomat*. He has authored over 400 op-eds, reports and monographs on national security issues and is a frequent guest on CNN, Fox News, CNBC and many other news outlets.

Bård Larsen is a political commentator, author, and historian. He is working as a fellow at the Norwegian think tank Civita. His main subjects are authoritarianism, human rights, and democratic erosion. He graduated from the University of Oslo on a thesis about the Armenian Genocide.

Seth Davin Norrholm, Ph.D. is an Associate Professor of Psychiatry and Behavioral Sciences at Emory University School of Medicine, a full-time faculty member in the Emory Neuroscience Graduate Program, and a member of the Emory Clinical Psychology Graduate Program. Dr. Norrholm has spent 20 years studying trauma-, stressor-, anxiety-, depressive-, and substance use-related disorders and has published over 90 peer-reviewed research articles and book chapters. An expert in human fear, Dr. Norrholm specializes in addressing fears associated with primary psychiatric diagnoses and personality disorders. Dr. Norrholm has been featured on NBC, ABC, PBS, CNN.com, Politico.com, *The Huffington Post*, Yahoo.com, *USA Today*, WebMD, The History Channel, and *Scientific American*.

Richard Painter has been the S. Walter Richey Professor of Corporate Law at the University of Minnesota Law School since 2007. From February 2005 to July 2007, he was associate counsel to the president in the White House Counsel's office, serving as the chief ethics lawyer for President George W. Bush. Currently, he's a candidate for U.S. Senate in Minnesota.

David M. Reiss, M.D. obtained a B.S. degree in Chemical Engineering and his M.D. from Northwestern University, followed by a psychiatric residency at U.C. San Diego. For over 30 years, he has maintained a private practice in California performing medical-legal evaluations and providing psychotherapeutic and psychopharmacological treatment. Dr. Reiss has been a psychiatric hospital Medical Director and continues to be an attending psychiatrist at hospitals in the New York/New England area. Dr. Reiss has worked with the media for 10 years, writing and being interviewed many times regarding issues directly and indirectly related to mental health and psychosocial/political phenomena.

Harry Segal graduated with a BA and MA in English Literature from Columbia (1990); He received a Ph.D. in English Literature Yale University and second doctorate in Clinical Psychology from the University of Michigan in 1990. He completed a post-doctoral fellowship in the Department of Psychiatry, University of Michigan Medical School, and joined the psychology faculty at Cornell in 1998. His work has focused on the clinical assessment of narrative and, more recently, models of the self. His publications include empirical studies on adolescent suicidality and depression, borderline personality disorder, and theoretical work on the creative process in fiction.

Thomas Singer, M.D., is a psychiatrist and Jungian analyst in private practice in San Francisco. He is the editor of a series of books which explore cultural complexes in different parts of the world, including Australia (*Placing Psyche*), Latin America (*Listening to Latin America*), Europe (*Europe's Many Souls*), and North America (*The Cultural Complex*). He is working on a book about cultural complexes in Asia. He has edited *Psyche and the City*, *The Vision Thing*, co-edited the Ancient Greece, Modern Psyche series and co-authored *A Fan's Guide to Baseball Fever*. He serves as President of National ARAS, which explores symbolic imagery from around the world. His most recent chapters include "Trump and the American Selfie" in *A Clear and Present Danger* and "Trump and the American Collective Psyche" in *The Dangerous Case of Donald Trump*.

Rosemary Sword is codeveloper of *Time Perspective Therapy* and co-author of related books such as *The Time Cure,* Wiley 2012; *Time Perspective Theory,* Springer, 2015; *Living and Loving Better,* McFarland, 2017; and *The Dangerous Case of Donald Trump, Macmillan, 2017*. Sword and Zimbardo write a popular column for *Psychology Today* and contribute to *AppealPower.com* (European Union online journal), *Psychology in Practice,* a new Polish psychological journal, and *Happify.com*. She is also developer of *Aetas: Mind Balancing Apps* (discoveraetas.com) and a private practice time perspective therapist.

Leanne Watt, Ph.D., M.A. is a clinical psychologist working in private practice for the last 25 years. She is a graduate of UCLA School of Medicine's post-doctoral fellowship program in clinical psychology. Dr. Watt completed an NIH post-doctoral research fellowship in neuropsychology at Keck School of Medicine of USC. She received her Ph.D. in clinical psychology from The School of Psychology at Fuller Theological Seminary (FTS) and completed a masters degree in theology from FTS.

Jacqueline J. West, Ph.D. With a BS from Stanford University and a Ph.D. in Psychology from the University of California, she trained to be a Jungian Analyst with the Inter-regional Society of Jungian Analysts. She has served as President and Training Director of the New Mexico Society and as President of the North

American Societies of Jungian Analysts. She is co-author, along with Nancy Dougherty, of *The Matrix and Meaning of Character: An Archetypal and Developmental Perspective* and has published several articles about Alpha Narcissism and the American psyche. She lectures and teaches widely on archetypal psychology and its interplay with art and politics.

Philip Zimbardo, Ph.D., professor emeritus at Stanford University, is a scholar, educator and researcher. Zimbardo is perhaps best known for his landmark Stanford prison study. Among his more than 500 publications are the bestsellers *The Lucifer Effect,* and *The Dangerous Case of Donald Trump*, as well as such notable psychology textbooks as *Psychology: Core Concepts, 8th edition* and *Psychology and Life,* now in its 20th edition. He is founder and president of *The Heroic Imagination Project* (heroicimagination.org), a world-wide nonprofit teaching people of all ages how to take wise and effective action in challenging situations.